A Subversive Voice in

A Subversive Voice in

CHINA

THE FICTIONAL WORLD OF MO YAN

Shelley W. Chan

CAMBRIA
PRESS

Amherst, New York

Cover image reproduced with the permission of Kalsang Norbu (格桑罗布).

Requests for permission should be directed to permissions@cambriapress.com,
or mailed to:
Cambria Press
20 Northpointe Parkway, Suite 188
Amherst, NY 14228

Library of Congress Cataloging-in-Publication Data

Chan, Shelley W.
  A subversive voice in China : the fictional world of Mo Yan / Shelley W. Chan.
    p. cm.
  Includes bibliographical references and index.
  ISBN 978-1-60497-719-6 (alk. paper)
1. Mo, Yan, 1955—Criticism and interpretation. I. Title.
  PL2886.O1684Z558 2010
  895.1'352—dc22

2010030384

To my late parents,
Chan Yau (陈友) (aka Chen Guoan 陈国安)
and Chiang Wai Yee (蒋惠怡) (aka Jiang Hua 蒋华),
as well as my lifetime teachers and mentors,
Professor Lu Shourong (卢守荣)
and Professor Qin Dezhuang (秦德庄)

TABLE OF CONTENTS

FOREWORD

"García Márquez wrote my novel!" So went Mo Yan's response to the widely held view that his early novels were Chinese versions of the Latin American "magic realism" style. As his English-language translator and someone who was a fan of Latin American fiction of the time, that struck me at the time as strange and quite audacious, but it took little for him to convince me that there was nothing derivative about his novel. While there are similarities between García Márquez's *One Hundred Years of Solitude* and Mo Yan's breakthrough novel *Red Sorghum*, mainly in their historical vision, their defamiliarizing narrative style, and their ability to get readers to accept the traditionally unacceptable, each created a fictional world that was national in its conception, international in its reach, and absolutely unique to its creator.

In the two decades since *Red Sorghum* burst onto China's literary scene, Mo Yan has proved to be one of the most prolific novelists of the post-Mao era and, in the view of many, its most accomplished and influential. His vast corpus—as many as a dozen big novels and more stories than I care to count—incorporates events and tales of virtually the entire twentieth century and a bit of the twenty-first. Heavily rural in setting, his novels' effect on his readers is unsettling. He seems to write to make them uncomfortable—in their lives, in their views of Chinese history, in their excesses, and in their prospects for the future. This he accomplishes through biting satire, graphic violence, epic historical fallacies, and a belief that Chinese society seems to be moving backward.

Shelley Chan has devoted much of her scholarly career to an examination, explication, and appreciation of the fictional works of China's most popular and widely read novelist. By putting an analysis of Mo Yan's fictional output in the context of his life as peasant, laborer, PLA officer, and full-time writer, she helps open up new windows into China's post Cultural Revolution social history. In the process, her sophisticated literary analysis reveals aspects, sometimes hidden, that go to the core of Mo Yan's literary project.

Scholarship is not advocacy, of course, at least it should not be, and Professor Chan, while an admirer of Mo Yan, is not uncritical in her in-depth study. Her objectivity and balanced approach do justice both to her subject and to literary scholarship. I frequently recommend Mo Yan to friends, colleagues, and just about anyone who wants a good read. Now I am happy to recommend this book—the first full-length study in English of my favorite author to anyone who wants the perfect complement to their reading of Mo Yan's novels.

—Howard Goldblatt
Research Professor of Chinese
University of Notre Dame

ACKNOWLEDGMENTS

I would like to thank Kalsang Norbu (格桑罗布) for his generous permission to use his new painting, "Red Carpet," as the cover of this book. I am greatly indebted to Professor Howard Goldblatt of the University of Notre Dame for his mentorship, intellectual stimulation, and acute reading of the earlier version of this work. Thanks also go to Professor Victoria Cass, Professor Stephen Snyder, and Professor Christopher Braider of the University of Colorado at Boulder, and Professor Joseph S. M. Lau (刘绍铭) of Lingnan University, Hong Kong, not only for their precious time and valuable comments but also for their advice and support during the course of my research.

I am grateful to May-lee Chai (翟梅莉) and Dr. Jacqueline Frischknecht for reading parts of my work and for their constant support. Special thanks go to Nicole Elizabeth Barnes, a warmhearted fellow student and friend, who insisted on reading the manuscript even though she herself was heavily pressed with work. Her friendship, encouragement, and inspiration are the best gifts a friend can ever offer.

I also remain indebted to my family and friends near and far for their understanding and support over the years.

Portions of chapters 1, 3, and 4 were published under the following titles, and thanks go to the reviewers and editors:

"From Fatherland to Motherland: On Mo Yan's *Red Sorghum* and *Big Breasts and Full Hips*," *World Literature Today* 74, no. 3 (Summer 2000): 495–499.

" 'It Is Hard Not to Write Satire': In A World of Vice and Folly," *American Journal of Chinese Studies* 13, no. 2 (2006): 233–259.

"Notes on *Life and Death Are Wearing Me Out*," *Orientierungen— Zeitschrift zur Kultur Asiens: Chinesische Gegenwartsliteratur: Zwischen Plagiat und Markt?* [Orientations—Journal for Asian Culture: Contemporary Chinese Literature: Between Plagiarism and Market Place?] (2009): 95–105.

Special thanks also go to the anonymous reviewers for their incisive comments, suggestions, and criticism, and to the editors and staff members of Cambria Press for their patience and diligent work.

Last but not least, I would also like to express my gratitude to Howard Y. F. Choy (蔡元丰), my husband, classmate, friend, and comrade. I have been enormously motivated by the feeling of working hard in concert with my loved one.

I dedicate this book to my late parents, Chan Yau (陈友) (aka Chen Guoan 陈国安) and Chiang Wai Yee (蒋惠怡) (aka Jiang Hua 蒋华), who not only gave me my life but also taught me how to be a good person. I also dedicate this book to my lifetime teachers and mentors, Professor Lu Shourong (卢守荣) and Professor Qin Dezhuang (秦德庄), who taught me English in their spare time when I was deprived of the right of receiving higher education in China simply because I walked with crutches and who have continued to encourage, support, and care about me in the past decades.

A Subversive Voice in

HUNGER AND LONELINESS

MO YAN'S MUSES IN BECOMING A WRITER

The twentieth century witnessed an unprecedented explosion of literature in the West. Fiction writing, for instance, progressed into a sophisticated enterprise that resulted in an enormous production of theories as well as the emergence of various schools of criticism. In addition, the development of literature was not only interdisciplinary but also international—writers in Europe, North America, and Latin America all strongly influenced by one another with their works.

While literature in the West enjoyed steady growth with multiple voices, in China its progress followed a roundabout course. Having a long history, traditional Chinese literature was known for its maturity, richness, and sophistication; hence, it had for many years been rather self-centered and self-sufficient, showing no interest in or any need for interaction with the literature of other countries. At the turn of the twentieth century, however, with the introduction of foreign cultures and the translation of foreign literary works, the May Fourth Movement[1] changed the autonomous nature of Chinese literature. Literary critics successfully identified echoes of

Western trends in the works of the most celebrated writers of that period, such as Lu Xun (鲁迅, 1881–1936), Guo Moruo (郭沫若, 1892–1978), Mao Dun (茅盾, 1896–1981), Cao Yu (曹禺, 1910–1996), and Ba Jin (巴金, 1904–2005). With the establishment of the People's Republic in 1949, however, China once again closed its doors to the outside world. Except for the works of some Soviet writers, such as Maksim Gorky (1868–1936), Alexander Serafimovich (1863–1949), and Nikolai Alexeevich Ostrovsky (1904–1936), foreign literature was by and large shut out. In fact, from the time that Mao Zedong (毛泽东, 1893–1976), the supreme leader of China, spoke at the Yan'an Forum on Art and Literature in 1942 until the late 1970s, literature—in terms of both topics and writing techniques—was under the strict control of the political party. Basically, highly politicized literature was the only officially approved form of creative writing, and it was used as a tool to educate people, shape their ways of thinking, and promote the official system of beliefs and values.

The literary monoglossia and the personality cult surrounding Mao Zedong reached an extreme during the Great Proletarian Cultural Revolution (1966–1976),[2] when formulaic and propagandist literature became dominant. Similar to the case of the performing arts, in which only eight "revolutionary model plays" were allowed to be staged throughout the entire country,[3] almost all literary works—except those by government-paid writers—were labeled as "poisonous weeds" and were either suppressed or repudiated.

With the death of Mao Zedong in 1976, the Gang of Four—which had actually controlled politics in Mao's declining years—was removed from power, and a new era began in Chinese history.[4] A revived interest in translations of Western works spread all over the mainland. Books by and about Friedrich Nietzsche (1844–1900), Jean Paul Sartre (1905–1980), Sigmund Freud (1856–1939), Milan Kundera (1929–), Gabriel García Márquez (1927–), and others enjoyed a large and enthusiastic readership, especially among students. Under such circumstances, literature and art regained a life of their own. The newly emancipated Chinese writers and artists began to move away from and even abandon the political ideology that had been imposed on them for nearly three decades, and they rejuvenated literature and art with new subject matter and writing styles. The open-door policy that came about after the Maoist era allowed the Chinese to see—much to their astonishment—the tremendous changes that had taken place in the outside world while they were isolated. This also spurred intellectuals into embarking on a painstaking introspection process regarding the events of the recent past. They began to question the Maoist legacy and to reexamine their history, culture, and the notion of "Chineseness" *per se*.

Consequently, the Chinese literary world began to flourish in the late 1970s. Different styles of production—especially in fiction writing—shifted rapidly, and the tastes of writers in this period changed remarkably. Novelists were interested in trying a variety of new styles of writing—both borrowed (such as stream of consciousness) and domestic (such as root seeking), which examines tradition and culture and searches for the roots of the Chinese people. Many gifted writers emerged in the 1980s, 1990s, and 2000s; some are now famous not only nationally but also internationally. Standing out in this talented group is Mo Yan (莫言, 1955–), the most prolific writer in present-day China as well as one of the country's most prominent avant-gardists, whose literary productions have enjoyed an enormous readership and have captured a great deal of critical attention not only in Mainland China, Hong Kong, and Taiwan but also in many other countries.

Mo Yan has published eleven novels to date: *Honggaoliang jiazu* (红高粱家族) [The red sorghum family] (1987), *Tiantang suantai zhi ge* (天堂蒜苔之歌) [The garlic ballads] (1988), *Shisan bu* (十三步) [Thirteen steps] (1989), *Jiuguo* (酒国) [The republic of wine] (1992), *Shicao jiazu* (食草家族) [The herbivorous family] (1994), *Fengru feitun* (丰乳肥臀) [Big breasts and wide hips] (1996), *Hong shulin* (红树林) [Red grove] (1999), *Tanxiang xing* (檀香刑) [Sandalwood punishment] (2001), *Sishiyi pao* (四十一炮) [Forty-one bombs] (2003), *Shengsi pilao* (生死疲劳) [Life and death are wearing me out] (2006), and *Wa* (蛙) [Frog] (2009). In addition to these novels, he has produced a large corpus of novellas and short stories. Thus far, five of Mo Yan's novels and a considerable number of his novellas, short stories, and essays have been translated into English; his works have also been translated into many other languages, including French, German, Italian, Spanish, Japanese, Korean, and Vietnamese. One of his novels, *The Red Sorghum Family*, was adapted for film by the internationally acclaimed director Zhang Yimou (张艺谋), and the film won the Golden Bear Award at the 1988 Berlin International Film Festival; this was the first major international prize awarded to a post-Mao Chinese film. Moreover, the novel was selected by the magazine *World Literature Today* as one of the "Top 40" of its first seventy-five years of publication and as the best of the year 1987. Zhang Yimou also adapted Mo Yan's "Shifu yuelaiyue youmo" (师傅越来越幽默) [Shifu, you'll do anything for a laugh] for the silver screen as a film entitled *Xingfu shiguang* (幸福时光) [Happy times], which won its director the Fipresci Prize and the Silver Spike at the Valladolid International Film Festival in 2000. In addition, the movie *Nuan* (暖), adapted by director Huo Jianqi (霍建起) from Mo Yan's novella "Baigou qiuqianjia" (白狗秋千架) [White dog and the swings], received the Tokyo Grand Prix–the Governor of Tokyo Award, at the 16th Tokyo International Film Festival in 2003. Mo Yan himself has frequently won various prestigious awards, including the inaugural Newman Prize for Chinese Literature in 2009, the first major American award for Chinese literature. Emerging in the mid-1980s as a young experimental writer, Mo Yan has since become a veteran and one of the most celebrated writers of Chinese literature today—recognized for his diligence and artistic achievements. Considered by many to be the most successful fiction writer in China, his talent, rich with creative enthusiasm, continues to flourish. Whereas writers of one generation after another have gradually stopped writing or have moved on to other professions, Mo Yan has continued his writing career, surprising readers and critics with a new masterpiece every two to three years.

Categorized by critics as a root seeker, a modernist, an expressionist, and a writer of magical realism, Mo Yan is a multifaceted novelist whose works cannot be easily pigeonholed. He is far more complex than any one of the above-mentioned labels would suggest, and the discussion of his importance can be extended to many dimensions—for instance, literature, society, history, politics, and language. Indeed, Mo Yan's complexity is comparable to that of Lu Xun, the most important exponent of May Fourth literature and China's most-discussed twentieth-century writer, whose works—especially his fictional writings—have become classics of modern Chinese literature. Mo Yan himself has said that Lu Xun is one of the writers from whom he has gained great inspiration. In a book Mo Yan edited in 1999, *Suokongli de fangjian: yingxiang wo de shibu duanpian xiaoshuo* (锁孔里的房间：影响我的10部短篇小说) [A room seen through the keyhole: Ten short stories that have influenced me], he collected ten stories, each by a celebrated writer: Polish author Henryk Sienkiewicz (1846–1916), Argentinean author Julio Cortázar (1914–1984), James Joyce (1882–1941), D. H. Lawrence (1885–1930), Gabriel García Márquez (1927–), William Faulkner (1897–1962), Ivan Sergievich Turgenev (1818–1883), Franz Kafka (1883–1924), Japanese writer Tsutomu Minakami (1919–2004), and Lu Xun (1881–1936).[5] As this list demonstrates, Lu Xun is the only Chinese writer Mo Yan feels has significantly influenced his own writings.

An examination of Mo Yan's fiction reveals that he has inherited the literary characteristics of Lu Xun's work (either consciously or unconsciously) that by and large represent mainstream May Fourth literature; in this way, Mo Yan bridges the rupture between the May Fourth period and the new literature of the postrevolutionary era. At the same time, however, Mo Yan does not live in the shadow of Lu Xun: he has certainly developed his own singular writing style, one that makes him unique and makes him stand out from his contemporaries. In other words, although Lu Xun's influence is evident in Mo Yan's work, Mo Yan's work has such a strong style of its own that he would never be thought of as a modern-day Lu Xun. Keeping in mind that the personal experiences and social circumstances of Mo Yan as a writer are very different from those of Lu Xun, it is of little significance to make a comparison in terms of the quality of their oeuvres, as has been done with Mo Yan and William Faulkner.[6] It is valuable, however, to note how Mo Yan—who among his peers is the writer most influenced by Lu Xun—adopts Lu Xun as his model and yet simultaneously maintains his own identity.

Moreover, it is also worth mentioning that Mo Yan carries on Lu Xun's tradition of fighting against cultural maladies, social injustice, and political failure in both Maoist and post-Mao China, where the political party established by Mao is still in power. Although Lu Xun's fictional works are largely characterized by cultural and social criticism, Mo Yan's novels, novellas, and short stories exhibit a much more obvious disapproval with respect to recent and current political circumstances in China. This is certainly not a light undertaking for a long-term army writer who has been part of the state apparatus. This book will examine Mo Yan's inheritance and development of Lu Xun's literary spirit as well as how he challenges the official ideology as reflected in revolutionary literature. Given the latter examination, discussions of his subversiveness and dissension in a broad sense are only natural for this study.

This book is thus a thematic study of Mo Yan's fictional creations within the framework of his continuity with and innovations on Lu Xun's work against the background of post-Mao China. Because Mo Yan has already been studied broadly under the rubrics of various theories, a close examination of the texts may be of benefit to readers. Rather than attempt an exhaustive analysis of Mo Yan's fiction, this volume conducts a focused textual study of some representative works in support of the analysis and presents a discussion of several important themes in his books. Mo Yan's oeuvre is so complex and rich, however, that no single study could possibly cover every work; one can only make selections. Four themes, therefore, serve as focal points for the chapters of this work: (1) Mo Yan's representation of history, (2) his paradoxical nostalgia, (3) his fancy for writing about violence, (4) and his employment of satire. Through an examination of these themes, this study serves to uncover the energy, imagination, innovation, mission, and passion of this important post-Mao writer through a close reading of his novels and stories. I hope to contribute to the field of Chinese literary criticism by illuminating an image of Mo Yan as at once a successor and a developer of Lu Xun's legacy and by demonstrating that Mo Yan's accomplishment is a combination of the May Fourth literary spirit and his own brilliance. Even though Lu Xun is known for both his essays and works of fiction, only his fictional works are examined in this study in juxtaposition to Mo Yan's work because Mo Yan is primarily a writer of fiction.

Mo Yan, whose real name is Guan Moye (管谟业), was born to a peasant family in Northeast Gaomi (高密) Township of Shandong (山东) Province, China, in 1955.[7] His mother gave birth to more than half a dozen children, only four of whom survived. Mo Yan is the youngest; he has two older brothers and one older sister. Living in an extended family with fourteen members—his parents, grandparents, and his uncle's family with four children—Mo Yan was somewhat neglected in his childhood. His father, who had completed four years of education, was considered an intellectual in his village and worked as an accountant until he retired in 1982. His mother was an illiterate housewife with a rural background who suffered from poor health, among other hardships.

Many factors played a role in the process of Mo Yan's becoming a writer, not the least of which was the influence of his family members. His grandparents were ordinary peasants, not at all prototypes of the Granddad and Grandma characters, the all-conquering heroes in his debut novel, *The Red Sorghum Family*. Though illiterate, his grandfather was actually Mo Yan's first teacher: he was a consummate storyteller. His tales revealed a world of fantasy to the young Mo Yan, who learned much about the unofficial history of China through anecdotes and stories about gods, spirits, foxes, and ghosts. Those stories later became a rich source of inspiration for Mo Yan's writing, especially for the legendary stories or fairy tales about his hometown. Mo Yan's grandmother, although not as unrestrained and daring as the character Grandma in *The Red Sorghum Family*, was a tough and capable woman who was highly respected by other women in the village. Guan Moxian (管谟贤), his oldest brother, also played an important role in Mo Yan's development into a writer. Guan Moxian was always the pride of his village because he was its only high school student and later the only college student from his hometown. As a student in the Chinese department of Huadong (华东) Normal University in Shanghai (上海) at the beginning of the 1960s, Guan Moxian naturally became Mo Yan's model. After a few years of elementary school education, however,

Mo Yan was forced to drop out of school at age twelve to work as a physical laborer alongside adults. Although extremely exhausted after the daily hard work, Mo Yan was starved for books, and his oldest brother's used textbooks, magazines, and even homework assignments became his source of intellectual nourishment as well as a means of self-education. At the beginning of his writing career, Mo Yan sent his stories to his brother for comments. At first, Guan Moxian discouraged him from writing fiction, even though he could see that his brother's potential as a good writer. As a middle-aged teacher, Guan Moxian had experienced countless political campaigns and seen too many examples of the miserable fate of intellectuals, including writers. He warned Mo Yan: "There are thousands of paths in this world, but never take the one leading to literature!" ("世上道路千万条，就是不能走文学这一条!")[8] When he saw that Mo Yan was persistent in his literary creations, however, and especially because he knew that his brother was depressed after some of his stories had been returned by publishers, Guan Moxian decided to support his younger brother in his writing career. Once he wrote to Mo Yan, advising that "in order to become a known writer, you must have your own unique style; following others (Chinese or foreign) will not lead to a bright future." ("要想成为名作家，必须具有自己独特的风格，跟在别人（不管是中国人还是外国人）后边走老路，是不会有出息的。)[9] The geographical location of Mo Yan's hometown is a second factor that should be noted. The Shandong peninsula is the birthplace of Confucius (551–479 BC), Mencius (372–289 BC), and Pu Songling (蒲松龄, 1640–1715),[10] and the areas is thus deeply influenced both by Confucian tradition and rich folklore. Moreover, it has been a crucial locale for politicians and strategists from ancient times to the modern period due to its geographical advantages. A major battlefield of the anti-Japanese war during the Second World War, this region was also infested by gangsters and bandits because of its special geographical location. Gaomi County was the hometown of Yan Ying (晏婴, ?–500 BCE), the famous prime minister of the Qi (齐) State, and Zheng Xuan (郑玄, 127–200), the celebrated Confucian classicist. Moreover, it is a place with unique folk culture and art, especially well known for its *jianzhi* (剪纸) [paper cuts]. Geographically, Gaomi County is located on the Jiaodong (胶东) peninsula, where summer floods are characteristic and as a result, long-stalked crops such as sorghum reap extra benefits from nature. Though the region is famous for its strong sorghum liquor, the vast red sorghum fields have also provided outlaws with an arena for their deeds, good and bad. These heroic figures serve as prototypes for some of Mo Yan's characters, and their acts of indiscretion contribute to these characters' richness, vividness, and liveliness.

Political circumstances in Mainland China have contributed abundantly to Mo Yan's creations as well. First of all, the Communist Party carried out meticulous examinations of class status, and the classification of people's social origins and family backgrounds was prevalent in China: Mo Yan's family members were categorized as middle peasants. Proletarians included workers, lower-middle peasants, and poor peasants, and the objects of their dictatorship were capitalists, landlords, and counterrevolutionaries, and so forth. Peasants were fundamentally divided into five categories: landlords, rich peasants, middle peasants, lower-middle peasants, and poor peasants. The last two categories enjoyed the highest political prestige, while the first two were labeled as class enemies.[11] Middle peasants, generally believed to be able to sustain themselves and their families, were "the objects of unity and education" ("团结教育的对象");[12] they were marginalized and alienated politically even though materially they were not much better off than the poor and lower-middle peasants. In order to live a safe and peaceful life, middle peasants had to earn the trust of party members and of other peasants who were poorer than they; any wrongdoing could easily lead to political discrimination. In an essay describing his hometown experience, Mo Yan recounts the following memory of his childhood: When he was twelve years old, he once labored on a construction site for sixty days, breaking stones at first and pumping the bellows for the blacksmiths later. One day, the young Mo Yan was so hungry that he uprooted a radish from the field of the production brigade. As soon as he started eating the radish, a poor and lower-middle peasant caught him and beat him up before sending him to the leader of the construction site, who called together all two hundred or so laborers and forced Mo Yan to admit his error in front of Mao Zedong's portrait. Down on his knees in front of the portrait of the then supreme authority, the young Mo Yan stammered: "Chairman Mao ... I stole a radish ... I committed a crime ... I deserve ten thousand deaths..." ("毛主席......我偷了一个红萝卜......犯了罪......罪该万死......"). When he went home, a cruel beating by his parents awaited him.[13] The reason for this beating, according to Mo Yan, was that

> on the one hand, the fact that I admitted my error to Mao's portrait in public hurt my parents' self-respect, and on the other hand, my family's social status was upper-middle peasant and we had to behave ourselves in order to rest content with temporary ease and comfort. (My translation)
>
> 一是因为我在毛泽东像前当众请罪伤了他们的自尊心，二是因为我家出身是上中农，必须老老实实，才能苟且偷生。
>
> (Mo Yan, "To Transcend Hometown," in *The Wall that can Sing: Selected Essays of Mo Yan*, 236)

This episode was later written into his novella "Toumingde hongluobo" (透明的红萝卜) [A transparent red radish] and the short story "Kuhe" (枯河) [Dry river].

The experience of hunger, a significant motif in Mo Yan's writing, was his major motivation to become a writer. Mo Yan experienced Mao Zedong's Three Red Banners and the three years of great famine that resulted from this political movement. Formulated in 1958, the Three Red Banners comprised the General Line for Socialist Construction, the Great Leap Forward, and the People's Communes. To meet the ambitions of Mao, rural cadres all over the country overstated their achievements:

> The grain-production figures had been disastrously overinflated. The announced total for 1958 of 375 million tons of grain had to be revised downward to 250 million tons (Western economists later guessed that actual production was around 215 million tons). Not only had no cadres dared to report shortfalls of the procurement quota they had been given out of fear of being labeled "rightists" or "defeatists," but many of the best-trained statisticians from state bureaus, having been removed in the 1957 antirightist campaign

(along with the most able demographers), were no longer around to issue words of caution even had they dared. (Jonathan D. Spence, *The Search for Modern China*, 580)

One of Mao's fantasies was the nationwide steel smelting campaign. One million local backyard steel furnaces were set up, scattered all over China, and every family was ordered to submit all kinds of metal products—only to produce steel of such poor quality that it had no use at all. Because cooking utensils were among the items confiscated, people were unable to cook at home and instead had to dine in public dining halls. In Mo Yan's "Tiehai" (铁孩) [Iron child], the history of steel smelting and public dining is turned into a surrealistic and ironic story. These policies of Mao led, in John Fairbank's words, to "an all-time first-class man-made famine"[14] that, according to Jonathan Spence, "claimed 20 million lives or more between 1959 and 1962. Many others died shortly thereafter from the effects of the Great Leap—especially children, weakened by years of progressive malnutrition."[15]

Mo Yan was one of these children who suffered from the general lack of food and from malnutrition in the late 1950s and early 1960s. He lived in a large family and there was never enough food to go around, so the young Mo Yan was always hungry. He cried at nearly every meal because he never had enough to eat; he longed to become a writer once he learned that a writer could have meaty dumplings as often as he wanted.[16] Mo Yan's deep memory of this large-scale famine has become a rich source for his writing, both fictional and biographical. Interestingly, this experience has led him to ponder the phenomenon of the extravagance of gluttony in contemporary China—a theme (discussed more fully later) that is reflected in his novels *The Republic of Wine* and *Forty-One Bombs*.

Mo Yan was obliged to drop out of school as a fifth-grader for political reasons. During the early stage of the Cultural Revolution, Mo Yan—inspired by the revolutionary news from his older brother—took part in the editorial work of a "rebel" school newspaper which flouted the authority of his school's teachers. Consequently, Mo Yan was kicked out of school at the age of twelve and began his life as a peasant, working all day long in the field as the adults did. When the representatives of the lower and poor peasants entered and were stationed in schools, Mo Yan was denied the opportunity of going back to school because he was from a middle-peasant family. In spite of the hard labor he was forced to endure, however, Mo Yan's enthusiasm for reading did not wane; on the contrary, his hunger for books greatly increased. In addition to his older brother's textbooks, he read every book he could get his hands on, regardless of its subject. The more Mo Yan read, the more he grew to dislike boring manual labor, and the greater his desire became to leave the countryside. Even though he had completed only five years of elementary school education, he dreamed of going to college. University entrance examinations had been abandoned during the Cultural Revolution, however, and entry into colleges was now only possible through the recommendations of lower and poor peasants, which was out of the question for Mo Yan. As a result, the only way out of his life of hard labor was to join the People's Liberation Army (PLA), although accomplishing this was not much easier than going to school because family backgrounds were equally important for military conscription. Mo Yan and his family tried persistently, and in 1976 he finally enlisted and realized his dream of leaving his rural hometown.

This golden opportunity was, in fact, a major turning point in Mo Yan's life. He bid farewell to hunger forever—and most importantly—in the army, he was able to study. As many others had done, Mo Yan lied about his age and academic credentials: he claimed to be a senior high school student when he filled out the personnel form. The same year Mo Yan enlisted, the Gang of Four was arrested, and the university entrance examinations resumed. Looking at Mo Yan's personal information and believing him to be a high school graduate, the army leaders told him to prepare for the examination. But because he had not actually finished his elementary education, Mo Yan was faced with a dilemma: this was his only chance to realize his dream of going back to school, but he knew it would be nearly impossible to prepare adequately for the examination in six months. Nevertheless, he was determined to try his luck. He worked extremely hard, only to find after much preparation that he did not in fact qualify to take the exam—he was by then one year over the age limit. Deeply disappointed, Mo Yan started contributing fiction to literary magazines. Unfortunately, there were no signs of success in the first few years.

Despite the fact that Mo Yan was unable to sit for the university entrance examination, the army leaders still believed that he was more capable than many other soldiers and assigned him to teach in a literacy campaign. At the same time, he was also appointed to work as a librarian. Taking advantage of this opportunity, Mo Yan read voraciously and continued writing fiction. In 1981 his debut short story "Chunye yu feifei" (春夜雨霏霏) [The incessant rain on a spring night] was published in *Lian chi* (莲池) [Lotus pond], a literary magazine based in Hebei (河北) Province; the story is about a newlywed wife who misses her solider husband. After that, Mo Yan published several short stories here and there, but none of them seemed to evoke any response among readers until 1983, when *Lotus Pond* printed one of his stories, "Minjian yinyue" (民间音乐) [Folk Music], which attracted some attention in literary circles. In crafting this romance between a young blind musician and the proprietress of a restaurant, Mo Yan abandoned the more traditional realistic forms and tried to create a misty—even absurd—aura. This piece is an example of his earliest experimentation.

The year 1984 marked another important turning point in Mo Yan's life. The PLA Art Institute, the army's highest art institution, decided to form a literary department and enroll students. When Mo Yan heard the news, the deadline to sign up had already passed, so he took with him several published stories and went to see Xu Huaizhong (徐怀中), a famous army writer and the new department's first chairperson. Xu was particularly impressed by "Folk Music" and allowed him to take the entrance examination, promising to enroll him even if he failed. Fortunately, Mo Yan validated the faith that Xu had placed in him: he passed the examination with a high score. Finally, Mo Yan was admitted to university. "Chairman Xu Huaizhong changed my fate!" ("徐怀中主任改变了我的命运！") Mo Yan has written.[17] During his first semester at the

Art Institute, Mo Yan was enlightened by the lectures of many well-known writers, including Wang Meng (王蒙), Zhang Chengzhi (张承志), Ding Ling (丁玲), and Liu Baiyu (刘白羽). In his own words,

> I gained a lot during that semester. Not until then did I know what "literature" meant. I determined to do something ... At that time I was so addicted to writing that I felt guilty if I stopped writing for a single day. The desire to write was so strong.... (My translation)
>
> 这一学期收获很大，方知文学是怎么回事，决心搞出一点名堂来 ...... 那时似乎已经成癖，一天不写东西，感到对不住自己，创作欲极强...... 。(He Lihua, "The Footprints of the Red Sorghum Singer," in *Research Materials about Mo Yan*, 17)

Soon thereafter, Mo Yan published the novella "A Transparent Red Radish," which brought him immediate recognition. During his two years of study at the Art Institute (from 1984 to 1986), Mo Yan produced several powerful novellas and short stories. In March 1986, the novella "Honggaoliang" (红高粱) [Red sorghum] was published by *Renmin wenxue* (人民文学) [People's literature], the most important official literary magazine in China; the piece was quickly reprinted by many other magazines.[18] Mo Yan was also admitted into the Chinese Writers Association that same month, which meant that his identity as a writer was now formally established. The year 1986 was an extremely productive one for Mo Yan: he finished four other novellas and put them together with "Red Sorghum" to form his first novel, *The Red Sorghum Family*, which was published in 1987. By this time, he was already regarded as one of the most important writers in post-Mao China; his rise was the most meteoric among contemporary Chinese authors.

After graduating from the PLA Art Institute in the summer of 1986, Mo Yan stayed in the army and continued to write. In September 1988, he was admitted to a master's program at the Beijing Lu Xun Literary Institute.

As a result of China's open-door policy after Mao's death in 1976, Mo Yan had the opportunity to read translations of foreign literary works. He has never denied the influences of foreign literature on him—in fact, he once declared that "Chinese literature cannot be separated from world literature."[19] In his preface to the previously mentioned book, *A Room Seen through the Keyhole: Ten Short Stories that Have Influenced Me*, Mo Yan briefly recollects his encounters with stories by these writers, all foreign except Lu Xun, and how each of them inspired his own writing. Mo Yan's favorite foreign author is William Faulkner. In a 1993 essay titled "Shuoshuo Fukena zhege laotou" (说说福克纳这个老头) [Talk about the old fellow Faulkner] and in a speech he gave at the University of California, Berkeley, in 2000, Mo Yan disclosed how much his Northeast Gaomi Township was a result of stimulation by Faulkner's Yoknapatawpha County.[20] He frankly admitted that prior to reading Faulkner, he had written in accordance with teaching materials used in the classroom.

> After reading Faulkner, I felt as if I had awakened from a dream. So one could write nonsense like this, so the trifles in the countryside could be used as fiction topics! His Yoknapatawpha County showed me that a writer could not only fabricate his characters and his stories, but could make up a geographical locale as well. (My translation)
>
> 读了福克纳之后，我感到如梦初醒，原来小说可以这样地胡说八道，原来农村里发生的那些鸡毛蒜皮的小事也可以堂而皇之地写成小说。他的约克纳帕塔法县尤其让我明白了，一个作家，不但可以虚构人物，虚构故事，而且可以虚构地理。(Mo Yan, "How Are You, Uncle Faulkner?," in *Mo Yan's Selected Prose*, 296–297)

Gabriel García Márquez also seems to have had a great influence on Mo Yan. His Macondo Town in *One Hundred Years of Solitude* was as inspirational to the Chinese writer as Faulkner's Yoknapatawpha County. As a point of departure, Mo Yan began to explore, imagine, (re)create, and transcend his hometown, Northeast Gaomi Township, which has been an inexhaustible source for his creativity. Combining legendary heroic ancestors from historical records with his own imagination, Mo Yan tried to "establish a republic of literature" (创建一个文学的共和国)，in his own words, and he himself, "was of course the sovereign of this republic" (当然我就是这个共和国开国的皇帝。).[21] This literary kingdom, rich in symbolic significance and therefore more than a geographical locale, signifies a landmark in his writing career and provides readers of contemporary Chinese literature with a vast imaginative space.

David Der-wei Wang (王德威) believes that "Mo Yan ... provide[s] the most important historical space in contemporary Mainland Chinese fiction."[22] Wang goes on to define his notion of "historical space" and to explain its importance in Mo Yan's fictional universe:

> The "historical space" to which I refer includes, but is not restricted to, the traditional dialectical discourse on space, time, history, and the ontological hometown (*yuanxiang*). "Historical space" refers to how writers like Mo Yan three-dimensionalize a linear historical narrative and imagination, and how they locate concrete people, events, and places into a flowing, kaleidoscopic historical coordinate ... With Northeast Gaomi, Mo Yan has established a contrast of values, juxtaposing city and country, development and backwardness, civilization and nature ... Mo Yan's ontological hometown, as found in the pages of his fiction, is a product of narration, the fruits of his historical imagination. Saying that Mo Yan's "root-seeking" works represent the reappearance of various styles and features of a certain geographic environment would not do as much justice to them as saying that they represent the central symbol of another time and space, thus fulfilling the category of dialectical historicism. (David Der-wei Wang, "The Literary World of Mo Yan," in *World Literature Today*, 488)

In fact, the terms "historical space" and "historical imagination" are appropriate not only for Mo Yan's "root-seeking" stories but for his other works as well, if the idea of history is to be treated in a broad sense. The following discussion shows that "another time and space" always exist in Mo Yan's narration, a trait of dialectical narrativity.

Chinese literature underwent a tremendous shift in the early twentieth century with the milestone of the May Fourth Movement. Many important writers emerged from the movement, each with his or her own distinct style, but in general May Fourth literature can be divided into two major categories, one of which is decisively more influential than the other. Mainstream May Fourth literature, led and represented by Lu Xun, was an elite and mission-driven literature that attempted to address and transform multiple maladies of the nascent republic, including the negative aspects of China's long history as well as crises the country faced from foreign forces. The complement to this kind of didactic literature was market-oriented popular literature, such as the sentimental fiction of the Mandarin Duck and Butterfly school, the apolitical nature of which led to its condemnation by the May Fourth leftists and their successors as ideologically insensitive, politically backward, and culturally decadent. As a result, popular literature and its important writers have by and large been neglected by literary critics in Mainland China. Because the present study does not attempt to carry out research on this second—but not secondary—category of the May Fourth literary phenomenon, I have treated the works of Lu Xun and his followers as the primary representatives of May Fourth literature in the discussion of Mo Yan's continuity and discontinuity of the spirit of that particular historical period.

May Fourth literature is heavily loaded with the intellectuals' sense of obligation to save the nation and change society, a sentiment that is best exemplified by Lu Xun's legendary slide-show incident, a well-known episode in Lu Xun mythology. (For years, people believed that the slide-show incident had indeed taken place until recently when some scholars argued that there was no evidence to prove that it happened.) The young Lu Xun went to Sendai, Japan, to study Western medicine in 1904 because he distrusted traditional Chinese medicine because it failed to cure his father's tuberculosis and save the old man's life. One day, a Japanese instructor finished his lecture earlier than usual, so he showed documentary slides to his students of the execution of a Chinese spy during the Russo-Japanese war fought on Chinese soil (1904–1905). At the center of the execution scene was a Chinese man who was accused of having spied on the Japanese for the Russians and therefore faced decapitation by the Japanese. Around him stood a group of Chinese people, apparently strong and healthy, who were watching their fellow countryman's execution in silence. Greatly shocked by the slide show, Lu Xun came to believe that it was more important to heal people spiritually than to cure their physical bodies. Consequently, he decided to quit medical school to pen works in hopes of awakening people from their spiritual numbness through his writing. Lu Xun used a metaphor— the iron house—in the preface to his short story collection *Nahan* (呐喊) [Call to arms] in order to describe the suffocating Chinese society in which people were asleep, unaware of the necessity of fighting for the future of their own nation and, indeed, of fighting for themselves.[23] Generally speaking, Lu Xun and other May Fourth intellectuals attributed the weakness of their country vis-à-vis foreign powers (as well as all other societal flaws) to the Confucian tradition that had dominated China for thousands of years. This resulted in the May Fourth intellectuals' adoption of what Lin Yü-sheng (林毓生) calls "totalistic iconoclasm"—a rejection of the heritage of the past as a cultural, social, and political totality.[24] With the explosion of human adversities as a major motif of May Fourth literature, the elite May Fourth writers, from their positions in the upper social strata, showed their humanistic concerns toward people who were suffering from all kinds of hardships, especially toward those living in more backward rural areas; the writers used their literary works for cultural and social criticism.

Heavily influenced by the May Fourth spirit, Mao Zedong and his party continued to radically reject the old culture; the notorious Cultural Revolution, launched by Mao in 1966, was the peak of this rejection.[25] Interestingly, Mo Yan carries on the iconoclasm of his May Fourth predecessors, but in his case the target of criticism is Maoist discourse itself. Showing deep sympathy for his peasant counterparts. Mo Yan places himself among ordinary Chinese people and examines the sources of the calamities they suffer from a nonelite point of view: this is one of the most important differences between Mo Yan and Lu Xun. Although they held deep sympathy for the Chinese people, especially for those in rural areas, Lu Xun and his May Fourth comrades, as intellectuals and elites, nevertheless exhibited a somewhat self-righteous attitude, whether consciously or not. Mo Yan, however, is totally devoid of this self-pride and of any sense of being a superior spokesman because he sees himself as one of the people whom he is both speaking for and criticizing. Although he does not necessarily attempt to turn his work into a weapon as Lu Xun did, Mo Yan nevertheless speaks for his fellow citizens and thus transforms his fiction into social criticism. Moreover, his writings move in the direction of political or national allegory; this is especially true of the fiction he has produced in later stages of his career. At the same time, however, Mo Yan distinguishes himself from the May Fourth intellectuals as well as from his own contemporaries by his wild imagination, unique employment of language, and an increasingly noticeable playfulness in his later works. These qualities prevent his works from becoming mere exposé; they display the pure pleasure of writing. In other words, for Mo Yan, sometimes writing is just for the sake of writing.

As a thematic study of Mo Yan, this book concentrates on four important foci in Mo Yan's fiction. The current section has set the stage by presenting a general picture of the literary situation in China and a brief biographical introduction, which serve as context for Mo Yan's emergence as a fiction writer who both inherited and advanced the legacy of Lu Xun, the precursor and leader of the May Fourth literary movement.

The first chapter discusses Mo Yan's representation of history, focusing on three of his novels: *The Red Sorghum Family*, *Big Breasts and Wide Hips*, and *Life and Death Are Wearing Me Out*. The first two works are family histories placed in the context of modern Chinese history, and the third is a story about a landlord who was executed and reincarnated during the reign of the ruling party. This chapter examines the ways in which Mo Yan challenges the political orthodoxy by depicting the life of "minor figures" from "below" in a milieu where historical narrative is dominated by the world from "above," to borrow Georg Lukács' terms.[26] In other words, chapter 1 reveals how Mo Yan's historical figures are free from ideological dogma within a highly politicized grand narrative. It also analyzes the author's skeptical attitude, which defies a materialistic conception of progressing history; Mo Yan holds the view that history is regressive and degenerative. In addition, the chapter addresses the changes in Mo Yan's conception of history during the decades between these three historical novels: the author's notion shifts from a nostalgic, masculinized ancestor worship in *The Red Sorghum Family* to a problematization of history *per se* represented by a philogynous writing style in *Big Breasts and Wide Hips* and later shifts to a parody of Buddhism's six realms of reincarnation loaded with comic vision in *Life and Death Are Wearing Me Out*.

Chapter 2 explores Mo Yan's paradoxical nostalgia toward his hometown, Northeast Gaomi Township. A comparison of Mo Yan's "White Dog and the Swings" with Lu Xun's two stories "Guxiang" (故乡) [My old home] and "Zhufu" (祝福) [The new-year sacrifice] delineates the similarities and differences between Mo Yan and Lu Xun in terms of their criticism of intellectuals, especially those who return to their hometown after a relatively long sojourn elsewhere. The chapter also examines other stories set in Mo Yan's hometown in order to investigate, on the one hand, how the depiction of rural life is condensed and concretized in Northeast Gaomi Township, and on the other hand, how this township has transcended its status as an ordinary homeland for the author, who has turned it into a conceptual plane of existence, a timeless and boundless stage on which he is free to perform.

Chapter 3 studies the extensive descriptions of violence in Mo Yan's works. The graphic scene of flaying a human still alive in *The Red Sorghum Family* marks the beginning of his use of violent narrative; ever since then, violence has been a major recurring theme in his stories and novels—domestic violence is represented by "Dry River" and *The Garlic Ballads*, and extreme cruelty related to the fate of the nation is represented in *The Red Sorghum Family* and *Sandalwood Punishment*. In addition, Mo Yan questions the legitimacy of violence committed in the name of revolution by depicting such violence in disturbingly graphic detail; *Big Breasts and Wide Hips* is a good example of this. Violence between human beings and animals is also featured, and typical cases can be found in *Life and Death Are Wearing Me Out* and *Forty-One Bombs*, among others. Like some other major post-Mao writers, such as Yu Hua (余华), who is known for his explicit and vivid depictions of violence, Mo Yan reveals his absorption of and deep disappointment with reality as well as with the history of the land in which he and his ancestors have dwelled. At the same time, the novelist seems to unconsciously present himself as a case study demonstrating the human tendency toward bloodthirstiness.

The fourth chapter makes a strong case for classifying Mo Yan's oeuvre as highly sophisticated satire. This chapter is composed of three sections, each focusing on one specific aspect of Mo Yan's work: cannibalism, vulgarity, and the grotesque. The investigation displays Mo Yan's condemnation of social, political, and cultural maladies and human weaknesses with a postmodern playfulness and shows how he turns one of his novels, *The Republic of Wine*, into a political allegory. The author's courage to ridicule irrationality and injustice as well as his satiric techniques lend themselves to a thorough analysis. This fourth chapter aims to reveal Mo Yan's brilliance as a satirist—adding one more laurel to his list of achievements.

CHAPTER 1

HISTORY

FROM FATHERLAND TO MOTHERLAND TO PLAYLAND

In the mid-1980s, Mo Yan was largely responsible for originating the trend among post-Mao Chinese novelists of writing historical fiction, particularly the genre of family history. His book *The Red Sorghum Family* was one of the earliest novels depicting the romances and sufferings of one family's ancestors, the grandparents of the first-person narrator. *Big Breasts and Wide Hips*, which appeared nearly ten years after the first novel, is again a family story interwoven with the modern history of China.[27] Interestingly, Mo Yan seems to have formed a habit of producing one historical novel (covering a relatively long time span) roughly every ten years—after *The Red Sorghum Family* in 1987 and *Big Breasts and Wide Hips* in 1996, Mo Yan published another historical novel, *Life and Death Are Wearing Me Out*, in 2006. Unlike the previous two works, which cover a range of history approximately from the republican period to the 1970s or the 1980s, *Life and Death Are Wearing Me Out* is set exclusively in the Communist era, recounting Chinese history from 1950 to 2000. The discussion in this chapter addresses not only the ways in which Mo Yan inherits and develops Lu Xun's critical attitude toward history but also how Mo Yan's conception of history changes during the decade between *The Red Sorghum Family* and *Big Breasts and Wide Hips* and between that work and *Life and Death Are Wearing Me Out*. On the one hand, Mo Yan attempts to demoralize, so to speak, the moralized history and to go against the official ideology. On the other hand, he tries to problematize history itself by subverting the binary opposition between good and evil, an opposition that had been set up in the old model of historical fiction. Characters are no longer treated as mere embodiments of such positive values as filial piety, faithfulness, and righteousness, or of such negative values as betrayal, disloyalty, and dishonesty. Instead, the characterization of the individuals in Mo Yan's novels is true to life, full of mixed qualities and human complexities.

In addition, Mo Yan blurs the boundary between history and fiction, confirming Hayden White's observation that "history is no less a form of fiction than the novel is a form of historical representation."[28] For Mo Yan, history is not necessarily progressing. By the same token, the writer denounces the degeneration of the human race. Interestingly, women, romantic attachments, and human sexuality play positive roles in his historiography. In *Big Breasts and Wide Hips*, he even adopts a philogynous way of writing: he writes adoringly about the female body throughout the book. Put otherwise, Mo Yan vulgarizes the grand narrative of history, making characters from "below" the central figures of his stories and presenting them as larger than life. Georg Lukács' remark about Walter Scott could easily have been made about Mo Yan: "He writes *from* the people, not *for* the people; he writes from their experiences, from their soul."[29]

The opening sentences of *Sanguo yanyi* (三国演义) [Romance of the three kingdoms] read, "The empire, long divided, must unite; long united, must divide. Thus it has ever been" (话说天下大势，分久必合，合久必分。).[30] This neatly summarizes the traditional Chinese belief that history is circular, repetitive. The Chinese also believe that retribution for sin—or more precisely, causality in its karmic sense—is the basic operating code in this circular pattern, and therefore moral admonition plays an essential role in life. Furthermore, the Chinese have faith in the correspondence of a moral order with the natural order: heaven aids the good rulers and punishes the tyrants. As a result of these mores, the writing of history was long based on morality and had a strong didactic function.

However, in the late nineteenth and early twentieth centuries, the country was forced by foreign military power and technology, such as the Sino-Japanese War of 1894–1895, to open up to the world, and Darwinism—together with other Western concepts—was introduced in China. As the notion of evolution by natural selection and the law of the survival of the fittest gained precedence, a linear and progressive comprehension of history gradually replaced the traditional circularity. A materialist and Darwinian manner came to prevail: history is a progression, a straightforward teleological evolution. According to this belief, history is like an album of facts that are forever true about the past; it is the record of past reality. Historical records, moreover, have an important admonishing function: the past should serve to provide present and future generations with experiences and lessons to help them avoid repeating past mistakes. A binary opposition of new and old, progressive and regressive, revolutionary and reactionary replaced the old system of circularity.

Unlike traditional historians who attempted to explain history with grand narratives, Mo Yan writes historical fiction that is consonant with "Nietzsche's insistence in *The Use and Abuse of History* … that the 'historical' is an aesthetic creation whose truth is dramatic rather than objective."[31] By embracing a skeptical attitude toward the progressive conception of history and challenging it, Mo Yan's historical fiction deviates from orthodox literary practice. Unlike the revolutionary history produced during the time of the Maoist monologue—history that submitted to the official ideology, that carried out the official narrative, and that was filled with class struggle and collectivism—history under Mo Yan's pen is full of desire and imagination, constructed by the élan vital of individuals.

THE RED SORGHUM FAMILY: A SUBLIME FATHERLAND

In 1987 Mo Yan published *The Red Sorghum Family*, a novel set in his hometown, Northeast Gaomi Township of Shandong Province. Relating the story of a peasant family from 1923 to 1976, this novel is about the hardships, loves, hatreds, and adventures of the peasants of Shandong. The book immediately attracted the attention of Chinese readers and critics, and its author gained international acclaim when the novel was adapted for the silver screen; the film version won the Golden Bear Award in 1988 at the Berlin International Film Festival.[32]

Hayden White suggests that

> historians do not have to report their truths about the real world in narrative form ... They [refuse] to tell a story about the past, or rather, they [do] not tell a story with well-marked beginning, middle, and end phases; they [do] not impose upon the processes that [interest] them the form that we normally associate with storytelling. While they certainly [narrate] their accounts of the reality that they [perceive], or [think] they [perceive], to exist within or behind the evidence they [have] examined, they [do] not narrativize that reality, [do] not impose upon it the form of a story. (Hayden White, *The Content of the Form*, 2)

Although Mo Yan is a novelist writing a historical novel, his mentality is similar to that of the historians discussed by White. Proudly recollecting the heroic achievements of his grandparents, the first-person narrator opens the story of his family in the year 1939, when his father and grandfather set out to ambush the Japanese. The story's point of departure is thus the Chinese resistance against Japanese invaders during World War II.

The beginning of the novel is seemingly conventional but actually highly experimental: "The ninth day of the eighth lunar month, 1939" (一九三九年古历八月初九).[33] To start a story with a concrete date is a traditional way of writing historical fiction; the combination of Chinese lunar and Western solar calendrical systems, however, is itself a gesture that obscures and mystifies history. The original Chinese term Mo Yan uses for "lunar calendar" in the novel is *guli* (古历) [literally "ancient calendar"] instead of *nongli* (农历) [literally "farmers' calendar"]; the latter is a more common word for "lunar calendar" in China. The character *gu* (古) [ancient], which indicates that the world being narrated is a past temporal moment distanced from yet connected with the modern time of 1939, further complicates and thus mystifies history.

The memories of dates have been dominated by the orthodox political discourse on the mainland for many years. For instance, years such as 1921, 1927, 1949, 1957, 1958, and 1966 as well as dates like July 1, August 1, and October 1 all carry special meanings in the collective memory. The Chinese Communist Party was established on July 1, 1921; the People's Liberation Army was set up on August 1, 1927; and the People's Republic of China was founded on October 1, 1949. The years 1957 and 1958 witnessed Mao's antirightist campaign (the political framing of thousands of intellectuals and other people) and the nationwide Great Leap Forward movement respectively. The year 1966 marked the beginning of the ten-year disaster of the Cultural Revolution. Although this association of weighted meaning with specific dates is by no means an invention of the government that came to power after 1949 (Chinese historians had tended to chronologize history for thousands of years), the reader of modern Chinese literature has become particularly sensitive to important dates in recent history due to the process of successful conditioning. As a result, dates in revolutionary literature have a mission to carry history forward in a progressive manner.

By beginning his novel with a date that is apparently clear but that upon closer examination becomes highly complex and ambiguous, Mo Yan creates a context of alienation for the reader. The date has been turned into an empty signifier by its ambiguity. This strategy is at once a continuation and a modification of Lu Xun's practice of relegating history to the trash heap and even canceling it out entirely. In Lu Xun's "Kuangren riji" (狂人日记) [A madman's diary], the madman sees the words *chi ren* (吃人) [eating people] "between the lines" (字缝里) of a history that "*has no chronology* and scrawled all over each page are the words 'Confucian Virtue and Morality'" (这历史没有年代，歪歪斜斜

的每叶上都写着"仁义道德"几个字。).[34] Time is of no significance to this madman because for him all the thousands of years of Chinese history can be summed up in these two characters. In other words, for him the only "truth" resides in the phrase "eating people." Mo Yan, rather than totally ignoring time, actually parodies history. Lunar or solar, the date he uses to begin his novel is noted in terms of actual calendrical time, and the setting he chooses for his story is also historically accurate: the Japanese invasion of China and the resistance of the Chinese people during the Second World War are all historical realities. However, "while events did occur in the real empirical past, we name and constitute those events as historical facts by selection and narrative positioning."[35] The historical fact for Mo Yan in this case is the ambush carried out by the narrator's father, who was at the time a teenager and "a bandit's offspring" (土匪种),[36] and by the narrator's grandfather, who is a bandit, a murderer, and an adulterer.

Mo Yan's writing of the common people's history stands in direct contrast to the norm upheld by the writings of Mao Zedong's time. In 1945 Mao claimed: "The people, and the people alone, are the motive force in the making of world history" (人民，只有人民，才是创造世界历史的动力。).[37] After they assumed power in 1949, however, the Communists seemed to propagate the idea that history is created and pushed forward not by ordinary people but by great men who are the only force capable of bringing order to chaos and saving humankind. This great force, not surprisingly, comprised Mao and the Communist Party in which he was the central figure. As a result, the revolutionary canon, including historical fiction—beginning in 1949 and continuing until the new historical fiction emerged in the 1980s—served to glorify the party's past by highlighting the hardships they had overcome in order to establish the People's Republic, to endorse the socialist present by pointing out the need for continual revolution, and to interpret the Communist future by drawing a rosy picture in which everything and everyone would be perfect. The heroes and heroines, then, are exclusively Communists who lead the Chinese people to fight against evil forces such as the Japanese as well as the *Kuomintang* (KMT) or *Guomindang* (国民党) [Nationalist

Party of China]—the opponent of the Communists. In revolutionary fiction, Mao and his Communist Party are the sole force that battles the enemy while ordinary people are only inspired and educated by them to save China. The opposition members are considered betrayers or cowards who cause difficulties and demand sacrifices. In the end, however, these enemies will be punished, and the force of justice (i.e., the Communist camp) will always prevail. For Mo Yan, however, even a nonentity without any pretentious dogma can be a hero in history. In fact, *The Red Sorghum Family* turns the anti-Japanese war, a frequently recurring motif in revolutionary historical novels, into a family saga in which the hero and heroine are the family's outlaw ancestors who by no means fit the traditional revolutionary standards. At the same time, both the Communist and the KMT troops are ironically described as unfriendly at best and cowardly at worst. In this way, the novel centralizes/maximizes the common people and marginalizes/minimizes the political forces in terms of the grand historical framework, thus reversing completely the Maoist discourse of the three preceding decades.

The Red Sorghum Family falls into the category of historiographic metafiction, for it self-consciously draws attention (1) to its own blurring of the boundary between history and fiction, (2) to its rendering reality incomprehensible, (3) to the fact that its language is an arbitrarily codifying system, and (4) to its unfaithfulness to history. Starting his novel with an empty signifier is one of Mo Yan's narrative strategies, a trope that sets a metafictional tone for the whole novel. Moreover, its structure challenges the progressive mentality of historical fiction. The novel's time frame ranges from 1923 to 1976; the opening scene takes place in 1939, and the story line is sometimes difficult to follow as it jumps casually from the past to the present or as it moves back and forth between the near past and the remote past. These shifts are more than flashbacks: they constitute a representation of the arbitrariness of history.

Similarly, the use of an omnipresent and mysterious first-person narrator in this novel exposes an eccentric attitude toward history. Traditionally and logically, a first-person narrator should have limited knowledge concerning what has happened or is happening. In other words, a first-person narrator should not be omniscient. The I-narrator in *The Red Sorghum Family*, however, knows virtually everything about his grand-parents and parents. This makes his reliability as a narrator question-able; an unreliable narrator is characteristic of a metafictional novel. Furthermore, this narration serves to link together the disjointed, imagi-nary family history. More precisely, the narrator's omnipresent eyes look through the temporal and spatial distances and sew up fragments of his-tory. This ambiguous I-narrator knows every detail of his family history; his knowledge even surpasses that of his own father:

> [Father] never knew how many sexual comedies my grandma had performed on this dirt path, but I knew. And he never knew that her naked body, pure as glossy white jade, had lain on the black soil beneath the shadows of sorghum stalks, but I knew. (Mo Yan, *The Red Sorghum Family*, trans. Howard Goldblatt, 6)
>
> 父亲不知道我的奶奶在这条土路上主演过多少风流喜剧，我知道。父亲也不知道在高粱阴影遮掩着的黑土上，曾经躺过奶奶洁白如玉的光滑肉体，我也知道。
>
> (Mo Yan, *The Red Sorghum Family*, 5)

Amazingly, the narrator also knows that "[a] steel pellet once lodged between two of [grandma's] back teeth when she was eating wild rabbit, and no amount of prying could dislodge it" (奶奶的后槽牙缝里，夹着一粒高粱米粒大的铁砂子，那是吃野兔肉时塞进去的，怎么抠也抠不出来)[38] and that "scattered sorghum dances on Grandma's face, one grain landing between her slightly parted lips to rest on flawless white teeth" (飞散的高粱米在奶奶脸上弹跳着，有一粒竟蹦到她微微翕开的双唇间，搁在她清白的牙齿上。).[39] These passages illustrate that this ageless "I" is everywhere, intruding upon and manipulating the representation of history: "Father was too young then to describe the sight in such flowery terms—that's my doing" (我父亲那时还小，想不到这些花言巧语，这是我想的。).[40] Although the narrator seems to magically know many things he should not know, at the same time he appears ignorant of some things he logically should know. For instance, after describing briefly how his father and grandfather set out for an ambush, the narrator says:

> That was how Father rushed toward the uncarved granite marker that would rise above his grave in the bright-red sorghum fields of his hometown. A bare-assed little boy once led a white billy goat up to the wee-covered grave, and as it grazed in unhurried contentment, the boy pissed furiously on the grave and sang out: "The sorghum is red—the Japanese are coming—compatriots, get ready—fire your rifles and cannons—"
> Someone said that the little goatherd was me, but I don't know. (Mo Yan, *The Red Sorghum Family*, trans. Howard Goldblatt, 3–4)

> 父亲就这样奔向了耸立在故乡通红的高粱地里属于他的那块无字的青石墓碑。他的坟头上已经枯草瑟瑟，曾经有一个光屁股的男孩牵着一只雪白的山羊来到这里，山羊不紧不忙地啃着坟头上的草，男孩子站在墓碑上，怒气冲冲地撒上一泡尿，然后放声歌唱：高粱红了——日本来了——同胞们准备好——开枪开炮——
> 有人说这个放羊的男孩就是我，我不知道是不是我。
> (Mo Yan, *The Red Sorghum Family*, 2)

For this reason, Howard Y. F. Choy (蔡元丰) asserts that "in Mo Yan's anachronistic historiography, history is less 'knowable' than sensible."[41] By displaying his uncertain identity and obscuring his ability of knowing, the narrator symbolizes a minimization of history that has played a key role in the party's political education in Communist China.

Another characteristic of the novel is Mo Yan's representation of history through a subversion of the binary opposition commonly found in revolutionary fiction. The recording of the family history begins with the blurring of the boundaries between past and present, between living and dead, and between good and bad. According to Mo Yan, Northeast Gaomi Township is a locale with paradoxical features because it "is easily the most beautiful and most repulsive, most unusual and most common, most sacred and most corrupt, most heroic and most bastardly, hardest-drinking and hardest-loving place in the world" ([高密东北乡] 无疑

是地球上最美丽最丑陋、最超脱最世俗、最圣洁最龌龊、最英雄好汉最王八蛋、最能喝酒最能爱的地方。).[42] Against the backdrop of this enigmatic land, Mo Yan fabricates a father image—Granddad—with conflicting attributes: he is at once a laborer, a murderer, an adulterer, a bandit, and a national hero fighting against the Japanese invaders.

Granddad Yu Zhan'ao (余占鳌) is an unusual man with an unrestrained temperament. At the age of sixteen, he kills the monk who has had an affair with Yu's widowed mother and escapes from his hometown to become a sedan bearer. When the bearers transport a bride (the narrator's grandmother) on her wedding day, Yu kills a robber who demanded money from the sedan bearers and who has attempted to kidnap and rape the bride. Three days later, he deflowers Grandma and kills her legal husband and father-in-law. Yu later lives openly with this woman who is not his wife. He also later kills the bandit who had attempted to rape Grandma. At one point, Granddad urinates into a wine crock, an act of rebellion which (unintentionally and ironically) results in a wine of especially good quality. Later he recruits troops and becomes the celebrated Commander Yu, who is in fact a bandit chieftain. He leads his poorly armed troops to fight against the Japanese without submitting himself to either the Communist- or nationalist-led forces. In his words, "Who's a bandit? Who isn't a bandit? Anyone who fights the Japanese is a national hero" ("谁是土匪？谁不是土匪？能打日本就是中国的大英雄。").[43]

The image of such a character provides a completely new reading experience for Chinese readers. Before and during the Cultural Revolution, communist fictional characters were always stereotypically and unambiguously good or bad. Chinese readers, therefore, were accustomed to revolutionary heroes who were depicted as flat, stylistic characters rather than as realistic, complex human beings. In other words, the heroes in revolutionary literature are deprived of all human needs and desires that might be regarded as vulgar, and the characters' lives serve only to fulfill the goals required by this kind of fiction—goals such as presenting moral examples. It is never difficult for the reader to distinguish a "bad" character from a "good" one: a bad character is always a completely evil, villainous person with no redeeming feature whatsoever. Mo Yan's image of Granddad was nothing short of iconoclastic in China in the 1980s precisely because this character blurs and even erases these moral boundaries. Interestingly, the paradoxical characteristics of good and evil found in the Granddad character actually enhance this figure's charisma.

The portrait of Grandma, too, is unconventional to a large extent. No less complicated than Granddad, she is a woman defiant of traditional moral values, one who is determined to decide her own fate. The most beautiful girl in the village, she is selected at the age of sixteen by the wealthiest resident to marry his son, who is a leper. When she learns that her parents have married her to a leper in exchange for a mule, Grandma revolts by committing adultery with Granddad, who later kills both the leper and his father. She takes over her leper husband's family brewery, managing a very successful business with the help of Uncle Arhat, who has worked for the brewery all his life (and is later believed to have had an affair with the young Grandma). She encourages Granddad and Father to ambush the Japanese so as to avenge Uncle Arhat, who is skinned alive by the invaders. On the day of the ambush, she carries lunch to the ambuscade and is killed by Japanese gunfire. Her interior monologue—or her self-justification—in her final moments is the best summary of her short life:

> Have I sinned? Would it have been right to share my pillow with a leper and produce a misshapen, putrid monster to contaminate this beautiful world? What is chastity then? What is the correct path? What is goodness? What is evil? You never told me, so I had to decide on my own. I loved happiness, I loved strength, I loved beauty, it was my body, and I used it as I thought fitting. Sin doesn't frighten me, nor does punishment. I'm not afraid of your eighteen levels of hell. I did what I had to do, I managed as I thought proper. I fear nothing. (Mo Yan, *The Red Sorghum Family*, trans. Howard Goldblatt, 72)

> 天，你认为我有罪吗？你认为我跟一个麻风病人同枕交颈，生出一窝癞皮烂肉的魔鬼，使这个美丽的世界污秽不堪是对还是错？天，什么叫贞节？什么叫正道？什么是善良？什么是邪恶？你一直没有告诉过我，我只有按着我自己的想法去

办，我爱幸福，我爱力量，我爱美，我的身体是我的，我为自己做主，我不怕罪，不怕罚，我不怕进你的十八层地域。我该做的都做了，该干的都干了，我什么都不怕。

(Mo Yan, *The Red Sorghum Family*, 91)

The first-person narrator's judgment of Grandma's non-traditional views is positive:

> In some significant aspects, heroes are born, not made. Heroic qualities flow through a person's veins like an undercurrent, ready to be translated into action. During her first sixteen years, Grandma's days had been devoted to embroidery, needlework, paper cutouts, foot binding, the endless glossing of her hair, and all other manner of domestic things in the company of neighbor girls. What, then, was the source of her ability and courage to deal with the events she encountered in her adult years? How was she able to temper herself to the point where even in the face of danger she could conquer her fears and force herself to act heroically? I'm not sure I know. (Mo Yan, *The Red Sorghum Family*, trans. Howard Goldblatt, 89)

> 在某种意义上，英雄是天生的，英雄气质是一股潜在的暗流，遇到外界的诱因，便转化为英雄的行为。我奶奶当时年仅一十六岁，从小刺花绣草，精研女红，绣花的尖针，铰花的剪刀，裹脚的长布，梳头的桂花油，等等女孩儿的玩艺伴她度日过年。她接触的也不过是东邻姐姐，西邻妹妹，何以生成了后来她处理重大变故的能力和胆魄？何以锻炼出她临危虽惧，但终能咬牙挺住的英雄性格？这都是难以说清的事。 (Mo Yan, *The Red Sorghum Family*, 110)

And again:

> Only Grandma would have had the audacity to place a plum tree on the back of a deer. Whenever I see one of Grandma's cutouts, my admiration for her surges anew. If she could have become a writer, she would have put many of her literary peers to shame. She was endowed with the golden lips and jade teeth of genius. She said a katydid perched on top of its cage, and that's what it did; she said a plum tree grew from the back of a deer, and that's

where it grew.   (Mo Yan, *The Red Sorghum Family*, trans. Howard Goldblatt, 132)

> 只有［奶奶］才敢把梅花树栽到鹿背上。每当我看到奶奶的剪纸时，敬佩之意就油然而生。我奶奶要是搞了文学这一行，会把一大群文学家踩出屎来。她就是造物主，她就是金口玉牙，她说蝈蝈出笼蝈蝈就出笼，她说鹿背上长树鹿背上就长树。   (Mo Yan, *The Red Sorghum Family*, 166)

Finally:

> I believe she could have done anything she desired, for she was a hero of the resistance, a trailblazer for liberation of the self, a model of women's independence. (Mo Yan, *The Red Sorghum Family*, trans. Howard Goldblatt, 14)

> 我深信，我奶奶什么事都敢干，只要她愿意。她老人家不仅仅是抗日的英雄，也是个性解放的先驱，妇女自立的典范。
> (Mo Yan, *The Red Sorghum Family*, 14)[44]

The narrator's admiration for his grandparents discloses the fact that Mo Yan does not see a progressive development in history; rather, he adopts a regressive point of view. Although the narrator is proud of his forebears, he senses a degeneration of humankind:

> The people of my father's generation ... killed, ... looted, and ... defended their country in a valiant, stirring ballet that makes us unfilial descendants who now occupy the land pale by comparison. Surrounded by progress, I feel a nagging sense of our species' regression. (Mo Yan, *The Red Sorghum Family*, trans. Howard Goldblatt, 4)

> 我的父老乡亲们......杀人越货，精忠报国，他们演出过一幕幕英勇悲壮的舞剧，使我们这些活着的不肖子孙相形见绌，在进步的同时，我真切感到种的退化。
> (Mo Yan, *The Red Sorghum Family*, 2)

Here "progress" is a bitingly sarcastic reference to the "civilized" modern society in which the narrator exists. After ten years away from his hometown, the narrator returns to collect materials for a writing project—his family history. The more he learns about his grandparents, the more he is ashamed of himself and the more he is aware of the hypocrisy of his own generation. He realizes that he is a man "affecting the hypocritical display of affection I had learned from high society, with a body immersed so long in the filth of urban life that a foul stench oozed from my pores" (带着机智的上流社会传染给我的虚情假意，带着被肮脏的都市生活臭水泡得每个毛孔都散发着扑鼻恶臭的肉体).[45] The narrator cannot help but compare his generation with the people of his grandparents' time, and the result is the firm belief that he and his contemporaries are somehow degenerate and inferior: "The young men of [Granddad's] generation were as sturdy as Northeast Gaomi sorghum, which is more than can be said about us weaklings who succeeded them" (我爷爷辈的好汉们，都有高密东北乡人高粱般鲜明的性格，非我们这些孱弱的后辈能比).[46] "Grandma, compared with you, I am like a shriveled insect that has gone hungry for three long years" (奶奶，你孙子跟你相比，显得像个饿了三年的白虱子一样干瘪。).[47]

The degeneration characteristic of modern people is symbolized by the decline of the sorghum. The pure red sorghum of earlier days is a metaphor for the spontaneity and strength of the characters; when the narrator returns to his hometown, he can no longer see any red sorghum. Instead, what is waiting for him is hybrid sorghum, which he loathes:

> Hybrid sorghum never seems to ripen. Its gray-green eyes seem never to be fully opened. I ... look out at those ugly bastards that occupy the domain of the red sorghum. They assume the name of sorghum, but are bereft of tall, straight stalks; they assume the name of sorghum, but are devoid of the dazzling sorghum color. Lacking the soul and bearing of sorghum, they pollute the pure air of Northeast Gaomi Township with their dark, gloomy, ambiguous faces. (Mo Yan, *The Red Sorghum Family*, trans. Howard Goldblatt, 358)

杂种高粱好像永远都不会成熟。它永远半闭着那些灰绿色的
眼睛。我……看着这些丑陋的杂种，七长八短地占据了红
高粱的地盘。它们空有高粱的名称，但没有高粱挺拔的高
杆；它们空有高粱的名称，但没有高粱辉煌的颜色。它们真
正缺少的，是高粱的灵魂和风度。它们用它们晦暗不清、模
棱两可的狭长脸庞污染着高密东北乡纯净的空气。

(Mo Yan, *The Red Sorghum Family*, 495)

As a matter of fact, both the color red and sorghum as a potent symbol contribute greatly to the narrative power of the novel. On the one hand, the sorghum plant signifies human life: Granddad and Grandma challenge traditional values by means of an illicit sexual act in the sorghum field, where Grandma conceives the narrator's father. Likewise, when the Japanese soldiers massacre the villagers, their horses tread on the sorghum crops; human death is echoed in the destruction of the plant. On the other hand, the color red represents both wine and blood and thus is a symbol of vitality and masculine power—a symbol closely associated with the theme of violence throughout the book, as the following episode shows.

The Japanese soldiers open a cut on Uncle Arhat's bald head because he has refused to take Grandma's mules to the construction site and work for the Japanese invaders. Grandma, to avoid being raped by the Japanese, smears Arhat's blood on her own face, pretending to be insane. After the deceased Uncle Arhat has been taken away with the two mules, Grandma washes her bloody face in a wine vat. Later, when Granddad and the Nationalist Detachment Leader Leng (冷) are planning the ambush, Grandma fills cups with the wine and says, "Uncle Arhat's blood is in this wine … If you're honorable men you'll drink it, then go out and destroy the Jap convoy" (这酒里有罗汉大叔的血，是男人就喝了，后日一起把鬼子汽车打了).[48]

Drinking wine mixed with a rooster's blood is traditional ritual behavior among members of secret societies on certain important occasions. It is interesting that the fowl must be male, suggestive of a borrowing of the bird's masculine vigor. This ritual is echoed in the novel, but here, the blood mingled with sorghum wine is from a *human* male body. If the issue of cannibalism is set aside, this act of drinking wine mixed with blood not only enhances human energy (just as the rooster's blood does) but also represents an internalization of the victim's spirit—a connection between the living and the dead which generates courage within the living for the task of revenge.

The color red is an important code in Mo Yan's writings—his fiction features red sorghum, a red radish, the red moon, red locusts, and a red dog, among other red items: a symbolism that at once creates a special visual effect and conveys a strong narrative message. More importantly, Mo Yan is subverting the Communist narrative by rewriting the meaning of the color red, demystifying the sacramentalized color of the revolutionary period. In traditional Chinese culture, red is a lucky color and is thus the color used for major celebrations, such as the new year and weddings. The Communist Party then harnessed this color of positive significance and used it to symbolize courage, hope, and the blood of revolutionary martyrs.[49] Red is not the only color Mo Yan uses for effect, however. In his newer novel, *Life and Death Are Wearing Me Out*, the color blue replaces red as the dominant color of the book, creating a peculiar artistic effect with respect to the protagonist. The color red (along with other colors) is discussed more fully later in this book, but at this point it is worth noting that Mo Yan's use of colors is characteristic of his unique interpretations of the material world and of his artistically bold narrative strategies. For instance, the reader encounters a red dog, a green dog, and a blue dog in *The Red Sorghum Family*; and the blood that gushes from Grandma's body is both red and green. In short, Mo Yan uses color in an unconventional and unrealistic way in order to enrich the subjective feelings of his characters.

Mo Yan's notion of the degeneration of humankind in a rapidly developing environment not only challenges the progressive conception of history since the turn of the twentieth century but also subverts the historical materialism of Communist ideology. In this respect, Mo Yan is unique among his contemporaries. Since the mid-1980s, history has become a topic of interest for writers, including Su Tong (苏童), Ge Fei (格非), Ye Zhaoyan (叶兆言), and Li Rui (李锐), to mention just a few. They examine history from different perspectives, but they all attempt to break away from the cliché of revolutionary historical fiction. Mo Yan, however, is the only author who self-consciously questions the fundamentals of a linear and progressive understanding of history; he casts doubt, likewise, on the Maoist conception of a grand history that is driven by a pivotal force with a supreme figure at its center.

Brimming with nostalgia and a deep veneration of the ancestors as well as of the history they have created, *The Red Sorghum Family* is a bold challenge to Communist propaganda. One critic believes that the promotion of heroism—a Communist ideal—in *The Red Sorghum Family* disqualifies the novel from categorization as an alternative to official history. On the contrary, this critic contends the work is committed to and entangles itself in Maoist discourse.[50] I would argue, however, that heroism is in no way an innovation of the Communists, who actually borrow the notion from the past; heroism has been a tradition for major historical works such as *Romance of the Three Kingdoms* written in the fourteenth century. What makes Mo Yan's novel subversive is the fact that its hero is from the bottom of the social and political hierarchy, whereas in the revolutionary historical fiction of the Mao era, heroes are leaders held up as examples. Ironically, Mo Yan's writing is a better illustration of ordinary people as the force of history than the revolutionary literature centered on Mao's lofty-but-never-realized slogan.

Nevertheless, Mo Yan's creation of a fatherland replete with masculine power and beauty is, to a certain extent, coincident with the Maoist patriarchy. Gender hierarchy pervades the book and the father figure is dominant throughout the novel; even Douguan (豆官), the narrator's father, is a hardened little person at the age of fourteen. Masculinity in this novel is highly concentrated and is embodied in Douguan's wounded male organ. After the ambush, the Japanese launch a reprisal raid that results in the deaths of nearly all the villagers. After eating human corpses, the village dogs begin attacking those still alive, and Douguan is bitten in his genitals, "leaving an elliptical testicle the size of a quail's egg hanging by a thin, nearly transparent thread. When Granddad moved him, the little red thing dropped into the crotch of his pants" (使一个椭圆形的、鹌鹑蛋大小的卵子掉了出来，仅有的一条白色的细线与原先的组织联络着，爷爷一动，那暗红色的小玩艺儿就掉在父亲裤裆里了。).[51] It is a deadly blow to Granddad:

> Granddad cupped it in the palm of his hand. It seemed to weigh a thousand pounds, the way he was bent over. His large, rough hand shook as though the thing were burning a hole in it.
>
>   …
>
> "It's all over…. Everything ended in that instant…." Granddad mumbled in a voice that quavered like an old, old man's.
>
> (Mo Yan, *The Red Sorghum Family*, trans. Howard Goldblatt, 221)

> 爷爷捡起它来，放在手心里托着。这小东西好像有千斤重，把爷爷腰都坠弯了。爷爷那只粗糙的大手好像被它烫得直发颤抖。
>
>   ……
>
> "完啦……这一下真完了……" 爷爷用与他的年龄相差甚远的苍老声音念叨着。
>
> (Mo Yan, *The Red Sorghum Family*, 288)

Granddad takes Douguan to a doctor and forces the man to sew the testicle back for the boy, as he does not want to "bring the Yu line to an end" (断了我姓余的后代).[52] Explaining to Granddad that it is impossible to connect blood vessels, the doctor tries to console him by saying that the one remaining testicle might function. Granddad is so worried about his son's virility that he says, "[Douguan] might as well be dead if that thing's useless" (要是那个不中用了，保住条命又有什么用。).[53] Qianer (倩儿) [Beauty], Douguan's playmate who later becomes his wife, is told by a woman in the village to play with his penis in order to check its functionality. At this point, it is worth scrutinizing Mo Yan's detailed description of the boy's healed organ as well as Granddad's reaction to the scene:

> In the light streaming into the room she looked at his injured, grotesque penis. The head, wild and proud, had an air of defiance. Timidly she held it in her sweaty hand and felt it gradually get warmer and thicker. It began to throb, just like her heart.
>
>   …

Granddad rushed into the shack, then rushed out again like a man crazed ... "Single-stalk garlic is the hottest!" he said almost incoherently. "Single-stalk garlic *is* the hottest!"

Granddad fired three shots in the air, then brought his hands together in front of his chest and screamed: "Heaven has eyes!" (Mo Yan, *The Red Sorghum Family*, trans. Howard Goldblatt, 226–227)

在明亮的光线下，母亲看到父亲的鸡子因为受伤变得丑陋不堪，鸡头上带着生死不怕、疯疯癫癫的野蛮表情。她小心翼翼地用汗津津的手握住它，感到它渐渐热起来，渐渐在她手心里膨胀起来，并像心跳一样在她手里跳动着。

......

爷爷钻进窝棚。

爷爷像发疯一样跑出窝棚，......语无伦次地说着："是独头蒜！是独头蒜！"

爷爷对着天空，连放三枪，然后双手合什，大声喊叫："苍天有眼！" (Mo Yan, *The Red Sorghum Family*, 295–296)

This attitude reflects the importance of the male duty to carry on the family line, and the episode also reveals the author's own tendency toward phallocentrism in his work. To Granddad, his son's life would be void of meaning if the boy had been castrated. Moreover, at the end of the story, the narrator's ancestors tell him to look for the only stalk of pure red sorghum at any price, for it is his talisman as well as their "family's glorious totem and a symbol of the heroic spirit of Northeast Gaomi Township" (我们家族的光荣的图腾和我们高密东北乡传统精神的象征).[54] The upright pure red sorghum, a phallic image, also contributes to the phallocentric tendency of the book. Even the female protagonist, Grandma, is masculinized and her grandson, the narrator, endorses her with the phrase "a hero among women" (*nüzhong haojie*, 女中豪杰),[55] a designation which implies that she is a man-like woman whose pursuit of freedom is rare among women.

In spite of Grandma's independent personality, she is in other ways a traditional woman who longs for "a good husband, handsome and well educated, a man who would treat her gently..." (一个识字解文、眉清

目秀、知冷知热的好女婿).[56] She also yearns to "lose her anxieties and loneliness in the arms of a strong and noble young man" (躺在一个伟岸的男子怀抱里缓解焦虑消除孤寂).[57] Obviously, her ability to control her own fate is limited, but she does manage to choose a man for herself; her emancipation is by and large fulfilled through illegitimate intercourse with Granddad in the sorghum field. Prior to that encounter, she is determined to defend her chastity after marrying the leper, and she successfully does so on the first two nights, armed with a pair of sharp scissors. According to tradition, a bride visits her paternal home on the third day of her marriage; on her way back there, Grandma is abducted by one of the young sedan bearers—Granddad—and taken to the sorghum field, where after a brief struggle, she makes a present of her chastity to him. Noticeably, Grandma does not initially offer herself to the man; it is Granddad who forces himself upon her. She tries to resist until she recognizes him as the sedan-chair carrier—then she gives in and even submits to him because she had been impressed by his fearless efforts to save her from the bandit a few days earlier. This episode is further evidence of the phallocentrism of the novel inasmuch as even Grandma's choice to resist her legal husband is trumped by what at least begins as an attempted rape by another man. Consequently, Grandma's brilliance and uniqueness serve only as a foil to set off the heroic image of Granddad. In other words, her independence, if any, is limited and subject to the standards set by masculine power.

Moreover, Grandma's voice is silenced, for she is deprived of life at the age of thirty, and the writing of her family history is carried on by her husband, her son, and her grandson. Ironically, this "hero among women" becomes a victim of men—her husband, her son, and the Japanese soldiers. Without being aware of it, Grandma's husband and son actually cause her death by exposing her to Japanese gunfire in the ambush. It is Granddad who has had her bring lunch to the ambuscade: Yu Zhan'ao tells Douguan, "Go tell your mom to have the women make some fistcakes, and tell her I want lunch here by noon. Say *I want her to bring it herself*" ("回家告诉你娘，让她找人擀抹饼，正晌午时，一定送到，让你娘

亲自来送。").[58] When lunchtime arrives, Douguan, her son, cries out at the sight of her and makes her the first victim in the battle:

> Father was the first to see her. While the others were following the slow progress of the trucks with unblinking eyes, some secret force told him to look to the west, where he spotted her floating toward them like a gorgeous red butterfly. "Mom—"
> His shout was like a command: a hail of bullets tore through the air from three machine guns mounted on the Japanese trucks. The sound was dull and muted, like the gloomy barking of dogs on a rainy night. Father watched as two shells opened holes in the breast of Grandma's jacket. She cried out in ecstasy, then crumpled to the ground, her carrying pole falling across her back. (Mo Yan, *The Red Sorghum Family*, trans. Howard Goldblatt, 63–64)

> 还是我的父亲最先发现我的奶奶，父亲靠着某种神秘力量的启示，在大家都目不转睛地盯着缓缓逼近的汽车时，他往西一歪头，看到奶奶像鲜红的大蝴蝶一样款款地飞过来。父亲高叫一声:"娘——"
> 父亲的叫声，像下达了一道命令，从日本人的汽车上，射出了一阵密集的子弹。日本人的三顶歪把子机枪架在汽车顶上。枪声沉闷，像雨夜中阴沉的狗叫。父亲眼见着我奶奶胸膛上的衣服啪啪裂开两个洞。奶奶欢快地叫了一声，就一头栽倒，扁担落地，压在她的背上。
> (Mo Yan, *The Red Sorghum Family*, 80)

At this point, Mo Yan's Grandma is reminiscent of Lu Xun's Zijun (子君) in his "Shangshi" (伤逝) [Regret for the past]. Written in 1925, Lu Xun's short story is about a young woman's tragedy after she moves in with a man. A somewhat educated woman who has been influenced by the "new culture," the enlightened Zijun declares, "I'm my own mistress. None of them has any right to interfere with me!" ("我是我自己的，他们谁也没有干涉我的权利!").[59] Accordingly, she is bold enough to ignore both strong objections from her family and severe discrimination by society. But after just a few months of cohabitation, the man is overwhelmed by the anxieties of everyday life and tells Zijun that he does not love her anymore. Zijun has no way out but to leave him, and she eventually dies in sadness and desperation. The two women, Grandma and Zijun, manifest marked similarities. For example, Grandma asserts that "it was my body, and I used it as I thought fitting," and Zijun claims that she is her own mistress. As a woman dwelling in a rural area, Grandma enjoys more sexual freedom than the May Fourth city woman Zijun (as previously mentioned, her grandson is able to relate the "sexual comedies [she] had performed on this dirt path"[60]); nevertheless, Grandma ultimately shares the fate of dying for the sake of a man with her May Fourth sister Zijun, who is victimized by history.

In short, in spite of its daring experiments and innovations, *The Red Sorghum Family* is a work that arguably upholds traditionally androcentric social structures.

BIG BREASTS AND WIDE HIPS—
A MATRIARCHAL MOTHERLAND

A reader accustomed to the solemn historical aura framed in the masculine kingdom of *The Red Sorghum Family* will be surprised not only by the much more overtly cynical attitude toward history in *Big Breasts and Wide Hips* (published almost ten years later than *The Red Sorghum Family*) but also by a tendency toward philogyny (i.e., adoring or worshiping women) in this lengthy work of over five hundred thousand words. In this novel, Mo Yan continues the experiment begun in his earlier work, blurring the boundary between good and evil even further in this later representation of history. To be precise, the author directly questions the self-appointed hero type of the Communist Party in the Maoist legacy.

Big Breasts and Wide Hips, like *The Red Sorghum Family*, is the story of a peasant family—the Shangguan (上官) family—that covers a longer time span than the earlier work. This novel is set in history from the year 1900 up to the post-Mao period, and its characters live through two foreign forays into China: the German construction of the Jiaoji (胶济) railway in Shandong Province at the turn of the twentieth century and the Japanese invasion during the Second World War. The Shangguan family, which according to the story, is from Mo Yan's hometown, dominantly features one important female image: Mother. This mother, with her full breasts and big hips, overshadows all of the male characters in the book and transforms Northeast Gaomi Township into a motherland (as opposed to a fatherland). Moreover, the other female figures in the story all exhibit strong personalities. Almost all of the men, traditionally considered the driving force of history in a male-oriented society like China's, are playfully mocked by the author.

The first chapter of the novel is about childbirth, where a paradoxical sequence of events unfolds—it is Mother's eighth delivery, and at the same time, the Shangguan family's donkey is also in labor. Because Mother has already given birth to seven daughters, she is eagerly awaiting a son. Her mother-in-law is no less anxious for a grandson, yet pays more attention to their donkey. The birthing scenes of both the donkey and the woman are juxtaposed with brutal killings by Japanese soldiers, who attempt to attack the village but are turned away by a guerrilla band led by characters named Sha Yueliang (沙月亮) and Sima Ku (司马库). Sha and Sima, who happen to belong to opposing political camps; both become Mother's sons-in-law later in the story. Finally a pair of twins is born, a girl and a boy, but the midwife, who is killed by the Japanese out in the yard soon after aiding in the births, has declared both babies dead. A Japanese doctor saves the babies and treats Mother, however, while a war correspondent takes pictures of the scene to be published in Japanese newspapers for propaganda purposes.

Once again Mo Yan dates this event with a mixture of Western and Chinese lunar calendar dates: "On the morning of the fifth day of the fifth lunar month, 1939…" (一九三九年古历五月初五日上午).[61] A formula that here, as in *The Red Sorghum Family*, mystifies history, this mixture is only one of the author's hybridizations in this novel. The twin babies further this hybrid theme because of their mixed racial parentage (their biological father is a Swedish pastor who has lived in Northeast Gaomi Township for several decades), as does the newborn mule (being the offspring of a horse and a donkey), and the amalgamation of birth and death denotes a history written in blood. All of these hybridizations mock the established conception of a pure and solemn history.

Like Grandma in *The Red Sorghum Family*, Mother in this novel is forced to be disrespectful of the traditional values imposed upon women. Mother's biographical information is narrated as a flashback at the end of the novel. In 1900 when the German soldiers had committed a massacre in her village, she was only six months old; her parents died in the massacre, but she was saved by an aunt and uncle who raised her as if she were their own daughter. Her aunt bound the girl's feet at the age of five. She survived the pain, and "her small and exquisite lotus feet were the number one treasures of Northeast Gaomi Township" (她的小脚......小巧玲珑，是高密东北乡第一宝物).[62] Naturally, she also became the most beautiful girl in the village, as a pair of "three-inch golden lotuses" (三寸金莲) was the most important standard of beauty at that time. Three years after marrying into the Shangguan family, however, the young woman was still unable to bear children. A woman's ultimate function in traditional Chinese society was to bear her husband children, especially sons, in order to carry on the family line. Because she could not become pregnant—in fact, her husband was sterile—Mother was abused by him as well as by his mother. Consequently, she had no alternative but to sleep with other men secretly in a "search for a better donor" (寻觅个好男人借种).[63]

In an arrangement made by her aunt, the first man Mother slept with was her own uncle, her aunt's husband. Over the years, she slept with five men and gave birth to six daughters; her seventh daughter was the result of a rape by four soldiers. However, the insults and abuse from her husband's family never stopped because none of these seven births produced a son. At last, her eighth pregnancy resulted in the birth of twins: a girl first and then a boy. This family itself represents one of the story's hybrids, as does the son, the only bearer of the family line, who is considered a half-breed because of his mixed racial parentage. By assigning his protagonist such an embarrassing birth, the author derides the traditional value attributed to a pure lineage as well as the dignity of Chineseness. The figure of the son seems to symbolize the idea that only when an ancient tradition absorbs the genes of foreign culture is it possible to obtain the advantage of hybridization and to shake off the tendency of *yinsheng yangshuai* (阴盛阳衰)—that is, "*yin* rising with *yang* declining," or in other words, the imbalance of the female being stronger and more powerful than the male. But the son, Shangguan Jintong (上官金童), does not benefit from this hybridization; instead, his character both embodies and ridicules the weakening and debility of the *yang* force of Chinese male citizens.

As Peter Brooks observed, "getting the body into writing is a primary concern of literature throughout the ages. And conversely, getting writing onto the body is a sign of the attempt to make the material body into a signifying body."[64] The title of the novel, *Big Breasts and Wide Hips*, reveals that Mo Yan is driven by an impulse to incorporate the body into his historiography—to write history on the body and the body into history. Postrevolutionary writers attempted to rediscover national and regional history through an approach to history that diverged from the official historiography, but Mo Yan, after making a similar attempt in his debut novel, *The Red Sorghum Family*, experimented further in *Big Breasts and Wide Hips*. Not only did he abandon the heroic male image and make women the important driving force of history, but he also went so far as to highlight the female body, a controversial move that could make him vulnerable to harsh criticism, given the fact that the body had been strictly taboo in both Confucian and Communist China. Indeed, there were many negative responses to this novel.

Big breasts and wide hips are physical characteristics not only of Mother but also of her daughters. Although the title mentions both body parts, in fact, the central bodily image of the book is that of the breast. The author asserts that the breast symbolizes "love … poetry … the highest realm of heaven and the rich soil under golden waves of wheat" (那是爱、那是诗、那是无限高远的天空和翻滚着金黄色麦浪的丰厚大地).[65] It also represents "tumultuous life, [and] … surging passion" (骚动的生命、......澎湃的激情).[66] Whereas *The Red Sorghum Family* was written with a phallus motif, this novel was written with a breast theme. In *The Red Sorghum Family*, Grandma is shot in her breast. The narrator gives the following description of her death:

> Grandma lies on the ground, the warmth of her breast slowly dissipating. She is dimly aware that her son is undoing her jacket,

that he is covering the wound over her breast with his hand, then the wound beneath her breast. Her blood stains his hand red, then green; her unsullied breast is stained green by her own blood, then red. Bullets have pierced her noble breast, exposing the pink honeycomb beneath it, and Father is in agony as he looks down at it. (Mo Yan, *The Red Sorghum Family*, trans. Howard Goldblatt, 67)

奶奶躺着，胸脯上的灼烧感逐渐减弱。她恍然觉得儿子解开了自己的衣服，儿子用手捂住她乳房上的一个枪眼，又捂住她乳下的一个枪眼。奶奶的血把父亲的手染红了，又染绿了；奶奶洁白的胸脯被自己的血染绿了，又染红了。枪弹射穿了奶奶高贵的乳房，暴露出了淡红色的蜂窝状组织。父亲看着奶奶的乳房，万分痛苦。

(Mo Yan, *The Red Sorghum Family*, 84–85)

The breasts of both women bear historical meanings. Whereas Grandma's breast is disfigured by Japanese bullets and thus transformed into a signifier for the end of an unusual woman's life amidst the national crisis, the breast in *Big Breasts and Wide Hips* not only symbolizes the suffering body of the female protagonist and of the story's other female characters but also represents a feminine force that is vital to history and that, in the novelist's hands, overrides the historically superior masculine power. The breast in *The Red Sorghum Family* is literally a breast, the locus of Grandma's physical demise and a symbol of death; whereas the breast in *Big Breasts and Wide Hips* is literally a means to nurture the next generation and a pervasive symbol of feminine vitality, marking the novelist's own shifting perceptions of history. The breast, a component of the physical body, ceases to be itself and serves at once as the object and agent of writing in the author's representation of history.

When Peter Brooks discusses the earliest experience of the body, for example, the experiences of an infant in relation to its mother's body, he quotes the psychoanalyst Melanie Klein (1882–1960) and states that "for Melanie Klein and her followers, the mother's body, and particularly the breast, provides the original object of symbolization, and then the field of exploration for the child's developing 'epistemophilic impulse,' the urge to know."[67] All of Mother's children and grandchildren, including a boy with no biological connection to Mother but whom she raised (i.e., Sima Liang, 司马粮, the son of Sima Ku and his concubine), begin identifying and learning about the world from this woman. Because she has sons-in-law with different political backgrounds—Sha Yueliang, the commander of a guerrilla band against the Japanese, who turns out to be a "traitor"; Sima Ku, an anti-Japanese hero in the nationalist army, who was executed by the Communists after 1949; and Lu Liren （鲁立人), a Communist officer—Mother's life is heavily imprinted with historical and political complexities. As a result, her breasts, with which she has nursed the children, serve to cancel the boundaries between different political forces. Mother's breasts have the same function as the All-Souls Grave in *The Red Sorghum Family*, where Communists, nationalists, Chinese, Japanese, and even dogs and wolves are buried together and where they are all reduced to white bones after several years, a state of final equality that highlights the absurdity and meaninglessness of political struggle and nationalism.

To Shangguan Jintong—the protagonist, the narrator, and Mother's only son—breasts are a forceful element throughout his life. From infancy, he displays a powerful desire to monopolize his mother's breasts, and this desire develops into a fetishistic obsession that dominates his entire life. Milk is the only food that agrees with him even after he reaches school age. Moreover, he is desirous not only of his own mother's breasts but also of the breasts of his sister and of all other women. The fact that Mo Yan chooses a feminized man (and not one of Mother's eight daughters) as his narrator is arguably the novelist's attempt to ridicule the declining *yang* phenomenon, through which Mo Yan implies that modern China has been metaphorically castrated. Several examples illustrate this point.

When Shangguan Jintong is seven years old, his mother is determined to wean him. He, however, immediately turns to the breasts of his eldest sister, even though she is not lactating.[68] This episode demonstrates the fact that Shangguan Jintong is actually obsessed with the breast *per se* rather than with the milk, although he is disappointed that "she'd had no milk, and her nipple had been covered by a layer of cold, odorific grime; just thinking about that brought feelings of despair" (她的乳房没

有乳汁，乳头上有腥冷的灰垢，想到此我感到极度绝望).[69] To put it another way, by refusing to consume any food except milk, Shangguan Jintong acquires the breast. The following two passages illustrate the protagonist's fetishistic tendency:

> Seeing the Bird Fairy's [his third sister's] coat reminded me of Laidi's [his eldest sister's] coat, which in turn reminded me of Laidi's breasts, and they reminded me of the Bird Fairy's breasts. Among Shangguan women, the Bird Fairy's breasts had to be considered top of the line. They were delicate, lovely, perky, with slightly upturned nipples as nimble as the mouth of a hedgehog. (Mo Yan, *Big Breasts and Wide Hips*, trans. Howard Goldblatt, 200)

> 从鸟仙的袍子我想到上官来弟的袍子，从上官来弟的袍子想到上官来弟的乳房，从上官来弟的乳房又想到鸟仙的乳房。鸟仙的乳房是上官家的乳房系列中的上等品，它们清秀伶俐，有着刺猬嘴巴一样灵巧而微微上翘的乳头。
>
> (Mo Yan, *Big Breasts and Wide Hips*, 181)

> Pandi [his fifth sister] was drenched, her thin clothes sticking to her skin; I was attracted to the sight of her full, high-arching breasts … Datelike nipples quivered under her blouse, and I could barely keep from rushing over to bite and fondle them. I didn't have the nerve. (Mo Yan, *Big Breasts and Wide Hips*, trans. Howard Goldblatt, 211)

> 上官盼弟浑身湿漉漉的，单薄的衣服紧贴在身上，肥大的乳房沉甸甸地下垂着，诱惑着我的眼睛。……她的枣子般的乳头在布衬衣里蠕动着，我多么想扑上去咬咬那奶头、摸摸那乳房啊，但是我不敢……。
>
> (Mo Yan, *Big Breasts and Wide Hips*, 192)

He dares not give in to his desire because his fifth sister has a violent temper and would probably slap his face. However, he is unable to resist the temptation and finally makes up his mind: "Maybe it would be worth it. I went over and hid from view beneath a pear tree, biting my lip and wishing I were braver" (宁愿挨耳光，我也要摸摸你！我躲在梨树下，牙咬着下唇，下定了决心。).[70]

In addition to various fantastic depictions of the breasts, the author provides the reader with several bizarre scenes. The first begins when the child Shangguan Jintong is selected to be the Snow Prince of the annual Snow Market, or Snow Festival, the biggest regional event of the year. It is a ritual in silence, during which no one is supposed to speak a word; otherwise there would be calamity. The last and most important duty of the Snow Prince is to bless the women from his home-town by stroking their breasts, as "the 'Snow Festival' was actually one for women. Snow, like a quilt covering the earth, provides the earth with moisture and vigor. Snow is the water of fertility, the symbol of winter, and the message of spring as well..." ("雪节"其实是女人的节日，雪像被子遮盖大地，让大地滋润，孕育生机，雪是生育之水，是冬天的象征更是春天的信息......).[71] The Snow Prince is expected to bury his hands in a basin of snow, then bless "all women wanting to bear a child in the coming year and those who wanted their milk to fill their young, healthy breasts" (那些祈求来年生子的女人，那些祈求奶水旺盛、乳房健康的女人).[72] Shangguan Jintong, the Snow Prince, and the narrator, describes the ritual:

> As I grasped them, I said a silent prayer of good wishes. One squeeze: May you have pudgy male triplets. Two squeezes: May your milk gush like a fountain. Three squeezes: May your milk be as wonderfully sweet as morning dew. (Mo Yan, *Big Breasts and Wide Hips*, trans. Howard Goldblatt, 330)
>
> 我抓着它们，心里默念着最美好的祝愿。捏一下，祝你一胎生三个胖孩子。捏两下，祝你的奶水像喷泉。捏三下，祝你的奶汁味道甜美。(Mo Yan, *Big Breasts and Wide Hips*, 329)

In a single day, the boy fondles at least one hundred and twenty pairs of breasts, "gaining layer upon layer of feelings and impressions of women's breasts, like turning the pages of a book" (若干的关于乳房的感觉和印象层层叠叠，像一本书，可以一页页翻阅).[73]

A similar episode occurs later in the book. In the 1980s, in hopes of healing the adult Shangguan Jintong's neurosis, Sima Liang, who had shared Mother's breasts with the infant Shangguan Jintong, hires hundreds of women to expose their breasts to Jintong, who is permitted to touch and even suck them.

Like a gynecologist specializing in breasts, Shangguan Jintong was performing breast examinations for the women. He would observe the profiles first, then fondle and fiddle the breasts to check their sensitivity toward stimulation, and feel them to see if there were any lumps. Finally, he placed his nose on the bosom to smell its fragrance, then kissed and sucked it. (My translation)

上官金童像一个妇产科的乳房专家，为女人们做着乳房的常规检查。先大致地观看外形，然后用双手抚摸，撩拨，检查对刺激的敏锐程度，摸摸里边有无包块。最后，把鼻子插在乳沟里闻香，用嘴吻一遍，轮流嘬一下。

(Mo Yan, *Big Breasts and Wide Hips*, 561)

In order to rescue Jintong from the destructive consequences of his obsession, the wealthy Sima Liang invests in a brassiere shop and appoints Jintong as manager: "You're an expert where women's breasts are concerned, so who in the world could possibly be more qualified than you in selling brassieres?" (你是乳房专家，乳房专家卖乳罩，是全世界最合适的人选。).[74]

When Shangguan Jintong's morbidity reaches an extreme, the object of his desire becomes a grotesque form of the breast. He is amazed for the first time by the breast of Duru Lao Jin (独乳老金) [single-breasted Old Jin] during the Snow Festival when she exposes herself to receive the blessing of the Snow Prince. This woman has an abnormal right breast, the origin of her name. Several decades later, after serving a sentence of fifteen years' imprisonment, the forty-two-year-old Shangguan Jintong, now seriously ill, returns to his mother. When he is struggling for existence on the verge of death, the milk—or rather, the breast—of this fifty-year-old, single-breasted woman saves him. This misshapen image of the feminine rejuvenates the body of the adult Snow Prince but simultaneously condemns his diseased mind to a condition that is beyond curing.

It is significant that Jintong's infatuation with breasts has nothing to do with sex; Jintong never becomes sexually mature. The first of the very few sexual encounters in his adult life is his mating with the corpse of Long Qingping (龙青萍), a one-armed old maid at the age of thirty-nine who is the head of a state farm on which Jintong is a laborer. A hardened Communist on the surface, Long yearns for the love of a man, and Jintong becomes her target. On a rainy evening, Long begs Jintong—and even tries to force him—to make love to her, but is refused. In desperation, she shoots herself. Only out of sympathy and a sense of guilt does Jintong have intercourse with her body, which is not yet cold. Jintong pays for this bizarre sexual behavior with a fifteen-year prison sentence. When Mother finally realizes that her son needs to be trained into becoming a real man, she asks for help from single-breasted Old Jin, who seduces Jintong. Although Jintong has had sex with her once before, what really interests him is her grotesque single breast.

By the end of the novel, Shangguan Jintong has developed another illness: a form of photism. In his case, breasts of different shapes and colors fill his entire visual space, floating and flying and finally combining into one huge breast towering aloft between heaven and earth. By this time, the image of the breast has become a condensation of his life on the one hand and the symbol of the motherland on the other.

Big Breasts and Wide Hips is remarkable not only for its philogyny but also for its bitterly sarcastic attitude toward men. In *The Red Sorghum Family*, Mo Yan indicates that a degeneration of men is taking place through the generations and draws a distinct line between the ancestors and their descendants. As previously discussed, Granddad and red sorghum represent the glorious past with masculine beauty and charisma whereas the I-narrator and hybrid sorghum characterize the shameful present. The following passage demonstrates the novelist's antipathy toward the modern world as well as his yearning for the glorious past:

> As I stand amid the dense hybrid sorghum, I think of surpassingly beautiful scenes that will never again appear: In the deep autumn of the eighth month, under a high, magnificently clear sky, the land is covered by sorghum that forms a glittering sea

of blood. If the autumn rains are heavy, the fields turn into a swampy sea, the red tips of sorghum rising above the muddy yellow water, appealing stubbornly to the blue sky above. When the sun comes out, the surface of the sea shimmers, and heaven and earth are painted with extraordinarily rich, extraordinarily majestic colors.

That is the epitome of mankind and the beauty for which I yearn, for which I shall always yearn.

Surrounded by hybrid sorghum, whose snakelike leaves entwine themselves around my body, whose pervasive green poisons my thoughts, I am in shackles from which I cannot break free; I gasp and groan, and because I cannot free myself from my suffering I sink to the depths of despair. (Mo Yan, *The Red Sorghum Family*, trans. Howard Goldblatt, 358–359)

我站在杂种高粱的严密阵营中，思念着不复存在的瑰丽情景：八月深秋，天高气爽，遍野高粱红成洸洋的血海。如果秋水泛滥，高粱地成了一片汪洋，暗红色的高粱头颅擎在浑浊的黄水里，顽强地向苍天呼吁。如果太阳出来，照耀浩淼大水，天地间便充斥着异常丰富、异常壮丽的色彩。

这就是我向往着的、永远会向往着的人的极境和美的极境。

但是我被杂种高粱包围着，它们蛇一样的叶片缠绕着我的身体，它们遍体流通的暗绿色毒素毒害着我的思想，我在难以摆脱的羁绊中气喘吁吁，我为摆脱不了这种痛苦而沉浸到悲哀的绝底。(Mo Yan, *The Red Sorghum Family*, 495–496)

In *Big Breasts and Wide Hips*, however, Mo Yan mocks almost every man in this novel mercilessly. The protagonist, as previously mentioned, is a man who attaches himself to women's nipples throughout his life, to the great disappointment of his mother:

> "I finally understand that it's better to let a child die than let him turn into a worthless creature who can't take his mouth away from a woman's nipple!"
>
> ...
>
> "I don't need a son who refuses to grow up ... I want a man who stands up to piss!" (Mo Yan, *Big Breasts and Wide Hips*, trans. Howard Goldblatt, 478)

"现在我明白了，与其养活一个一辈子吊在女人奶头上的窝囊废，还不如让他死了好！"

......

"我已经不需要一个永远长不大的儿子，......我要一个真正站着撒尿的男人！"

(Mo Yan, *Big Breasts and Wide Hips*, 507–508)

Furthermore, Shangguan Jintong's nominal father and grandfather are little more than clowns whereas his grandmother is a strong, even masculine, woman: "Weak father, weak son, accomplishing little with their soft hands—limp wicks, fluffy cotton, always careless and given to cutting corners" (父子二人......活脱脱一对难兄难弟。......他们的手......轻飘飘,软绵绵，灯心草，败棉絮，......漫不经心，偷工减料。).[75] Then there is Mother's aunt, the woman who raised her; she is the head of the family whereas her husband, Big-Paw Yu (于), is a weak man:

> Everyone knew she [Mother's aunt] was the head of the household, and that Big-Paw Yu was good for gambling and bird-hunting only. The fifty acres of land, the two donkeys that worked it, the household chores, and the hiring of workers all fell to Mother's aunt, who was barely five feet tall and never weighed more than ninety pounds. That such a small woman could get so much done was a mystery to everyone. (Mo Yan, *Big Breasts and Wide Hips*, trans. Howard Goldblatt, 48–49)
>
> 谁都知道，于大巴掌家是女人当家。大姑夫除了赌钱、玩枪、打鸟之外，啥也不干，家里良田五十亩，养着两头骡子，家务活儿、地里的活儿［请人雇工，］都是大姑姑一手包揽。她身高不足一米五，体重不超过四十公斤，这么小的身体，竟能发挥出那么大的能量，的确是个奇迹。
>
> (Mo Yan, *Big Breasts and Wide Hips*, 611)

Interestingly, the only male hero in the novel is Sima Ku, Mother's second son-in-law, the nationalist officer and the head of the notorious landlord's restitution corps, an armed vigilante corps organized by runaway landlords to facilitate their return and the restoration of their power over peasants during the civil war of 1946–1949. In Mother's words: "He's a bastard, but he's also a man worthy of the name. In days past, a man like that would come around once every eight or ten years. I'm afraid we've seen the last of his kind" ("他是混蛋，也是条好汉。这样的人，从前的岁月里，隔上十年八年就会出一个，今后，怕是要绝种了。").[76] And again, "Sima Ku had his faults, plenty of them, but he lived his life like a man, and that's worth emulating" ("司马库千坏万坏，但到底是个好样的男人，你要向他学！").[77] Like Granddad in *The Red Sorghum Family*, Sima Ku is a figure who blurs the boundaries between good and bad. The complexity of this character embodies the complexity of history *per se*; and its politicization indicates the author's questioning of the historiography sanctioned by the political establishment.

Linda Hutcheon points out that

> historiographic metafiction plays upon the truth and lies of the historical record ... [C]ertain known historical details are deliberately falsified in order to foreground the possible mnemonic failures of recorded history and the constant potential for both deliberate and inadvertent error. (*A Poetics of Postmodernism: History, Theory, Fiction*, 114)

This novel exemplifies Hutcheon's observation. It certainly plays upon the official history that has been implanted in the Chinese people. By questioning the reliability and trustworthiness of the "historical record," the author challenges the Maoist legacy directly. Therefore, it is not surprising that a storm of criticism from the political left surrounded the publication of *Big Breasts and Wide Hips* in Mainland China, especially since the work was awarded a major prize by a literary magazine. Leftist critics regarded the book as both an attack on the communist leadership during and after the Sino-Japanese war and as a ringing endorsement of the nationalist government as represented by Sima Ku. As far as the left was concerned, this was a distortion of history. One critical article is simply titled "Distorting History, Uglifying Reality" (歪曲历史，丑化现实), and its author criticizes Mo Yan's novel thus: "The book's general inclination as well as its basic ideological content are a serious distortion and uglification of, and, in certain aspects, a complete contradiction to history and the life of our society" (作品的总体倾向和基本思想内容......是严重地歪曲历史和丑化社会生活的。在某些方面，甚至与历史和社会生活的真实截然相反。).[78] After citing details from the novel, the author comments, "Look, under the rule of the KMT, people lived such a 'happy and easy' life. It sounds like a 'time of peace and prosperity' for which people yearned. *Big Breasts and Wide Hips* not only reverses history and fabricates lies, but it also beautifies the Japanese fascists and the landlord's restitution corps, to the degree that it is sycophantic and shameless" (看，在国民党统治下，老百姓的日子过得多么 "美好舒心"，真是太平盛世，令人向往。《丰乳肥臀》颠倒历史，编造谎言，美化日本法西斯和地主还乡团已到了奴颜媚骨、荒诞无耻的程度。).[79] This critic especially dislikes Sima Ku: "[In the novel], ... such an immoral, womanizing man, who is the head of the landlord's restitution corps, is delineated as a hero. This is, indeed, we must say, a 'creation' and a 'miracle' in the history of contemporary Chinese literature" (......把这样一个眠花宿柳的淫棍、地主还乡团长描写成为一个英雄，应该说，这在中国当代文学史上确是一个 "创造" 和 "奇迹"。).[80] The leftists were also disappointed in the novel because the Communist soldiers are depicted as a group of "aimless men who pay no attention to policy and discipline ... and slaughter innocent people indiscriminately..." (毫无目标，毫无政策，毫无纪律的人，......滥杀无辜......).[81] One of the articles lambasting this novel even cites detailed "historical evidence" to disprove certain points in the work by giving concrete dates and statistical figures.[82] In the minds of the writers of this and similar articles, the official history is absolutely reliable and not open to question. Consequently, when someone such as Mo Yan tries to problematize the long-standing beautified history, he is accused of attempting to uglify and thus blaspheme it. In the view of the leftists, Mo Yan has lost his conscience and his sense of responsibility as a writer.

No matter how much Sima Ku has irritated the leftists by his heroic image and behavior, however, he is merely a single figure whose valor cannot make up for the incompetence and weakness of the other male characters, let alone compare with the heroism of a central icon such as Granddad in *The Red Sorghum Family*. The absence of a father figure distinguishes *Big Breasts and Wide Hips* not only from Mo Yan's earliest novel but also from works written by other authors under the influence of the Maoist ideology. To what extent has Mo Yan escaped the prison of the Maoist principles? I would argue that *Big Breasts and Wide Hips* is, overall, a departure from the patriarchal Communist ideology because the absence of a father image can largely be regarded as a challenge to one of the norms of *Mao wenti* (毛文体), or Maoist discourse.[83] The Communist Party has advocated gender equality in China and as a result, the social status of women has greatly improved over time; nonetheless, the consciousness of male superiority is still prevalent in all walks of society, including the supreme leadership of the central party. Men far outnumber women in important governmental and administrative positions. On formal occasions, such as plenary meetings of the Central Committee of the party, when the list of delegates' names is announced, the sex of a woman delegate is put in parentheses after her name. Likewise, the sex of female professionals, such as writers and doctors, is more often than not indicated by adding the character *nü* (女) to the characters indicating the profession—for instance, *nüzuojia* (女作家) or *nüyisheng* (女医生). The fact that only the female sex is highlighted is paradoxical and ironic given the communist call for gender equality. The gesture makes explicit the attempt to promote the social and political status of women in the new society, yet the gesture itself is discriminatory, for it implies a tolerant and even patronizing attitude on the part of men, the original "owners" of these professions—which are still primarily the domain of men. Although Jiang Qing, Mao's wife, exercised great power during Mao's later years, she effectively promoted her own individual image and influence and did not fight for the collective rights and interests of Chinese women. Consequently, Mao is still the greatest father figure representing male dominant power in China. Therefore, even though *Big Breasts and Wide Hips* cannot be regarded as truly feminist writing (the female characters are in need of feminine consciousness in general), it is certainly subversive and challenging inasmuch as it recounts the recent history of China—including the emergence of the Communist Party—in a story whose only manly hero is a nationalist.

Moreover, the extremely detailed descriptions of sex and the body would certainly have been intolerable in the revolutionary writings of Mao's time, and they remain heretical in the eyes of Maoist ideologues. In his discussion of sexuality and the Western tradition, Peter Brooks points out that "the erotic body both animates and disrupts the social order."[84] To be more precise, the erotic body has a Bakhtinian "carnivalesque" function of disrupting the social order, challenging the conservative orthodoxy, and subverting social hierarchy—and thus vitalizing society. In China, *Big Breasts and Wide Hips* has indeed caused discomfort in society, especially among the formalists, who regard the descriptions of sex and female genitalia in the book as "fierce floods and savage beasts"—that is, as great scourges. To them, the novel "has contaminated society, poisoned the minds [of readers], and harmed the reader with vulgar, obscene, dirty and ugly content" (竟以庸俗、淫秽、下流、丑恶的内容污染社会，毒害心灵，坑害读者。).[85] Mo Yan dedicated his novel to the soul of (his) mother, and the formalists regard this as a humiliation to all mothers and to Chinese women in general. Such comments are strikingly reminiscent of criticism leveled during the Cultural Revolution, when writers suffered badly from political persecution. The goal of this kind of criticism is to defend the sanctity of history, which is exactly what postmodern historical metafiction attempts to undermine.

LIFE AND DEATH ARE WEARING ME OUT— A TRAGIC PLAYLAND

Ten years after the publication of *Big Breasts and Wide Hips*, Mo Yan published another historical novel in 2006, *Life and Death Are Wearing Me Out*, which combines the real and the surreal by means of postmodern playfulness, viewing history from the perspectives of animals and casting China's recent history as an absurd tragicomedy. Changes in the author's understanding of history can again be detected in this work; this time the novelist parodies the Buddhist six realms, a cycle of rebirth or reincarnation, a trope which enables him to add comic elements to the story and to laugh at the absurdity and ridiculousness of history.

The novel opens on New Year's Day of 1950 in Shandong Province, when Ximen Nao (西门闹), a landlord executed during the nationwide land-reform movement begun in 1946, is reincarnated as a donkey. The dead Ximen Nao feels that he has been seriously wronged, for he had been a good landlord who had earned his land and property through hard work and had helped many poor people in his village. Therefore, although he is constantly being tortured, Ximen Nao persistently appeals to Lord Yama, the king of hell, to allow him to return to the human world and clear his name. Eventually, Lord Yama is moved by his persistence and allows him to go back. To his great surprise, however, he is not reborn as a human being as he had asked; instead, he is reborn as a baby donkey to the family of Lan Lian (蓝脸), or Blue Face, his former farmhand. After Ximen Nao was executed, his property, including his two concubines, was redistributed to the villagers. Although his legal wife, Lady Bai (白), remains single, his first concubine is married to Lan Lian and is now pregnant, and his second concubine has married Huang Tong (黄瞳), or Yellow-eyed Huang, the executioner who took Ximen Nao's life. After the death of the donkey, Ximen Nao goes on to be reincarnated as an ox, a boar, a dog, a monkey, and finally a human being again. In the system of Buddhist cosmology, all creatures are trapped and suffer within the wheel of life due to their sinful actions. In the novel, Ximen Nao's rebirths are all in the animal realm except for the last one (although he is eventually reincarnated as a human being, he suffers from a rare disease), and all are related to different political movements in the recent history of China, symbolizing the suffering of people who are trapped in man-made adversities with no escape.

Beginning with his *Sandalwood Punishment* (2001), Mo Yan has consciously returned to the format of classical literature. *Sandalwood Punishment* comprises three parts—the head of a phoenix, the abdomen of a pig, and the tail of a leopard—an employment of the method of writing *yuefu* (乐府) poems, whereas *Life and Death Are Wearing Me Out* is written in a traditional Chinese novelistic style, namely, the *zhanghui*

(章回) style, which divides the novel into many chapters, each of which is titled with a couplet that gives the reader an inkling of its contents. This traditional Chinese style, nevertheless, does not overpower the novel's many foreign influences. Over the course of his fifty years of rebirths, Ximen Nao undergoes a Kafka-esque metamorphosis as he is transformed into multiple animal forms before returning to his desired form as a human being. In the meantime, themes of human alienation and loneliness are skillfully interwoven in the persistence of the Don Quixote-type hero Lan Lian. The final reincarnation transforms the former Ximen Nao into a millennium baby, who is in fact a descendant of Ximen himself—a mature adult in the form of a child, this character is a reminiscence of Oskar Matzerath, the protagonist of *The Tin Drum* (Günter Wilhelm Grass, 1927–). Last but not least, in his third rebirth, Ximen Nao as a boar reminds the reader of George Orwell's (1903–1950) satirical allegory, *Animal Farm*. Crossing the boundaries of human and nonhuman, real and surreal, classical and modern, as well as Chinese and foreign, the novel is a comedy of language that displays the unbearable lightness of history in modern China.

Like Franz Kafka's (1883–1924) Gregor Samsa in *Metamorphosis*, who changes into an enormous insect overnight, Ximen Nao is first reborn as a donkey. The idea of a man's changing into a bug all of a sudden is certainly absurd and laughable; it is similarly funny to see Mo Yan's Ximen Nao, "a literate, well-educated member of the gentry class … be reborn as a white-hoofed donkey with floppy, tender lips" (...... 读过私塾、识字解文、堂堂的乡绅西门闹，竟成了一匹四蹄雪白、嘴巴粉嫩的小驴子。).[86] In the form of a bug, Kafka's Gregor experiences extreme loneliness as an Other and eventually dies when his younger sister, the person he cares about the most, loses her patience with him. Likewise, Ximen Nao as a donkey retains human feelings and ways of thinking; at the same time his existence confuses the boundary between human and nonhuman, for he also possesses animal instincts, characteristics, and abilities. As an ox, a boar, and a dog, he experiences a similar split of self without exception, manifesting a kind of schizophrenia that sets up the novel's comical elements.

Recounting China's recent history, which is characterized by endless political, social, and national turmoil, is a task doomed to be heavy; the writer inevitably must touch upon certain tragic topics. Yet Mo Yan's writings have become more and more playful, funny and dark at the same time. *Life and Death Are Wearing Me Out* is an excellent example. A tragicomic aura thoroughly imbues the novel as a result of the absurd combination of a confused human-animal mindset with the parody of political language. For instance, when the donkey is fighting with two mules over some food, he says: "Don't be so stingy, you bastards, there's enough there for all of us. Why hog it all? We have entered the age of communism, when mine is yours and yours is mine" ("你们这两个杂种，不要如此猖狂，有饭大家吃，休要吃独食。现在是共产主义时代，我的就是你的，你的就是我的，还分什么彼此。").[87] The idea of a donkey's freely using the principle of communism to convince other animals to share food with him is certainly amusing, and the irony is obvious: the communist ideology is so deeply rooted in every corner of the country that even a donkey thinks in a revolutionary way and acts a bit like the Red Guards—known for confiscating the property of wealthy people during the Cultural Revolution.

Another example comes from the boar. At a propaganda meeting promoting the revolutionary significance of raising pigs, a government officer shouts, "Every pig born is a cannon shell fired into the stronghold of the imperialists, revisionists, and reactionaries…" ("每一头生猪，都是一颗射向帝修反反动堡垒的炮弹……").[88] Piglet Sixteen, the leader of the pig farm who enjoys privileges because of his political status, considers this remark:

> That shout and gesture reminded this wise and experienced pig of a movie scene and had me wondering whether being shot from a cannon would be a dizzying and shuddering experience. And what would happen if a fat pig suddenly fell into the stronghold of the imperialists, revisionists, and reactionaries? They'd probably die of sheer joy. (Mo Yan, *Life and Death Are Wearing Me Out*, trans. Howard Goldblatt, 260–261)

他的声嗓和动作，让我这头见多识广的猪，联想到了一部著
名电影中的镜头。当然我也联想到，如果真能被安装到炮筒
中发射出去，在空中飞行的感觉，是不是也会是晕晕乎乎、
颤颤悠悠呢？而如果是一头肥猪，突然降落到帝修反的碉堡
里，还不把那些坏蛋乐死？

(Mo Yan, *Life and Death Are Wearing Me Out*, 237)

This statement reminds the reader of a similar claim in Yu Hua's novel *Huozhe* (活着) [To live], when the team leader announces that the protagonist Fugui's (福贵) family has successfully made iron during the Great Leap Forward Movement. The leader declared, "We'll be able to make three bombs out of this iron, and all of them are going to be dropped on Taiwan … We'll drop one on Chiang Kai-shek's bed, one on his kitchen table and one on his goat shed" ("这钢铁能造三颗炮弹，全部打到台湾去，一颗打在蒋介石床上，一颗打在蒋介石吃饭的桌子上，一颗打在蒋介石家的羊棚里。").[89] The comedy is in the sincerity and ignorance of the leader, who is one among many other Chinese people who truly believe that everything they have done contributes to the revolutionary cause. Now Mo Yan's piglet with its human consciousness is mocking human intelligence, imagining himself to be the cannon shell falling on the table of the enemies only to bring them great joy because a big fat pig would provide them with good food—especially in that particular time period, when the supply of daily necessities was limited in China and there were quotas on such basic items as grains, meat, fish, cooking oil, sugar, cloth, and so forth. The funny imaginary scene certainly makes the reader laugh, a fact which casts scornful sarcasm on Mao's fantasies.

Perhaps the most amusing episode in the novel also comes from the piglet's life on the occasion of Mao's death on September 9, 1976, the day after the Mid-Autumn Festival. While everybody is mourning the death of Mao, sincerely or not, Piglet Sixteen observes the following scene:

My moon, solemn and bleak, rose up for Mao Zedong. We saw him sitting on the moon—his bulk pressing down and altering its shape into an oval. He wore a red flag like a cape, held a cigarette in his fingers, and raised his heavy head slightly. A pensive look was frozen on his face. (Mo Yan, *Life and Death Are Wearing Me Out*, trans. Howard Goldblatt, 339–340)

这月亮悲壮苍凉，是专为逝世的毛泽东而来。我们看到毛泽东坐在月亮上—他肥胖的身体使月亮受压而成椭圆—身上披着红旗，手指夹着香烟，微仰着沉重的头颅，脸上是若有所思的表情。(Mo Yan, *Life and Death Are Wearing Me Out*, 319)

Later the pig wants to take a closer look at Mao, so he paddles into the river with his girlfriend, a sow named Little Flower, on his back. "Little Flower dug her hooves into my ribs and shouted 'Faster! Faster!' as if I were her horse" (小花......用后腿踢着我的肚子，嘴里连声喊叫着: "加油啊，加油!" 好像我是它胯下的一匹马。).[90] Then he goes on to describe how other animals, such as red carps, white eels, and turtles chase Mao and the moon, but they can never reach their goal.

The caricature of Mao sitting on the moon as a big crowd of nonhumans chases him is certainly one of the most amusing images of the political figure to appear in the literature of postrevolutionary China. Having lived as the most respected human leader on earth in mid-twentieth century, Mao continues to be a chief after his death, although this time his followers are animals. Whereas nonhumans are raised to a level higher than that of human beings, Mao is debased and mocked.

Paralleled with the reincarnations of Ximen Nao is the story of Lan Lian, a Don Quixote–type hero and the only self-employed, independent farmer in all China. Mao Zedong, in order to surpass the United Kingdom and the United States in terms of industrial and agricultural productions, launched the Three Red Banners movement in the 1950s, two elements of which were the notorious Great Leap Forward and the People's Commune. In 1955 and 1956, peasants all over China were organized into cooperatives, an initial step toward the communist collectivity (the nationwide campaign of the People's Commune). Then in 1958, as a program to support the Great Leap Forward, peasants were further organized into People's Communes, the exclusive social structure among Chinese peasants. In other words, individualism was totally dismissed. Socialist literary works have described how happy Chinese peasants were led by the Communist Party to pursue the collective life, but literature in the post-Mao era devotes much space to revealing how unwilling many Chinese peasants actually were to join the People's Communes during the three decades of their existence. It is a new experience in post-Mao literature, however, to encounter an individual farmer like Lan Lian, who insists on working on his own even after agricultural collectivization.

To many people, Lan Lian is mad, a man following his prototypes—Lu Xun's madman and Miguel de Cervantes' (1547–1616) Don Quixote—whose behavior is beyond the comprehension of the majority. Lu Xun's madman sees a cannibalistic culture in China's thousand years of history and entreats that the children be saved. He is one of the few people who are awake, and he is hoping to arouse the sleeping majority and break the iron house—a metaphor for feudal China—that imprisons and suffocates the masses. Eventually, however, the madman is cured; he emerges from his illusion and returns to the mainstream. Cervantes' hero is idealistic, suffering from his indulgence in illusions; he understands the world, life, and the situations he encounters differently from others and turns ordinary happenings into grand activities.

Lan Lian, however, does not live in illusions. Instead, he is a stubborn man with courage and loyalty—he is courageous enough to maintain loyalty to his own belief: "Even brothers are dividing up family property, so what good is putting strangers together to eat out of the same pot?" ("亲兄弟都要分家，一群杂姓人，混在一起，一个锅里摸勺子，哪里去找好?").[91] One can imagine how much hardship and pressure he has to endure for his refusal to be part of any socialist associations at a time when collectivism is enforced and any kind of individualism is a social sin. Unlike Lu Xun's madman and Cervantes' Don Quixote, Lan Lian sees his persistence well rewarded: he witnesses the end of the People's Communes after the Cultural Revolution, and he is vindicated in his beliefs.

Interestingly, Lu Xun's elite madman hopes to awaken the numb masses trapped in the iron house by enlightening and rescuing them from atop; Don Quixote is also an elite loner with knightly virtues, "refusing to accept the everyday world and instead insisting on changing it or at least treating it as if it were otherwise."[92] Lan Lian, in contrast, is a recluse from the bottom of the social ladder who attempts neither to change nor to rescue anyone. He simply insists on his own belief, which means, in the context of politicized China, risking his family and even his life. However, whereas both the madman and Don Quixote return to the social fold without having changed anything in reality, Lan Lian finally wins the battle as a single individual against the entire ideology-driven nation.

The comedy in Lan Lian's case resides in the interplay of a double absurdity. To the people of his own time, Lan Lian is laughable because he is obviously taking the narrow way leading to a dead end. To the reader of the novel, Lan Lian is the only sober person, and the people around him who suffer from uncontrollable revolutionary fanaticism are illogical and irrational to the point of being comical.

It is noticeable in this novel that Mo Yan's use of color has shifted. In previous works, such as *The Red Sorghum Family*, red is the color favored by the author and plays an important role in signifying the spirits of freedom and courage. In *Life and Death Are Wearing Me Out*, however, blue becomes the color that represents the positive values in his mind, whereas red begins to represent the illogicality and senselessness of the crazy era that Mo Yan is subjecting to ridicule. The blue birthmark on Lan Lian's face earns him his name, Blue Face, and distinguishes him from others. Moreover, both his son, Lan Jiefang (蓝解放), and his grandson, Lan Kaifang (蓝开放), are marked with a patch of blue on their faces. In the very beginning of the novel, too, Mo Yan describes the blue color on the faces of Ox Head and Horse Face, the hell attendants, as an "iridescent blue ... [a] noble color, one rarely seen in the world of mortals" (......耀眼的蓝色光芒......人世间很少见过这种高贵的蓝色).[93] Their blue faces are so unique that "...earthly dyes could never, not in a million years, paint faces with hues that noble or that pure" (......人间的颜料，永远也画不出他们这般高贵而纯粹的蓝脸。).[94] The author's questioning of the madness of revolution is demonstrated by his favoring blue at a time when red is the only correct color, a switch that signifies the novelist's contention that a color bestowed with a heavy political meaning is absurd.

The episode in which Lan Lian's face is painted red by Red Guards who are led by his stepson Ximen Jinlong (西门金龙, the biological son of Ximen Nao) is both comic and tragic. Lan Lian is denounced as a stubborn independent farmer while one side of his face—the side with no birthmark—is painted red by a Red Guard. Not satisfied with his stepfather's half-red and half-blue face, Jinlong orders Lan Lian's entire face painted red, paying no attention to how much the paint hurts the old man's eyes. He justifies his behavior in the name of revolution: "The whole nation is red, leaving no spot untouched" ("全国一片红，不留一处死角。").[95] Painting a man's face as if it were a wall is funny, but the cruelty behind the deeds is laid bare. Ximen Jinlong's statement foreshadows his accusation of his stepfather: "The whole country, awash in red, with only a single black dot, here in Ximen Village, and that black dot is you!" ("全国山河一片红了，只有咱西门屯有一个黑点，这个黑点就是你！").[96] Lan Lian retorts, "I'm fucking honored, the one black dot in all of China!" ("我真他娘的光荣，全中国的一个黑点！").[97] When Jinlong swears to convert his stepfather by saying, "We are going to erase that black dot" ("我们要抹掉你这个黑点"),[98] the older man insists, "I'm going to live, and live well. China's going to have to get used to this black spot!" ("我要好好活着，给全中国留下这个黑点！").[99] The colors in opposition, red versus blue and red versus black, are politicized into special codifying symbols to denote ideological antagonism, playing into the deep significance of colors as cultural codes in Chinese tradition and as political symbols in China's recent history.

The novelist not only elevates the color blue when red is the sole politically correct color but also salutes the moon while the whole country is worshiping the sun. Whereas the episode cited previously of Mao's sitting on the moon is an example of Mo Yan's playfulness, the other descriptions of the moon are often related to Lan Lian in a less playful way. Lu Xun's madman connects the moon with his perception of the world and of the people around him; Lan Lian, the only independent farmer in China, also shares a close bond with the moon. The highly politicized sun, a metaphor for Mao Zedong himself, became a holy and inviolable symbol during the Cultural Revolution. Lan Lian, who is regarded as an embarrassment to the country, is not permitted to work under the glorious sun. As a result, he works at night for decades with the moon as his best companion. Piglet Sixteen remembers what Lan Lian told him when he was an ox: "Ox, the sun is theirs, the moon is ours..." (牛啊，太阳是他们的，月亮是我们的。).[100] The binary opposition of "theirs" and "ours," represented by the sun and the moon respectively, demonstrates both the suppressive power of the revolution and its absurdity (the sun as the symbol of Mao becomes the supreme being).

When Lan Lian learns the news of his children's marriage, he cries to the moon:

> "Moon, you've accompanied me in my labors all these years, you're a lantern sent to me by the Old Man in the Sky. I've tilled the soil by your light, I've sown seeds by your light, and I've brought in harvests by your light … You say nothing, you are never angry or resentful, and I'm forever in your debt. So tonight permit me to drink to you as an expression of my gratitude. Moon, I've troubled you for so long!" (Mo Yan, *Life and Death Are Wearing Me Out*, trans. Howard Goldblatt, 306)
>
> "月亮，十几年来，都是你陪着我干活，你是老天爷送给我的灯笼。你照着我耕田锄地，照着我播种间苗，照着我收割脱粒......你不言不语，不怒不怨，我欠着你一大些感情。今夜，就让我祭你一壶酒，表表我的心，月亮，你辛苦了！"
> (Mo Yan, *Life and Death Are Wearing Me Out*, 287)

A comment made by Piglet Sixteen underscores the uniqueness of this character and his sentiments and also reveals the subversiveness of the novelist: "In an age when throngs of people sang the praises of the sun, it was unheard of for someone to hold such deep feelings for the moon" (在万众歌颂太阳的年代里，竟然有人与月亮建立了如此深厚的感情。).[101] Given, too, that the sun is regarded as the masculine *yang* element while the moon is the feminine *yin* element in Chinese tradition, Mo Yan's preference for the moon over the sun in this book can be understood as a continuation of his conception of history in *Big Breasts and Wide Hips*. Furthermore, the fact that Lan Lian, a man whom many of his contemporaries believe to be crazy, is closely connected with the moon reminds the reader of Lu Xun's own madman and his association with the moon.

Besides Lan Lian, another important character is the one who shares his name with the novel's author, Mo Yan. This is not the first time that Mo Yan assigns his own pen name to one of his characters. One early example is the three-year-old boy in his novel *The Herbivorous Family*, who tastes a watermelon contaminated by human feces. In *The Republic of Wine*, the correspondence between the character "Mo Yan" and the amateur writer Li Yidou (李一斗), together with Li's writing practices, forms a subplot in the detective story in which a case of cannibalism is investigated, turning the story into a political allegory. "Mo Yan" eventually becomes the mirror image of the detective, Ding Gou'er (丁钩儿), in the main plot, implying that the detective, too, is one of the participants in cannibalism. The fact that Mo Yan gives his own name to some of his characters demonstrates his harsh political and cultural criticism: no one can escape debasement, including himself. In this sense, Mo Yan is a follower of Lu Xun. Lu Xun's madman has a suspicion that he is eating his own sister's flesh, but Mo Yan goes so far as to equate himself with the cannibals. Thus, whereas Lu Xun criticizes the evil cultural feature from above, from the standpoint of an elite individual, ambiguously including himself as part of the criticized culture, Mo Yan's criticism is explicitly directed at the entire Chinese people, and he lends his own name to show unambiguously that he considers himself to be part of that group.

In *Life and Death Are Wearing Me Out*, the character "Mo Yan" forms an important part in the structure of the story. A resident of Ximen Village, he appears in the very beginning of the story although he has not been born yet. Chapter 4 records his birth, which is his first physical manifestation; in the previous three chapters, the narrator alerts the reader to the existence of this character by mentioning his future fictional writings. Of the book's fifty-eight chapters, only nine do not include this character. As the story develops, "Mo Yan" becomes increasingly important, and his writings either supplement the narrators' story line or are challenged and denied by the narrators. In other words, the two lines of text form a dialogue as each challenges the other's reliability. This "Mo Yan" character is more self-referential than the "Mo Yans" of other works, not only in terms of references to his works, such as "Lingyao" (灵药) [The cure] or "Baozha" (爆炸) [Explosions], but also in terms of his family status—the character, like the novelist himself, is from a middle-peasant family.

This "Mo Yan" character is degraded and made fun of whenever possible. Described as an ugly man who annoys almost everyone with his bad ideas and nasty behavior, he plays the role of a clown in a comedy. The fact that the author Mo Yan assigns this clown a birthday of October 1, the national day of the People's Republic of China, adds subtle meaning to the text and invites the reader to use their imagination to prescribe significance. "Mo Yan's" subtexts gradually merge with the main text and eventually take over in book 5, when this character becomes the sole narrator to complete the novel. This character, whose name literally means "do not speak," speaks garrulously in the novel and becomes dominant in the end. Mirroring the real author, whose language flows endlessly in his fictional world despite his pen name, this "Mo Yan," who does not necessarily carry out any mission of education or criticism, effectively renders the novel's structure more complex, enriches the text, and adds dimension to its playfulness. Known for his experimental writing skills, Mo Yan once again demonstrates his inexhaustible talent and rich imagination.

Mo Yan's attitude toward history has evolved throughout his writing career of the past three decades, as exemplified in *The Red Sorghum Family*, *Big Breasts and Wide Hips*, and *Life and Death Are Wearing Me Out*. If the first novel—an early experiment in subverting the binary opposition common in historical fiction as well as in other literary creations of Mao's time—reveals the nostalgic sentimentality of the writer, the second work shows no trace of his missing the good old days; rather, it goes further in its problematization of history *per se* by adopting a philogynous way of writing. *The Red Sorghum Family* may be understood as an endeavor to rescue masculinity. *Big Breasts and Wide Hips*, however, denies spiritual masculinity or confirms the loss of masculinity in China by illustrating the commonly cited *yinsheng yangshuai* phenomenon; the novel thus could be regarded as the author's negation of his previous work. From drinking wine (Granddad) to drinking milk (Shangguan Jintong), Mo Yan's characters undergo a shift from the Dionysian spirit to an Oedipal complex, indicating the writer's skepticism and sarcasm with respect to history as reflected in the "species' regression" presented in *The Red Sorghum Family*. Moreover, Shangguan Jintong's obsession with milk and the breast is a metaphor for the novelist's perception of the Chinese people, perhaps best described by the title of Sun Lung-kee's (孙隆基) 1995 book *Weiduannai de minzu* (未断奶的民族) [A people not yet weaned].[102] In this sense, the humiliating metaphor of the "sick man of East Asia," used during the late Qing dynasty and the early republican period when China was defeated by foreign imperial powers, is applicable to China again (or still).

Based on this view, Mo Yan is arguably not only problematizing history but also examining and questioning the ethos of the Chinese people and their culture. His willingness to look beyond particular evils, examine the modern Chinese character, and determine that it is fundamentally flawed sets him apart from other contemporary Chinese writers and makes him a successor of Lu Xun in his cultural criticism. In fact, Mo Yan is often thought to be even more remorseless and scornful than Lu Xun. The adult Shangguan Jintong, the modern "sick man," Mo Yan admits, is a typical product of his time—a deformity produced by a totalitarian society and long-term political pressure.[103] This character thus bears multifaceted significance as a critique of history, culture, society, and politics. Under the guise of cynicism, the character's creator, Mo Yan, has demonstrated his commitment to pondering the fate of his nation and fellow citizens.

When it comes to his latest historical novel, Mo Yan impresses the reader with even more explicit cynicism, presenting history as mere farce.

The comic, carnivalesque features of *Life and Death Are Wearing Me Out* serve as a unifying thread extending through the insufferably dark historical events of half a century—a thread that transforms what should be a heavy story into a light one that makes the reader laugh at the political circumstances, thus hopefully laughing away the fear caused by such historical trauma. Although the comic vision interacts with Mo Yan's "obsession with China,"[104] at times his playfulness moves beyond this obsession and falls into a dimension of pure enjoyment, that is, writing for writing's sake. His experiment of the two Mo Yans who reside on different diegetic planes and who eventually merge into a single Mo Yan is an example that supports this argument.

CHAPTER 2

HOME, BITTER-SWEET HOME

A PARADOXICAL NOSTALGIA

Given that Mo Yan served in the military for an extended period of time, the fact that he is not categorized as an army writer is perhaps surprising. Unlike Zhu Sujin (朱苏进), Zhou Meisen (周梅森), and the early Yan Lianke (阎连科), whose writings focus on soldiers and officers, Mo Yan writes primarily about the countryside, his hometown of Northeast Gaomi Township in particular. As a result, Mo Yan has been regarded as one of the *xungen* (寻根) [root-seeking] writers by influential critics both on the mainland and abroad, although some reviewers exclude him from this important movement of the mid-1980s.[105] The *xungen* movement, generally considered to have taken shape in 1984 and 1985,[106] drew support from local tradition in order to seek a new aesthetic interest in the subject matter as well as in the language of fictional creations. Looking for a breakthrough in fictional writing after *shanghen wenxue* (伤痕文学) [literature of the wounded], which displayed individual mental wounds and sufferings; *fansi wenxue* (反思文学) [literature of reflection], which criticized the ultraleftist trend of thought that led to the ten-year Cultural Revolution; and *gaige wenxue* (改革文学) [literature of reform], which exposed the problems of social and economic reforms, writers shifted their interest to a broader theme: culture. At the same time, when Colombian novelist Gabriel García Márquez was awarded the Nobel Prize in Literature in 1982, Chinese writers were greatly encouraged to pay attention to their cultural roots. García Márquez's *One Hundred Years of Solitude* provides an example of third-world literature breaking the monopoly of Western literary hegemony as well as that of an artistic work particular to an ethnic group created through the culture, feelings, and writing techniques of that people. In fact, none of the previous Nobel Prize winners in literature had stimulated such widespread and long-lasting interest among Chinese writers, who were greatly inspired by Márquez's success to mine the riches of their own culture.

By examining Chinese tradition, analyzing the cultural psyche of the Chinese people, and pondering the notion of Chineseness, *xungen* writers either sought a sense of national identity and a return to cultural spirit or adopted a rational and critical attitude toward tradition and culture. Moreover, the *xungen* movement can be understood as a reaction to Maoist orthodoxy as well as a reaction against the rulers of that time who advocated that the people of China look forward, partly in the hope that they would stop thinking about the unhappy recent past. A gesture of looking back, searching for roots is simultaneously a refusal to forget the past that has become both a treasure and a burden in the present and a reevaluation of Chinese culture and history.

To a certain extent, the "root-seeking" movement, which occurred in the post–Cultural Revolution chaos, is a kind of collective nostalgia—more often than not imaginary—of the Chinese writers who grew up in the midst of a cultural fracture: almost all traditional values had been repudiated over the course of the Cultural Revolution. Therefore, the nostalgic sentiment of the post-Mao writers is "a longing for continuity in a fragmented world," in Svetlana Boym's words.[107] The consciousness of roots is reflected in a return to the regional culture in which the *xungen* writers grew up or spent their formative years as rusticated but educated youth.[108] As a result of this trend, China's human-geographical map was largely carved up by writers employing different styles—writers who were either former "sent-down" young students from the city, such as Han Shaogong, who wrote about the Hunan (湖南) Province's geographical and human landscapes; or local intellectuals, such as Mo Yan, who was then firmly planted in the Shandong Province, the birthplace of Confucian culture.

A PARADOXICAL NOSTALGIA

Mo Yan's seeking roots is paradoxical—although he is nostalgic about the glorious past of his ancestors, he criticizes without remorse the inherent weakness of the Chinese people. On the one hand, Mo Yan's attack of cultural evil makes him a successor to Lu Xun, who was known for his constant denunciation of both Chinese tradition and existing social diseases. On the other hand, Mo Yan's longing for a return to the (imagined) past enables him to add a dimension of nostalgia to his cultural and social criticism, rendering him a far more complex writer. At this point, nostalgia is represented on two levels: the *remote* past, or the (imagined) history of the Chinese performing on the stage known as Northeast Gaomi Township, and the *recent* past, which comprises the spatial and temporal distances in which the novelist has had his own experience and which again makes use of his own hometown, this time a more concrete and real locale. Some Chinese critics believe Mo Yan to be "one of the writers who possess the best aesthetic vision in the entire root-seeking trend of thought" (在整个文化寻根思潮中，莫言是最具审美眼光的作家之一) because of his "discovery" of the ancestors' spontaneity, intuition, and independence, especially in *The Red Sorghum Family*.[109] "There is no doubt," claim these critics, "our ancestors had countless shortcomings that should be criticized and discarded, an insistent effort of writers since Lu Xun. However ... the forebears also had many praiseworthy virtues" (无疑，从社会历史文化的角度看，我们的祖先是有无数应该批判和扬弃的缺点，自从鲁迅以来的几代作家一直在做着这种艰苦卓绝的努力。然而......我们的祖先同样也有着许许多多值得赞美的精神。).[110] According to these critics, Mo Yan's fictional writing "distinguishes itself from other cultural fiction by means of its unique artistic pursuit; its insightful observation on and aesthetic handling of ancestral culture make it different from general cultural criticism" (...... 以自己独特的艺术追求而迥异于一般的文化小说，它对于祖先文化精神的独具眼光的审视和审美把握已不同于一般的文化批判。).[111]

What these critics point out is only partially correct. It is true that Mo Yan has recognized and expressed admiration for the ancestors, yet other root-seeking writers, such as Ah Cheng and Jia Pingwa, also discover "praiseworthy virtues" in Chinese tradition and handle such virtues aesthetically, developing an idyllic tradition from another important May Fourth writer, Shen Congwen (沈从文,1902–1988). Furthermore, Mo Yan's depiction of the past(s), especially in his later works, is harsh and stern, making the author one of the most unsympathetic Chinese writers in terms of cultural criticism and ultimately demonstrating him a true successor to Lu Xun. Indeed, Mo Yan's nostalgia for the past, complicated by his strong and sometimes scornful criticism of tradition, makes him an important root-seeking writer. Furthermore, this nostalgia is a result of his regressive conception of history, as discussed in the previous chapter. His discontent with modern culture echoes the Nietzschean aspiration of rejuvenating present-day life with the help of Dionysian power:

> What else, in the desolate waste of present-day culture, holds any promise of a sound, healthy future? In vain we look for a single powerfully branching root, a spot of earth that is fruitful: we see only dust, sand, dullness, and languor ...
>
> But what amazing change is wrought in that gloomy desert of our culture by the wand of Dionysos! All that is half-alive, rotten, broken and stunted the whirlwind wraps in a red cloud of dust and carries off like a vulture. Our distracted eyes look for all that has vanished and are confused, for what they see has risen from beneath the earth into the golden light, so full and green, so richly alive. (Friedrich Nietzsche, *The Birth of Tragedy and The Genealogy of Morals*, trans. Francis Golffing, 123–124)

As mentioned earlier, the Dionysian spirit finds its way into this post-Mao Chinese writer's novel *The Red Sorghum Family*, in which irrepressible people, represented by Granddad and Grandma, shock modern-day readers with their soul-stirring behavior.

As David Lowenthal asserts that "nostalgia [is] a pervasive, bitter-sweet feeling,"[112] so Mo Yan's nostalgia is a complex sense of at once loving and hating his hometown. In other words, it is not only a feeling of home-sickness, a longing to return home, but also a resentment toward home. Neither is it as simple as a diachronic dichotomy of the pleasant-past and the unpleasant-present that Charles A. A. Zwingmann has suggested;[113] it is rather a synchronic amalgamation in temporal, spatial, and sentimen-tal terms. As some critics aptly maintain, "our present usage of the word [nostalgia] is ... distinctly modern and metaphorical. The home we miss is no longer a geographically defined place but rather a state of mind."[114]

At the beginning of *The Red Sorghum Family*, the love-hate com-plex is made explicit through the monologue of the first-person narrator, which might also be taken as an authorial discourse that reveals the real author's vision:

> I had learned to love Northeast Gaomi Township with all my heart, and to hate it with unbridled fury. I didn't realize until I'd grown up that Northeast Gaomi Township is easily the most beau-tiful and most repulsive, most unusual and most common, most sacred and most corrupt, most heroic and most bastardly, hardest-drinking and hardest-loving place in the world. (Mo Yan, *The Red Sorghum Family*, trans. Howard Goldblatt, 4)
>
> 我曾经对高密东北乡极端热爱，曾经对高密东北乡极端仇恨，长大后......我终于悟到：高密东北乡无疑是地球上最美丽最丑陋、最超脱最世俗、最圣洁最龌龊、最英雄好汉最王八蛋、最能喝酒最能爱的地方。
>
> (Mo Yan, *The Red Sorghum Family*, 2)

Later, in 1992, Mo Yan confessed his paradoxical sentiments toward his old home in an essay:

> Eighteen years ago, when I was a thoroughgoing peasant working hard on the barren land of Northeast Gaomi Township, my hatred

toward that land was inveterate ... I could not imagine returning to it should I be so lucky to leave it one day ... Two years later, however, I was so excited when I stepped on the land of my old home again ... You may love or hate this land, on which you were born and brought up, under which the bones of your ancestors were buried, but you will never be able to break away from it ... While I was making an effort to be far away from my hometown, I was nevertheless getting closer to it unconsciously, step by step ... (My translation)

十八年前，当我［作］为一个地地道道的农民在高密东北乡贫瘠的土地上辛勤劳作时，我对那块土地充满了刻骨的仇恨。......当时我幻想着，假如有一天，我能幸运地逃离这块土地，我决不会再回来。......但两年后，当我重新踏上故乡的土地时，我的心情竟是那样的激动。......对于生你养你、埋葬着你祖先灵骨的那块土地，你可以爱它，也可以恨它，但你无法摆脱它。......就在我做着远离故乡的努力的同时，我却在一步步地、不自觉地向故乡靠拢。

(Mo Yan, "To Transcend Hometown,"
in The Wall that can Sing, 223–225)

On the one hand, the relocation from the countryside to the metropolis is a displacement for Mo Yan. The temporal and spatial distances have produced a past that he bears in memory. Moreover, the cultural, educational and intellectual differences between the two places have created a feeling of disharmony. As a result, he never feels that he belongs to the city; rather, he always remains an outsider, an Other. Mo Yan teases himself thus:

A country bumpkin like me, who didn't leave Northeast Gaomi Township until twenty years of age, would never become an elegant gentleman no matter how he dressed up. Similarly, no matter what garlands I have decorated my fiction with, it could only be sweet-potato fiction. (My translation)

我这个二十岁才离了高密东北乡的土包子，无论如何乔装打扮，也成不了文雅公子，我的小说无论装点什么样的花环，也只能是地瓜小说。

(Mo Yan, "To Transcend Hometown,"
in The Wall that can Sing, 225)

On the other hand, however, once out of the countryside and civilized or contaminated by the city, Mo Yan has no way back except, perhaps, through his imagination. Consequently, the sense of being estranged from both the past and the present begets a desire to write, and Northeast Gaomi Township has become the point of departure for his writing voyage as well as a rich source of material for his literary creations. At this point, Mo Yan shares a similar experience with the major native-soil (*xiangtu*, 乡土) writers of May Fourth literature, such as Lu Xun, Shen Congwen and Xiao Hong (萧红, 1911–1942). As Lu Town is for Lu Xun, Border Town for Shen Congwen, Hulan (呼兰) River for Xiao Hong, and even Yoknapatawpha County for Faulkner, so this impoverished Shandong village, Northeast Gaomi Township, has become Mo Yan's literary kingdom, the holder of his bittersweet memory, and a space for his reconstruction of the past. Since the past is lost, the writer has been engaging in a lifetime career of seeking, that is, writing, through which he painstakingly (re)visits, (re)discovers and (re)gains the past.

One critic rightly claims that "no nostalgic writing can be considered a 're-creation of the original scene.' Different from a written record that calls up memories of yesterday, nostalgia, as the fashion of contemporary China, uses the construction and embellishment of remembrance to assuage the present" (任何一种怀旧的书写，都并非"原画复现"，作为当下中国之时尚的怀旧，与其说是在书写记忆，追溯昨日，不如说是再度以记忆的构造与填充来抚慰今天。).[115] Nostalgia was once considered a disease in Western medicine, and bloodletting by opening the greater brachial veins was recommended if other treatments had proved ineffective.[116] For Mo Yan, writing has a healing function similar to that once attributed to bloodletting. The pain and resentment toward the past turn out to be a positive force for his writing. In his words, "I regard all the darkness and hardship I experienced during my twenty years in the country as a blessing from God" (二十年农村生活中，所有的黑暗和苦难，都是上帝对我的恩赐。).[117] He realizes that a physical parting from the hometown leads only to a spiritual return to it, a return which is necessary for him as a writer who hopes to develop his own style or "local color." Agreeing with Thomas

Wolfe, who claims that "the way to discover one's own country was to leave it ... [and that] the way to find America was to find it in one's heart, one's memory, and one's spirit, and in a foreign land,"[118] Mo Yan elaborates his own thoughts as follows:

> The so-called literary style does not merely refer to the using of dialect and slang or the writing of local scenery; it is a unique feature that fuses with the unique mentality and viewpoints of the writer. It must be unique from the language to the story, from the characters to the structure. To form such a style, the writer must leave his hometown to gain different life experiences. In so doing, the writer is able to discover the uniqueness of his hometown, be it advanced or backward, and the universality included in various kinds of uniqueness ... (My translation)

> 所谓的文学风格，并不仅仅是指搬用方言土语、描写地方景物，而是指一种溶铸着作家独特思维方式、独特思想观点的独特风貌，从语言到故事、从人物到结构，都是独特的、区别他人的。而要形成这样的风格，作家的确需要远离故乡，获得多样的感受，方能在参照中发现故乡的独特，先进的或是落后的；方能发现在诸多的独特性中所包含着的普遍性...... (Mo Yan, "To Transcend Hometown," in *The Wall that can Sing*, 243)

This uniqueness allows Mo Yan not only to record but also to (re)create his hometown, making it at once a realistic and imaginary place, and the text becomes a space for him to engage in his nostalgia. To Mo Yan, "hometown" is a literary-geographical concept that he can transcend freely with his wild imagination. It is by no means a bounded space that people can find on the map; instead, it is a place containing natural landscapes and human activities from everywhere, and the author uses whichever of these fits the stories and the plots. In Mo Yan's words, "I believe that a writer can continue his writing career when he is able to assimilate the lives of others and bring the interesting experiences far apart into your own 'hometown'" (我想一个作家能同化别人的生活，能把天南海北的有趣生活纳入自己的 "故乡"，就可以持续不断地写下去。).[119] In fact, the new territory, vitalized by a combination of the interesting experiences from the lives of others as well as from the writer's own life, serves to explore and display social and human complexities.

Although Mo Yan is considered to have inherited the May Fourth literary tradition, especially that of native-soil writers such as Lu Xun and Shen Congwen, he does not, however, take over the characteristics of May Fourth literature without incorporating his own uniqueness in his writing. One of Mo Yan's major thematic continuities with May Fourth literature is his focus on the miserable life in the countryside where peasants are victims of the social hierarchy—instead of the focus on matters of the new society that is characteristic of fictional writing in the three decades after 1949. What is new is that Mo Yan pinpoints the source of the peasants' suffering: the local party members or officials who abuse their rights. As a result of the officials' misbehavior, peasants' interests are largely neglected, their rights are severely violated, and they are often described as living under the oppression of local cadres. While Mo Yan's novel *The Garlic Ballads* and short story "Dry River" are good examples of how life is treated as if it were worthless, his later works, such as *Forty-One Bombs* and *Life and Death Are Wearing Me Out*, also contain accounts of party officials who are "more equal than others"—a George Orwell theme—enjoying special privileges and oppressing peasants. On top of this, Mo Yan also exhibits a marked difference from the May Fourth writers inasmuch as he writes from a perspective closer to that of the peasants and feels more obligated to speak on their behalf using his own experiences because he regards himself as one of them.

HOMETOWN—A THEME INHERITED FROM LU XUN

According to Mo Yan, in his novella "A Transparent Red Radish" and in his short stories "White Dog and the Swings" and "Dry River," all published in 1985, he first sets his fiction in Northeast Gaomi Township (in "White Dog and the Swings") and directly uses his hometown experiences for the first time (in "A Transparent Red Radish" and "Dry River").[120]

The first story set in Northeast Gaomi Township, Mo Yan's "White Dog and the Swings" is strongly reminiscent of Lu Xun's "My Old

Home" and "The New-Year Sacrifice." To begin with, the first-person narrator has several things in common with the narrators in Lu Xun's stories: he left the countryside for the city a long time ago and now upon his return to his hometown, sees his old home from a different perspective. According to Mo Yan himself, writing about one's hometown is something passed on by Lu Xun to all writers, and the idea of a person who has left his old home, wandered in a foreign land, and then returns to his hometown is a subject matter that was started by Lu Xun—one which has become an eternal motif that almost no writer can escape.[121] The first-person narrator of "White Dog and the Swings" leaves Northeast Gaomi Township for college in the city when he is nineteen years old. Ten years have passed, and "I" has been teaching at the college and is very likely to be promoted as a lecturer. On a hot summer afternoon, "I" returns to his hometown and reencounters Nuan (暖), his high school sweetheart. Nuan and "I" both dream of becoming members of the PLA Performing Arts Propaganda Team by means of their respective talents of singing and playing the flute. An accident, however, has left Nuan handicapped, blind in one eye: "I" invites Nuan to play on a swing, but the rope breaks—Nuan falls into a locust bush and her right eye is pierced by a thorn. After "I" goes to college, Nuan decides to discontinue their relationship because she believes, "I was already disfigured and unworthy of you; might as well suffer alone, no point making two people suffer…" ("我已经破了相，配不上你了，只叫一人寒，不叫二人单......").[122] Now when they reencounter one another on this summer day, what "I" sees is a woman carrying a huge bundle of sorghum leaves, "with her head parallel to the ground and her neck stuck way out, probably to lessen the pain of the load on her back" (她的头与地面平行着，脖子探出很长。是为了减轻肩头的痛苦吧？).[123] A "daughter of the lesser God," Nuan is marginalized and isolated by the villagers and doomed to marry a rough mute, with whom she has three mute sons. She has no one to talk to; the only listener is her white dog. By the end of the story, she manages to meet the narrator in the sorghum field and pleads with him to help her conceive a child capable of speaking. The story has an open ending: how "I" reacts when confronted with this plea remains unknown to the reader.

This story echoes Lu Xun's "My Old Home" and "The New-Year Sacrifice" in many ways. All three first-person narrators who have become "shizide" (识字的) [scholar] and "chumenren" (出门人) [one who travels], as Xianglin's (祥林) wife in "The New-Year Sacrifice" puts it,[124] are nostalgic when they return to their hometown after years of absence. They are actually "homeless" upon returning—two of them have to stay with their relatives because they have no homes in their hometowns, and the third is returning in order to sell his old house and to bid farewell to his old home. In other words, the nostalgia of these three uprooted intellectuals is imaginary; it is no more than an empty signifier. The past is but a lost one to which they can never return.

> Nostalgia, in fact, may depend precisely on the *irrecoverable* nature of the past for its emotional impact and appeal. It is the very pastness of the past, its inaccessibility, that likely accounts for a large part of nostalgia's power.... This is rarely the past as actually experienced, of course; it is the past as imagined, as idealized through memory and desire. (Linda Hutcheon, "Irony, Nostalgia, and the Postmodern")

The memories, especially those of the narrators of Mo Yan's story and of Lu Xun's "My Old Home," are indeed idealized. The I-narrator of "My Old Home," who is going to sell his family property in his hometown, is depressed on the way home because what he sees are "a few desolate villages, void of any sign of life, scattered far and near under the sombre yellow sky" (苍黄的天底下，远近横着几个萧索的荒村，没有一些活气。).[125] As a result, he denies this hometown: "Ah! Surely this was not the old home I had been remembering for the past twenty years? The old home I remembered was not in the least like this. My old home was much better" (阿！这不是我二十年来时时记得的故乡？我所记得的故乡全不如此。我的故乡好得多了。).[126] Obviously, the old home he *remembers* exists only in his memory, the reliability of which is highly suspect. Later, when this narrator meets his childhood playmate Runtu (闰土), this sense of disillusionment becomes stronger because the heroic little boy does not exist anymore. Now a middle-aged man like the narrator himself, Runtu has lost his charisma as a clever, agile country youth; in front of the narrator stands a simple, slow, and dull adult, a typical peasant who has been afflicted by the hardships of rural life. Even worse, this childhood friend has realized the class differences between himself and the narrator, who has always been superior to him as far as social status is concerned; Runtu has been unconscious of the fact until now. By addressing the narrator as "Master," Runtu humbly differentiates himself from his former friend and contributes to the narrator's sense of alienation by adding the social gap to the ironical difference between memory and reality.

There is no doubt that the narrator has been longing to return to the past, but he does not belong to this place anymore. Yet his disappointment in the old home is not so much with the place as it is with time itself. In other words, he is able to return to a place, but he can never return to a time. Moreover, irreversible time also changes his perception of the same old place. As a result, the place and time are combined to become a whole that becomes his spiritual home, a carrier of his nostalgia. During the process of writing the story, the narrator's nostalgia has in fact turned into the writer's disillusionment with respect to the past.

At this point, Lu Xun's comments on Xu Qinwen's (许钦文) first collection of short stories, *Guxiang* (故乡) [My old home], are appropriate for Lu Xun's own story of the same title:

> …before he could write native soil literature with his hands unfettered, he was already exiled from his hometown. Being driven off to a foreign land by life, he had to recall his "father's garden," a garden which did not exist any longer. It would feel better and self-consoling to recall something not in existence anymore than something that still exists but is unable to be accessed…. (My translation)

> ……在还未开手来写乡土文学之前，他却已被故乡所放逐，生活驱逐他到异地去了，他只好回忆"父亲的花园"，而且是已不存在的花园，因为回忆故乡的已不存在的事物，是比明明存在，而只有自己不能接近的事物较为舒适，也更能自慰的……。(Lu Xun, "Preface to the Second Collection of Short Stories in *Compendium of Modern Chinese Literature*," 6:247)

Xu Qinwen longs for his father's garden; likewise "I" in Lu Xun's "My Old Home" is nostalgic about the garden-like picture of Runtu that has been rooted in him since his childhood:

> a golden moon suspended in a deep blue sky and beneath it the seashore, planted as far as the eye could see with jade-green watermelons, while in their midst a boy of eleven or twelve, wearing a silver necklet and grasping a steel pitchfork in his hand, was thrusting with all his might at a *zha* which dodged the blow and escaped through his legs. (Lu Xun, "My Old Home," in *Lu Xun: Selected Works*, trans. Yang Xianyi and Gladys Yang, 1:91)

> 深蓝的天空中挂着一轮金黄的圆月，下面是海边的沙地，都种着一望无际的碧绿的西瓜，其间一个十一二岁的少年，项带银圈，手捏一柄钢叉，向一匹猹尽力的刺去，那猹却将身一扭，反从他的胯下逃走了。(Lu Xun, "My Old Home," in *The Collective Works of Lu Xun*, 1:477)

The longing for hometown scenery can also be found in Mo Yan's "White Dog and the Swings," in which "I" tells Nuan, "I felt very homesick, not only for the people here, but I missed the old river, the stone bridge, the fields, the red sorghum in the fields, the clean fresh air, the lovely sound of the birds singing …" ("我很想家，不但想家乡的人，还想家乡的小河，石桥，田野，田野里的红高粱，清新的空气，婉转的鸟啼……").[127] Standing in front of him, however, is a poor, shabbily clothed and grotesque Nuan, from whom he hears these words in a sarcastic tone: "What's there to miss in this beat-up place? You missed this broken down bridge? It's like a goddamn rice steamer in the sorghum fields, about to steam me to death" ("有什么好想的，这破地方。想这破桥？高粱地里像他妈X的蒸笼一样，快把人蒸熟了。").[128] *Absence makes the heart grow fonder* is the cliché in discussions of nostalgia; Jonathan Steinwand contended that "the unpresentable loss, painful as it may be, is thus transformed by nostalgic recollection into a beautiful form."[129] Indeed, the possible senses of pain and suffering in the past may have been filtered and numbed by time; only the actual or imagined feelings of warmth and happiness remain. Linda Hutcheon asserted that

> [nostalgia] operates through what Mikhail Bakhtin called an "historical inversion": the ideal that is *not* being lived now is projected into the past. It is "memorialized" as past, crystallized into precious moments selected by memory, but also by forgetting, and by desire's distortions and reorganization. ("Irony, Nostalgia, and the Postmodern")

This assessment is appropriate to the circumstances of the "I" narrators in both Lu Xun's and Mo Yan's stories. In fact, Mo Yan's "I" clearly appreciates the hard work Nuan is engaged in and knows that this would have been his lot, too, had he not left the countryside:

> I know all too well what it feels like to push your way through those dense and windless sorghum fields cutting leaves. Needless to say, your whole body is drenched with sweat and your lungs feel like they're going to explode, but the worst thing is the way the dry little hairs on the sorghum leaves scratch against your sweat-soaked skin. (Mo Yan, "White Dog and the Swings," in *Worlds of Modern Chinese Fiction*, trans. Michael S. Duke, 46–47)
>
> 我很清楚暑天里钻进密不透风的高粱地里打叶子的滋味，汗水遍身胸口发闷是不必说了，最苦的还是叶子上的细毛与你汗淋淋的皮肤接触。(Mo Yan, "White Dog and the Swings," in *Collected Works of Mo Yan*, 5:315)

Realizing how lucky he is to have escaped a life of such hard labor, he "heaved a relaxed sigh that I wasn't carrying that bundle" (我为自己轻松地叹了一口气。).[130]

This sigh is significant because it builds up a boundary between the two social classes represented by "I" and Nuan—that of the city intellectual and that of the peasant, respectively—and because the sigh represents the narrator's discovery of Nuan as an Other. Nuan's Otherness instantly weakens the sweetness of the narrator's nostalgia and increases his moral burden. As Yi-tsi Mei Feuerwerker (梅仪慈) suggested in her analysis of this story,

> what creates a dilemma for the intellectual I-narrator when he returns to visit the countryside after a ten-year absence, is not a split identity but his advanced class status and the question of his moral obligations toward those left behind. (*Ideology, Power, Text*, 210)

Indeed, this suggestion is applicable not only to "White Dog and the Swings" but also to Lu Xun's "My Old Home" and "The New-Year Sacrifice." All three I-narrators in question feel guilty and sorry for the fate of the people who have remained in their rural homes. Mo Yan's narrator, however, is trapped in a mood of more extreme unhappiness and helplessness.

Lu Xun's narrators are more fortunate, for after they have engaged in a bit of self-serving rationalization, their negative emotions are more or less relieved. The guilt afflicting their souls dissipates; they turn their backs on those who had aroused their sympathies and return to their civilized urban life. The narrator of "My Old Home," for example, may not be exactly optimistic, but at least he possesses some hope:

> Hope cannot be said to exist, nor can it be said not to exist. It is just like roads across the earth. For actually the earth had no roads to begin with, but when many men pass one way, a road is made. (Lu Xun, "My Old Home," in *Lu Xun: Selected Works*, trans. Yang Xianyi and Gladys Yang, 1:101)
>
> 希望是本无所谓有，无所谓无的。这正如地上的路；其实地上本没有路，走的人多了，也便成了路。(Lu Xun, "My Old Home," in *The Collective Works of Lu Xun*, 1:485)

In "The New-Year Sacrifice," the narrator encounters Xianglin's wife, a woman who has been married twice, widowed twice, and has lost her only son; she has been rejected by her fellow villagers because they think she will bring bad luck and she eventually dies as a beggar on New Year's Eve. The day before she dies, Xianglin's wife asks the narrator about the afterlife; he responds evasively, "I'm not sure" and justifies this answer because he believes it frees his conscience. The following day, he decides to leave his old home and enjoy some shark fin soup in the town. Lu Xun's criticism of this homecoming urbanite is discernable here; although the narrator feels uneasy about the death of the woman, he releases himself from the sentiment without trouble, forgetting his emotional discomfort in the happy explosion of firecrackers: "Enveloped in this medley of sound I relaxed; the doubt which had preyed on my mind from dawn till night was swept clean away by the festive atmosphere…" (我在这繁响的拥抱中，也懒散而且舒适，从半天以至初夜的疑虑，全给祝福的空气一扫而空了……).[131] An educated person, who has a responsibility to awaken the masses in the iron house, should be sensitive to and concerned the well-being of others. Ironically, however, this intellectual narrator shows more concern for the delicious shark fin soup that must not be missed than he does for the beggar's profound, soul-searching question. If Lu Xun harbors hope for the first-person narrator of "My Old Home"—who imagines that the future will be better for his nephew and for Runtu's son—the author's attitude toward the narrator of "The New-Year Sacrifice" is pessimistic. In this story, Lu Xun blames the intellectual. When the few people who are awake avoid their responsibility to wake the others up, they have in fact joined the sleeping crowd and suffocated in the iron house. The future is therefore hopeless. Lu Xun's criticism of the I-narrator of "The New-Year Sacrifice" arguably indicates that intellectuals, including himself, are in reality useless and helpless in changing the fate of the majority.

Compared to these two narrators, the narrator in Mo Yan's story suffers much more. He is indirectly responsible for Nuan's disfigurement, so there is no way for him to relieve himself from the accusations of his conscience. Even though he does not think of her much when he is away, he is burdened with guilt once he is back in the same village and encounters her again. No self-serving rationalization can help him out of his difficult position; his own fate is tied up with Nuan's. Yi-tsi Mei Feuerwerker argued that the "immediate, physical act … might possibly alleviate the horror of her situation and thereby redeem" the narrator,[132] but this is questionable: arguably, there will be no redemption for either party whether the "physical act" occurs or not. The story has two possible endings: "I" may agree to have sex with Nuan or he may refuse. If "I" refuses Nuan's plea, things will remain unchanged. But even if "I" agrees to physical intimacy with Nuan, and even if she successfully conceives a child who can speak, the triple qualities of her Otherness—she is a peasant, a woman, and (crucially) disabled—would require her to remain an Other. In fact, her deformity makes her an Other among Others: even her fellow peasants look down on her. The reaction of the narrator's uncle when he learns of his nephew's attempt to visit her is telling: "What'd you say you were going out there to see her for? Out there with the blind and the dumb, aren't you afraid people here will laugh at you? Fish are fish and fowl are fowl; you shouldn't stoop below your station!" (你说你去她家干么子，瞎的瞎，哑的哑，也不怕村里人笑话你。鱼找鱼，虾找虾，不要低了自己的身分啊！).[133] Nuan's fellow villagers show no sympathy toward her even when she is in the most miserable of circumstances, so a child capable of speaking would neither improve her situation in the village nor save her from her ultimate misfortune.

The story's open ending poses a dilemma for the narrator; neither choice is satisfactory. On the one hand, if he refuses Nuan, he will be even more heavily burdened with guilt and with a sense of obligation to her for the rest of his life. In addition, since he is predisposed to be a conscience-ridden intellectual in the text, he is not allowed to refuse this helpless woman's request. But on the other hand, his acquiescence would be equally problematic. Nuan is marginalized and socially inferior to our narrator, who is a physically healthy, urbanized man: the narrator is *gaojide* (高级的) [of high class] while Nuan is *dijide* (低级的) [of low class]. The idea of salvation through a "physical act" between a man of higher status (*gao*, 高) and a woman of lower status (*di*, 低) is irrational and ironic. At best, the act would be regarded as his taking advantage of her; at worst, it would be labeled male chauvinism.

By assigning the narrator responsibility for the miserable fate of "those left behind" (represented by Nuan), Mo Yan highlights the moral obligation of the intellectual with respect to the people in his hometown. This authorial move reveals Mo Yan's own refusal to stand aloof from his memories of the past. Furthermore, he puts his hero in a predicament at the story's end from which he has no hope of escaping: the plight of his narrator discloses Mo Yan's acknowledgment of his own painful quandary. The creation of the one-eyed Nuan, moreover, has significance in social, cultural, and literary dimensions. First of all, she reveals the unfavorable living conditions in the countryside; a few decades after the establishment of the People's Republic, the gap between urbanites and their rural contemporaries—like the one between Lu Xun's narrators and Runtu or Xianglin's wife—was not eliminated as promised.[134] Secondly, Nuan's character serves to disclose the ignorance, insensitivity, and indifference of ordinary people toward those living under less favorable circumstances—those, for example, who suffer from diseases or who have physical disabilities. The deformities of Nuan, her husband, and her children are an even stronger satire and cultural critique than the scar on the head of Lu Xun's Ah Q, who has been believed to represent the negative features of the Chinese people. Thirdly, Nuan's plea—which places the first-person narrator in a dilemma—is a powerful and efficient way to complicate the story, increase the tension in the text, and question the self-justification of the man from the higher class. This character's request transforms an ordinary homecoming story into a rich piece that invites the readers' participation—different readers will create different endings according to their own imaginations and understandings of life.

Mo Yan's "I" undergoes a process of self-justification, as does the narrator of "The New-Year Sacrifice." Visiting Nuan's family, "I" is at first shocked by the sight of her dumb and rude husband: "Although I'd heard from my eighth uncle that Nuan's husband was a mute, when confronted with the genuinely crazed aspect of the man, I couldn't help feeling immediately depressed" (我虽然从八叔的口里，知道了暖姑的丈夫是个哑巴，但见了真人狂状，心里仍然立刻沉甸甸的。).[135] Nevertheless, he attempts to think positively about Nuan's life and feels relieved on his way back to his uncle's home:

> As I walked I thought to myself: even though he is a mute that doesn't prevent him from being a man with a genuine personality.

Being married to him Nuan probably doesn't suffer too much; he can't talk, but after getting used to relying on hand signals and facial expressions they can break through that physiological barrier. Perhaps all those misgivings I had before were as groundless as the ancient man of Qi's phobia about the sky caving in. By the time I reached the bridge, I'd left off thinking of her problems and all I wanted to do was jump into the water and take a bath. (Mo Yan, "White Dog and the Swings," in *Worlds of Modern Chinese Fiction*, trans. Michael S. Duke, 60)

走着路，我想，他虽然哑，但仍不失为一条有性格的男子汉，暖姑嫁给他，想必也不会有太多的苦头吃，不能说话，日久天长习惯之后，凭借手势和眼神，也可以拆除生理缺陷造成的交流障碍。我种种软弱的想法，也许是犯着杞人忧天的毛病了。走到桥头间，已不去想她的事，只想跳进河里洗个澡。(Mo Yan, "White Dog and the Swings," in *Collected Works of Mo Yan*, 5:330)

Lu Xun ends "The New-Year Sacrifice" with the narrator's forgetting the unhappiness caused by the death of Xianglin's wife, expressing a discernable disapproval of the intellectual. Mo Yan does not let his narrator off so easily: this "I" has to face his own responsibility for a deed, albeit unintentional, committed in adolescence. He is brought into the sorghum field and listens to Nuan pour out her grievances and sufferings: "I hung my head very low and mumbled, 'Sis … Sis … it's all my fault, if I hadn't dragged you out to the swings that time …'" (我深深地垂下头，嗫嚅着：'姑……小姑……都怨我，那年，要不是我拉你去打秋千……'').[136] When Nuan asks him whether he would have wanted her if she had asked him to marry her, his reaction is heartfelt: "Seeing that look of wild abandon on her face, I was greatly moved: 'Of course I would, I certainly would'" (我看着她狂放的脸，感动地说：'一定会要的，一定会。').[137] The reader has reason to believe that this is not mere lip service and that the narrator is sincere. The more sincere he is, however, the more pained and guilty he feels. The intellectual's self-censure makes Mo Yan's story more than a criticism in Lu Xun's tradition; Mo Yan develops Lu Xun's motif to fit the new historical context of the post-Mao society.

In short, Mo Yan has inherited the nostalgic tradition of the May Fourth native-soil writers, especially that of Lu Xun. He simultaneously shows sympathy for the sufferings of those who are at the bottom of society and ridicules the negative features and human weaknesses they embody. Nevertheless, Mo Yan is more heavily burdened than his literary predecessors with an attachment, an obsession, a self-contradictory and penitential consciousness with respect to both his past and the class to which he once belonged.

A CHILD'S POINT OF VIEW

The other two stories set in Northeast Gaomi Township, "Dry River" and "A Transparent Red Radish," lay bare Mo Yan's paradoxical love-hate complex and bittersweet nostalgia for his hometown. They also showcase Mo Yan's employment of *tongnian shijiao* (童年视角) [a child's point of view], one of the narrative techniques he frequently uses, especially in the stories involving his hometown for which his childhood experiences serve as inspiration for his creation. This is a major reason for his closer literary engagement with and involvement in rural life than most of his May Fourth ancestors and even most of his contemporaries.

"Dry River" is a story about a country boy named Xiaohu (小虎) [little tiger], a son in an upper-middle peasant's family, who is good at tree climbing. When the daughter of the village party secretary asks him to get her a straight branch from a big tree, the unfortunate boy falls from the tree and hits the girl, who was waiting below. The outraged secretary gives him a hard kick in his chest that sends him flying. Then the boy's whole family—his father, mother, and brother—beat him severely, each in turn. His brother "headed for home dragging him in tow ... threw him on the ground, and gave him a hard kick right in the buttocks " (哥哥拖着他往家走。他的脚后跟划着坚硬的地面......哥哥把他扔在院子里，对准他的屁股用力踢了一脚......).[138] His mother had never hit him before, but this time her "thimbled hand slapped savagely at his ears..." (母亲......戴着铜顶针的手狠狠地抽到他的耳门子上。).[139] Then comes his father, who "pulled down a stiff hemp rope hanging from the eaves and plunged it into a pickling vat, then picked it up care-fully and held it away from his body as drops of muddy brine pitter-pattered from the rope. 'Strip off his pants!' father said to elder brother" (父亲......从房檐下摘下一根僵硬的麻绳子，放进咸菜缸里的盐水里泡了泡，小心翼翼地提出来，胳膊撑开去，绳子淅淅沥沥地滴着浊水。"把他的裤子剥下来！"父亲对着哥哥说。).[140] Mo Yan designs an extreme ending for the child Xiaohu, who is badly injured as a result of these beatings. Unable to bear further abuse, the boy sneaks out of the house at midnight and decides to drown himself in the icy river. He is imagining that by the next morning, he will

> sleep for all eternity ... greeting the rising sun with his buttocks, his face buried deep within the blue-black melon sprouts ... This bottom of his would be covered with scars and bruises, and with sunshine as well. The people would gaze upon it as if looking at a beautiful and radiant face .... (Mo Yan, "Dry River," in *Spring Bamboo*, trans. Jeanne Tai, 210)

> 他......长眠不醒......用屁股迎着初升的太阳，脸深深地埋在乌黑的瓜秧里。......这个屁股上布满伤痕，也布满阳光，百姓们看着它，好像看着一张明媚的面孔......。
>
> (Mo Yan, "Dry River,"
> in *Collected Works of Mo Yan*, 5:273–274)

It is worth asking why Xiaohu's family members go so far as to drive the boy to his death. Certainly Xiaohu's parents are not without parental affection toward their little son. When Xiaohu escapes from home at midnight, having made up his mind to kill himself, he hears his mother looking for and calling him in a sad voice: "From the top of the riverbank came mother's piteous cries: 'Xiaohuuuu—huuuu—fuuuu—huuuuer-a-la-la-la, my poor, poor child ai-ya-ya-ya...'" (河堤上响着母亲的惨叫声：虎——虎——虎——虎儿啦啦啦啦——我的苦命的孩呀呀呀呀——。).[141] Their torturing him after he accidentally hurts the daughter of the Party Secretary is in fact an outlet for them to vent their unhappiness and frustration with the difficul-ties they experience because they have been categorized as upper-middle peasants. As previously mentioned, among the five categories, landlords and rich peasants were regarded as class enemies, while lower-middle peasants and poor peasants were the mainstay of revolution. Middle peasants and upper-middle peasants were marginalized and alienated people who enjoyed little—if any—political privilege. As a result of their precarious social and political position, therefore, Xiaohu's parents had to be extremely cautious and endeavor to win the trust and favor of the party secretary and of the other village cadres—to the extent that they almost humiliate themselves from time to time. Once the party secretary makes fun of Xiaohu, and his father is happy about it because "if the party secretary likes to tease him, it means the man gets along with us, he's showing his regard for us" ("书记愿意逗他，说明跟咱能合得来，说明眼里有咱。").[142] After Xiaohu injures the girl, his father,

> down on his knees, … had begged pitifully: "Mr. Party Secretary, please forgive your worthless servant, sir, this son of a bitch, I'm sure going to beat the daylights out of him. Even ten of his dog lives aren't worth one of Xiaozhen's, I'll do anything to make her safe and well again, I'll even cut off a hunk of my flesh…."
> (Mo Yan, "Dry River," in *Spring Bamboo*, trans. Jeanne Tai, 220)

> 父亲跪着哀求：　"书记，您大人不见小人的怪，这个狗崽子，我一定狠揍。他十条狗命也不值小珍子一条命，只要小珍子平安无事，要我身上的肉我也割......。"
> (Mo Yan, "Dry River," in *Collected Works of Mo Yan*, 5:281)

Furthermore, Xiaohu's carelessness may ruin his brother's hopes of enlisting in the People's Liberation Army, which only recruits young people from families with clean and clear political backgrounds. This means a great deal to his brother, as it does to every family member, since Xiaohu's brother would be able to change his family's fate completely if he had a chance to enlist in the army and be promoted. In other words, Xiaohu destroys the hopes for the future of the entire family. However, for Xiaohu, who is too young to realize what terrible consequences his fall could have, the cruel punishment from those dear to him makes life unbearable and unlivable. His choice to destroy himself adds drama to the story and turns it into social exposé. The conversation among Xiaohu's family members after his harsh beating clearly discloses the predicaments faced by people like these peasant characters:

> Angrily mother said to father: "Why don't you kill me too? I don't want to go on living either. Just us both, me and my son, it's better to be dead anyway. It's all your dad's fault, that muddle-headed old fool, he knew very well the Communists were coming, but still he went and bought those twenty acres of soggy swampland that not even rabbits would shit on. So then they decided he was an upper-middle peasant, and now one, two, three generations later we're still living like outcasts, not quite demons but not quite human either." Elder brother said: "Then why did you marry into this family in the first place? All those poor and lower-middle peasants, why didn't you marry one of them instead?" Mother burst into tears and began to bawl and wail, even father broke down and sobbed, gasping and blubbering. (Mo Yan, "Dry River," in *Spring Bamboo*, trans. Jeanne Tai, 226)

> 母亲恼怒地对父亲说："你把我也打死算了，我也不想活了。你把俺娘们全打死算了，活着还赶不上死去利索。都是你那个老糊涂的爹，明知道共产党要来了，还去买了二十亩兔子不拉屎的涝洼地。划成一个上中农，一辈两辈三辈子啦，都这么人不人鬼不鬼地活着。"哥哥说："那你当初为什么要嫁给老中农？有多少贫下中农你不能嫁？"母亲放声恸哭起来，父亲也"嘻嘻嘻哈，嘻嘻嘻哈"地哭起来......。
> (Mo Yan, "Dry River," in *Collected Works of Mo Yan*, 5:284)

An open criticism of Communist class policies, this short story is heavily imprinted with political significance. Mo Yan admits that this piece is "a denunciation of the extreme leftist line: love does not exist in an abnormal society; it is the environment that makes people cruel and merciless" (我的《枯河》实则是一篇声讨极左路线的檄文，在不正常的社会中，是没有爱的，环境使人残酷无情。).[143]

Xiaohu, a victim of the politicized reality, is portrayed as a child who has a peculiar perception of the world—a perception far too gloomy for a child his age in normal surroundings. For instance, from the high tree he sees "limping down the road a little brown dog whose bowels had been scrunched open by the car's tires, its intestines trailing in the dirt like a long cord" (有一条被汽车轮子碾出了肠子的黄色小狗蹒跚在街上，狗肠子在尘土中拖着，像一条长长的绳索).[144] When he sees a young married woman's dead body, he feels that "death [is] something quite alluring" (......死是件很诱人的事情).[145] Later he decides to end his young life, and "the woman, death, and vaguely the little brown dog as well, all were coming toward him, without any anger or reproachfulness..." (小媳妇，死，依稀还有那条黄色小狗，都沿着遍布银辉的河底，无怨无怒地对着他来了。).[146] In Xiaohu's eyes, the world is ugly, and whenever he is teased or abused by adults, the only words that are squeezed through his clenched teeth are "dog shit!" ("狗屎！"),[147] "stinking dog shit!" ("臭狗屎！").[148] It is no surprise, given the boy's experience, that he is not sorry at all when he decides to leave the dog-shit world.

An interesting diegetic discrepancy that appears twice in the story, once early on and then again at the end of the story, is worth our attention. The story's very last sentence echoes the end of its opening paragraph, when the third-person narrator recounts how people look at Xiaohu's bottom as if watching a beautiful and radiant face after his death; the narration is oddly followed by "as if looking at me myself." In the interest of clarity, both segments where the diegetic discrepancy exists are reproduced here. The last sentence of the opening paragraph reads, "This bottom of *his* would be covered with scars and bruises, and with sunshine as well. The people would gaze upon it as if looking at a beautiful and radiant face, as if looking at *me myself*" (......他的......屁股上布满伤痕，也布满阳光，百姓们看着它，好像看着一张明媚的面孔，好像看着我自己。).[149] The story itself ends as follows:

> By the time people found *him he* was already dead. *His* parents stared blankly, their eyes like those of fishes ... Folks with faces as bleak as the desert gazed upon *his* sun-drenched buttocks ... as if looking at a beautiful and radiant face, as if looking at *me myself*.... (Mo Yan, "Dry River," in *Spring Bamboo*, trans. Jeanne Tai, 227; emphasis added)

> 人们找到他时，他已经死了......他的父母目光呆滞，犹如鱼类的眼睛......百姓们面如荒凉的沙漠，看着他

布满阳光的屁股......好像看着一张明媚的面孔，好像看着我自己......。 (Mo Yan, "Dry River," in *Collected Works of Mo Yan*, 5:285)

In a story told by a third-person narrative voice, the appearance of the first-person pronouns in the narration may lead the reader to associate the author himself with the character. In other words, the consciously or unconsciously used first-person pronoun (coupled with the reflexive pronoun) perhaps betrays the author's own somewhat mixed feelings with respect to his writing about his hometown.[150]

If the image of dog shit serves to represent a negative feeling toward the past, then that of the transparent red radish discloses a more positive, if abstract, side of nostalgia. "A Transparent Red Radish" is again a story about a country child. Heihai (黑孩) [Blackie] is a boy of about ten who has been abused by his stepmother. The village team leader sends him along with the stonemason to help on the communal construction site, where the stonemason falls in love with the young woman Chrysanthemum, who is from the neighboring village. The young couple treats Heihai well and is nice to him, and he likes them in return. While breaking stones one day, he gets hurt and is sent to help the blacksmiths instead. The younger blacksmith, a one-eyed man, is also in love with Chrysanthemum, but she does not feel the same way about him. On occasion, he orders Heihai to steal some sweet potatoes and radishes for late night snacking. One day, an ordinary radish suddenly appears to Heihai to be a magical object in the light of the forge. But the radish is thrown into the river by the young blacksmith who is in a bad mood, for he has the lower hand in the love triangle. Heihai's attempt to find the radish in the river fails, and after that he begins to act strangely. Instead of helping the stonemason in a fight with the young blacksmith, Heihai unexpectedly helps the latter, whom he dislikes—causing the stonemason to lose the fight and Chrysanthemum to be blinded in one eye.

This is the novella for which Mo Yan first became known. In the story, he transforms his experienced world into a nonexperienced one, which consists of peculiar and marvelous feelings and images. In his own words,

> The miraculous images and weird feelings all originate from my peculiar [childhood] experiences ... Life in a deformed mind must inevitably be abnormal. As a result, in the story, the red radish is transparent, the train is a crawling monster, hair dropping on the ground produces a sound, and a girl's scarf is a burning flame.... (My translation)
>
> 文中那些神奇的意象、古怪的感觉，盖源于我那段奇特经历。畸形的心灵必然会使生活变形，所以在文中，红萝卜是透明的，火车是匍伏的怪兽，头发丝儿落地訇然有声，姑娘的围巾是燃烧的火苗......。 (Mo Yan, "To Transend Hometown," in *The Wall that can Sing*, 236)

The reader, however, sees not only the transformation of the author's experience but also the sublimation of his experience through this transformation—a process which brings to light the utopian dimension of nostalgia. Like Xiaohu in "Dry River," Heihai is described as a child with distinct attributes. The hardships in his life gradually cause him to shut down part of his normal sensations to reality and drive him into a purely sensational world of his own creation—he has been alienated from others and moves into a nonhuman or superhuman existence. His physical senses of cold, pain and hunger, for instance, are numbed and even vestigial. People around him might easily think that he has a tendency to inflict self-abuse. For instance, he does not mind being naked to the waist in cold weather and refuses the coat that the old blacksmith has offered him. He insists on picking up—with his bare hand—a bore bit that has just been taken from the forge. What replaces these physical sensations is a highly developed ability of observation, through which the boy comprehends the world in his own way.

Mo Yan provides the reader with detailed descriptions of Heihai's facial features (eyes, mouth and ears) and expressions. He never says a single word: language is of no use to him since he does not need it to communicate with the mundane world. He is not a mute, yet he utters only three sounds throughout the story.[151] The first time is when he gets hurt breaking a stone: "He felt a numbness in his left index finger, and his left arm had a spasm. He suddenly burst out a syllable, like a whine, and also like a sigh" (他感到左手食指一阵麻木，左胳膊也不由自主地抽搐了一下，他的嘴里突然迸出了一个音节，像哀叫又像叹息。).[152] The second sound he makes is an exclamation when he sees the fire in the forge for the first time: "Heihai was so excited that he uttered an 'Oh!'" (黑孩兴奋地"噢"了一声。).[153] The third sound occurs at the most important moment of the story: he opens his mouth wide and draws a sigh when he sees the golden-transparent red radish lying on the anvil.[154]

Whereas his mouth is almost functionless in terms of speaking, Heihai's ears and eyes are highly attuned, and with them he experiences the external world selectively and transforms it into his peculiar and rich internal world. For instance, he does not hear the instructions of the commune leader on the construction site, but he hears the people he likes quite well—he has no trouble hearing Chrysanthemum and the stonemason, the young lovers who care about him. Moreover, Heihai hears what "normal" people never do: "The evaporating vapor knocking against the jute leaves and their dark red or light green stems produce a deafening noise. The sound of locusts flapping their wings is like that of a train speeding across an iron bridge" (逃逸的雾气碰撞着黄麻叶子和深红或是淡绿的茎秆，发出震耳欲聋的声响。蚂蚱剪动翅羽的声音像火车过铁桥。).[155] When Chrysanthemum brings him food, one of her hairs is on the steamed bread. She "picked it up with two fingers and flicked it away. The sound was so loud when the hair dropped onto the ground that Heihai heard it" (［姑娘］用两个指头拈起头发，轻轻一弹，头发落地时声音很响，黑孩听到了。).[156] The reader experiences the boy's amplified world, which is characterized by a selectiveness and an idealization particular to the author's nostalgic sentiment.

The transparent red radish is the central metaphor of the story. Initially it is simply one of the radishes Heihai picks from the radish field in carrying out the orders of the young blacksmith. Because the radish falls to the ground and becomes dirtied with iron filings, it is set aside casually on the anvil next to the forge. Heihai's imagination sublimates it into a mysterious object, a transformation which represents the boy's secret longing for beauty. The following is the marvelous picture Heihai sees:

> The smooth anvil was suffused with faint blue light. On the anvil with faint blue light, there was a golden red radish. The shape and size of the radish were about that of a big pear, which had a long tail with golden wool-like hair. The radish was sparkling and crystal-clear, transparent, dainty and exquisite. Inside the golden skin was a lively silver liquid. It had fine lines; from its beautiful curves it sent forth golden rays, some longer, some shorter. The long ones were like wheat awns, the short ones, eyelashes. Everything was in gold…. (My translation)

> 光滑的铁砧子，泛着青幽幽蓝幽幽的光。泛着青蓝幽幽光的铁砧子上，有一个金色的红萝卜。红萝卜的形状和大小都像一个大个阳梨，还拖着一条长尾巴，尾巴上的根根须须像金色的羊毛。红萝卜晶莹透明，玲珑剔透。透明的、金色的外壳里苞孕着活泼的银色液体。红萝卜的线条流畅优美，从美丽的弧线上泛出一圈金色的光芒。光芒有长有短，长的如麦芒，短的如睫毛，全是金色......。

> (Mo Yan, "A Transparent Red Radish,"
> in *Collected Works of Mo Yan*, 3:348)

The narrative reaches its climax at this point. The mysterious radish signifies Heihai's aesthesia as well as the novelist's own sweet memory and sublimation of his past. As Mo Yan admitted in a conversation with his teacher and a few young writers, life is full of colors, imagination, and an air of romance; happiness and ideas exist even in the hardest times of life. Life itself consists of a beauty of mystery, of philosophy, and of obscurity. What Mo Yan wants to seize is the color of beauty.[157] This is exactly what forms nostalgia: no matter how harsh the past may have been, there is something good and beautiful to be remembered, missed, and longed for. "Each particular trace of the past ultimately perishes, but collectively they are immortal. Whether it is celebrated or rejected, attended to or ignored, the past is omnipresent."[158] For Mo Yan, the collectiveness and omnipresence of the past is centered on and articulated by the metaphorical red radish.

The conflicts between the two worlds in this story create a tension in the narrative. Heihai is amazed by the golden radish and wants to get hold of it, but the young blacksmith, who is jealous of the stonemason, grabs it from the anvil. As soon as the blacksmith is about to bite the radish with his stained teeth, Heihai "jumped to his feet with a rare nimbleness, hung himself onto the blacksmith's arms with his own thin ones, and slid down to drop the radish" (黑孩以少有的敏捷跳起来，两只细胳膊插进小铁匠的臂弯里，身体悬空一挂，又嘟噜滑下来，萝卜落到了地上。).[159] The young blacksmith kicks him hard on his buttocks and again attempts to eat the radish. Heihai "threw a piece of coal cinder toward the blacksmith, which brushed past his cheek" (抓起一块煤渣投过去，煤渣擦着小铁匠腮边飞过).[160] When the furious blacksmith throws the radish into the river, "Heihai saw a long golden rainbow flying in front of his eyes, and he fell weakly between Stonemason and the girl" (黑孩的眼前出现了一道金色的长虹，他的身体软软地倒在小石匠和姑娘中间。).[161] The disappearance of the radish symbolizes Heihai's disillusionment. "That golden radish was plunged into the river, causing the water to splash in all directions. It floated for a while before sinking. At the river bottom it rolled slowly, then was buried by layers of sand" (那个金色的红萝卜砸在河面上，水花飞溅起来，萝卜漂了一会儿，便慢慢沉入水底。在水底下它慢慢滚动着，一层层黄沙很快就掩埋了它。).[162] The sand buried not only the radish but also Heihai's spirit: "Throughout the whole morning, Heihai was so distracted ... Heihai's eyes were covered by a mist, and he was very depressed" (整整一个上午，黑孩就像丢了魂一样......。黑孩的眼里蒙着一层淡淡的云翳，情绪非常低落。).[163] Heihai begins a journey in search of the radish, as if it had taken away his soul; he is sorely disappointed, however, for the dreamy radish never reappears. Following the radish's disappearance, Heihai gradually returns to the "normal" world of reality, in which he behaves abnormally—as previously mentioned, he unexpectedly helps the young blacksmith in the fight, accidentally causing injury and blindness to one of Chrysanthemum's eyes. The grotesque image of the one-eyed young blacksmith is mirrored by another abnormal bodily image, that of the now-blind Chrysanthemum;

the young woman's loss represents the cruelness of reality. Chrysanthemum's fate echoes that of the one-eyed Nuan in "White Dog and the Swings": Mo Yan consistently uses the one-eyed image to represent the imperfection of the past. From the moment of Chrysanthemum's blinding, the narrative goes into a decline as Heihai's illusory world is also gradually lost.

The author's subtle interior changes can also be detected in Mo Yan's treatment of Chrysanthemum's handkerchief. Before the golden radish appears, the handkerchief with which Chrysanthemum wraps Heihai's broken finger is an important prop that arouses the reader's expectations; yet it is eventually forgotten by the author himself and is somewhat overlooked by critics as well. The handkerchief appears for the first time after Heihai utters his first sound in the story. These two "firsts" are not coincidental: they create the expectation of communication between the little boy and the external world. The handkerchief has a red Chinese rose on it, which becomes stained with Heihai's blood. A red rose commonly symbolizes affection between the sexes, and the blood on this particular rose complicates its connotations. Heihai hides the handkerchief in a crack on the bridge pier, and he sits on the stone that was once Chrysanthemum's seat to stare at the item—both actions indicate that he cherishes the affections of this pretty woman. For a young boy, the symbol of a red rose with blood on it is ambiguous. His feelings toward her can be understood as a mixture of a yearning for love from an older sister, from a mother, and lastly, from a woman. According to one critic,

> Chrysanthemum is a beautiful hope and a sacrament in his mind, and so he hides her handkerchief in the bridge pier crack ... However, he is only willing to enjoy this joy deep in his inner heart. Once Chrysanthemum shows her pity and sympathy to him in public, he goes so far as to bite her on her wrist. (My translation)
>
> 菊子姑娘是他心目中的美好希冀和神圣物，他把她的手帕藏在桥墩上隐蔽的石缝里......。可是，他只愿意在内心深处

独享这一份愉悦，当菊子在众人面前公开地表示对他的怜悯和同情时，他竟在菊子的手腕上咬了一口。

(Xia Zhihou, "The Variability of the Color Red," in *Research Materials about Mo Yan*, ed. He Lihua and Yang Shousen, 223)

Xia also observes that when Heihai discovers the relationship between Chrysanthemum and the stonemason, he cannot bear it, which results in his unexpected help to the young blacksmith to defeat Stonemason. Xia concludes that both Heihai's love and hatred are narrow-minded.[164]

Such a Freudian reading is convenient, fashionable, and somewhat reasonable. It is true that the handkerchief with a red rose represents a positive sentiment in Heihai's consciousness. Because the handkerchief is from Chrysanthemum, who wraps his wounded finger with it, to see it as a symbol of Heihai's indistinct sexual impulse is acceptable. The conclusion, however, is not convincing. In fact, it falls into the trap of moral judgment, especially when Xia goes on to accuse the author himself of the same "narrow-mindedness."[165] How the Freudian reading leads to such a conclusion and the resulting accusation is questionable.

The handkerchief's role is to reveal the changes that take place in the writer's nostalgic sentiment during the process of writing. Initially, when it is used as a connection between Heihai and the world, it concretizes a relatively direct nostalgic feeling of the author. Later, "the handkerchief was no longer white, but the rose was still bright red" (手绢已经不白了，月季花还是鲜红的。).[166] The handkerchief that is not clean anymore can have more than one possible meaning. First, it may suggest the disappointment of the writer with the subject of his nostalgia: the real world, or more precisely, his hometown. The dirty handkerchief foreshadows the catastrophe of Chrysanthemum's blinding; both the stained piece of cloth and the blinded girl symbolize in turn the destruction of a beautiful world. Secondly, the handkerchief may well hint at the writer's fading memory of his concrete hometown and a shift toward a more spiritual and abstract world. The rose that is "still bright red" serves as a connection between the two worlds. The handkerchief is degraded from a clean one to a dirty one and is eventually forgotten by Heihai as well as by the author himself in the second part of the novella, but the golden red radish that takes its place is elevated from an ordinary state as a dirty object to a mysterious condition as an illusory entity. Mo Yan's transfer of attention from the handkerchief to the radish—from the concrete object to the surreal, imaginary one—is indicative of the process of idealization and abstraction that the author's hometown memory undergoes during his writing, although this process lasts only briefly.

HUNGER—THE MUSE

Another important motif in Mo Yan's fiction about his hometown is hunger. Again in the author's own words: "I never had enough food as a child, so my earliest memory is about food" (因为生出来就吃不饱，所以最早的记忆就与食物有关。).[167] Born in 1955, Mo Yan experienced the Great Leap Forward of the late fifties, the three-year famine of the early sixties, and the Cultural Revolution from 1966 to 1976. Throughout those two decades, peasants like Mo Yan and his family were afflicted with poverty and starvation. This experience has become a poignant tool in Mo Yan's writings. On more than one occasion, Mo Yan has recounted his experience of eating coal:

> In the spring of 1961, a load of glistening coal was delivered to our elementary school. We were so out of touch we didn't know what the stuff was. But one of the brighter kids picked up a piece, bit off a chunk, and started crunching away. The look of near rapture on his face meant it must have been delicious, so we rushed over, grabbed pieces of our own, and started crunching away. The more I ate, the better the stuff tasted, until it seemed absolutely delicious. Then some of the village adults who were looking on came up to see what we were eating with such gusto, and joined in. (Mo Yan, "Hunger and Loneliness: My Muses," preface to *Shifu, You'll Do Anything for a Laugh*, trans. Howard Goldblatt, ix)
>
> 一九六一年的春天，我们村子里的小学校里拉来了一车亮晶晶的煤块，我们孤陋寡闻，不知道这是什么东西。一个聪明的孩子拿起一块煤，咯嘣咯嘣地吃起来，看他吃得香甜

[的]样子，味道肯定很好。于是我们一拥而上，每人抢起一块煤， 咯嘣咯嘣吃起来。我感到那煤块越嚼越香，味道的确是好极了。看到我们吃得香甜，村子里的大人们也扑上来吃......。 (Mo Yan, "Hunger and Loneliness: My Muses," in *Mo Yan's Selected Prose*, 276)[168]

This episode sounds unreal, yet it is indeed the actual experience of Mo Yan, who subsequently made use of it in the short story "Tiehai" (铁孩) [Iron child], in which two boys eat iron.

The story is set in 1958, during the notorious Great Leap Forward campaign. At that time, the steel- and iron-smelting movement was sweeping across China, one of Mao Zedong's most unrealistic fantasies. The first-person narrator is a boy aged four or five, whose parents are laborers on the iron-smelting and railway-construction sites. Lured by an iron child, the boy begins a life of wandering and eating iron. Together they eat reinforcing bars, screws, cooking pans, and virtually anything made of iron. Eventually he, too, becomes an iron child. These two little boys, who begin to rust, scare the adults on the construction sites, who think that they have seen "iron demons." The story is a mixture of the real and the surreal. The opening sentence sets a realistic tone:

> During the Great Leap Forward Smelting Campaign, the government mobilized 200,000 laborers to build a twenty-five-mile rail line....
>
> Only four or five years old at the time, we were housed in a nursery school thrown up beside the public canteen.[169] (Mo Yan, "Iron Child," in *Shifu, You'll Do Anything for a Laugh*, trans. Howard Goldblatt, 97)[169]

大炼钢铁那年，政府动员了二十万民工，用了两个半月的时间，修筑了一条八十里长的铁路。......。

那时侯我们只有四五岁，生活在与"公共食堂"一起建成的"幼儿园"里。 (Mo Yan, "Iron Child," in *Collected Works of Mo Yan*, 5:439)

The smelting campaign and the public canteen during the Great Leap Forward movement are historical, but the story moves into the realm of the surreal when the iron child appears and lures the narrator to join him. The second part of the story witnesses a merging of the actual world with the fantastic one: a scene of the narrator's parents working and eating among their fellow workers on the construction site is juxtaposed with a scene in which the iron children eat iron. The boundary between reality and fantasy, like that between human and demon, is blurred. The story, an early attempt to place unfortunate events in a cheerful context (and thus a precedent for *Life and Death Are Wearing Me Out*), could easily have been oppressive; the Great Leap Forward movement and the steel-smelting campaign are a painful memory for the Chinese people. However, the author imbues the work with an air of magical humor and lightness inasmuch as these two little "iron demons" appear to be somehow cute and lovely; this rendering reduces the heaviness that could have dominated the story because of its political background and because of the horror usually associated with the sight of demons. The comic aspect makes the story all the more powerful because the comedy seems to erase the political trauma—but it actually condemns the absurdity of reality and human hardship.

Another short story directly related to the memory of hunger is "Liangshi" (粮食) [Grain], set during the nationwide famine of the early 1960s, a famine which was one of the immediate results of the Great Leap Forward. In the story, a woman is supporting a family of three children and an aged mother-in-law by herself. She has to feed them with the most unpalatable wild herbs and even a kind of white clay that can appease hunger but may cause death. Assigned to work at the mill, she follows the examples of other working women who smuggle grain out of the mill to feed their families. Unfortunately, the woman is caught by the storekeeper, who forces her to trade sex for grain. In order to avoid further sexual assaults, she eventually develops the skill of swallowing whole grains such as peas, corn, and sorghum without chewing them, then regurgitating them into a basin with water when she gets home. Consequently, the storekeeper has no way to discover any evidence. In this way, she is not only able to save the lives of all her children and of her mother-in-law, but she also enables them "to obtain sufficient proteins and vitamins. As a result, her mother-in-law lived a long life, and her children grew healthily" (......获得了足够的蛋白质和维生素。婆母得享高寿，孩子发育良好。).[170] Told by a third-person narrator situated at a distance, the tale sounds like another surrealistic piece up to this point; Mo Yan again makes good use of his storytelling talents as well as his rich imagination to fabricate a tale in such an ironic tone. The story, however, ends on an extradiegetic level with the comments of a first-person narrator, who may represent the author himself: "This is a true story, which occurred in Northeast Gaomi Township in the early sixties, from which I draw inspiration: Mother is great, grains are precious" (这是六十年代初期发生在高密东北乡的一个真实故事，这故事对我的启示是：母亲是伟大的，粮食是珍贵的。).[171] The jump between diegetic levels directs the reader to the real world and leads the story to its closing. The ending, however, is too light a conclusion to wrap up such a heavy story: that Mother is great and grains are precious is too ordinary a saying to be inspirational (qishi, 启示) to a first-person narrator or real author, at least one who describes such irrationality. Perhaps by intentionally diverting the reader to something lighter in the end, the author is drawing out the very weight of the story.[172]

AN IMAGINED NOSTALGIA

Whereas the stories discussed above are all about Mo Yan's bittersweet memories of his hometown, his debut novel *The Red Sorghum Family* is filled with romantic imagination. Although he makes his *lian-xiang* (恋乡) / *yuan-xiang* (怨乡) [loving/hating one's hometown] complex explicit in this novel (as noted earlier in this chapter), Mo Yan actually demonstrates an anxious longing for the glorious history of Northeast Gaomi Township. He is, however, "miss[ing] things [he] ha[s] never lost,"[173] and his nostalgia "exists without any lived experience of the yearned-for-time,"[174] because the past he represents is a fantasized mirage to which he never belonged and will never be able to return. At this point, another May Fourth native-soil master comes to mind: Shen

Congwen, who also writes about his homeland, West Hunan Province, both in his fiction and in his autobiographical essays—particularly in *Xiangxing sanji* (湘行散记) [Random sketches on a trip to Hunan]. The remote and backward mountainous area is reconstructed as a place that is "both more and less than an imaginary kingdom like Faulkner's Yoknapatawpha."[175] Shen Congwen represents his hometown as an idyllic utopia; his "subjectivity ... transforms the places ... into those of his childhood and adolescence, which constitute the ideal country that will never change in his imagination."[176] As David Der-wei Wang has written: "[Shen's] nostalgia refers not so much to a representational effort to enliven the irretrievable past as to a creation of an imaginary past on behalf of the present."[177] What makes Mo Yan different from Shen Congwen is temporal distance: Mo Yan has never lived in the glorious past recounted in *The Red Sorghum Family*, a past which is totally imaginary, whereas Shen Congwen has experienced the world in his works, and he re-creates a beautified and purified past. As a result, the idea of "imaginary nostalgia" applies more to the work of Mo Yan than to that of Shen Congwen—at least as far as *The Red Sorghum Family* is concerned. This kind of nostalgia is the source of a sense of belatedness for Mo Yan, the regret that he was born too late to have lived during the "good old days." "Missing" a past he never experienced and therefore never truly lost leads to Mo Yan's fictional return to that very past.

To resist temporal irreversibility and a sense of belatedness, Mo Yan creates an omnipresent first-person narrator, discussed in the previous chapter, who crosses the temporal boundary on the one hand and recounts a homeland of heroes on the other. This narrator not only has the capacity to move freely back and forth between different scenes as other omnipresent narrators do in historiographical fiction, but he is nearly omniscient as well, knowing everything about the characters, situations, and events. Mo Yan's unconstrained and innovative style of writing can be identified from the creation of this narrator.

As described in the previous chapter, *The Red Sorghum Family* begins with a farewell scene, which takes place in 1939, when Father is fourteen years old. Grandma is seeing off Granddad and Father who are on their way to ambush a Japanese convoy. The narrator knows every detail of his parents' and grandparents' history, including things even his own father is ignorant of. He knows that his father feels chilled by the "warm fragrance of [grandma's] lined jacket" (奶奶的夹袄里散出的热烘烘的香味);[178] he is aware of the sexual escapades his grandma had engaged in on the dirt path, and more. He is not sure, however, who he himself is: he does not recognize the "bare-assed little boy"[179] singing an anti-Japanese song, even though "someone said that the little goatherd was me … I don't know."[180] This sense of uncertainty as to his identity, together with the narrator's omnipresence throughout the story, creates flexibility and freedom among narrative levels and results in an intrusion of the present into the past that highlights the novelist's attempt to recapture the times of yore.

The more the first-person narrator intrudes into history, the more dissatisfied he becomes with the present. In other words, his attempts to overcome his sense of belatedness result in the feeling that the present is inferior to the glorious past of his ancestors; this sense of inferiority, in turn, reinforces his nostalgia, his longing for the heroic and epochal days that he has missed. Interestingly, this narrator, mysterious and infinitely resourceful in recounting the story of his family, appears quite ordinary and real in the present. In order to write his family history, he returns to his village and carries out an investigation, gathering information from an old woman aged ninety-two who survived the Japanese massacre in 1939 as well as from the gazetteer of his old home. The narrator himself realizes that his hometown is the "most beautiful and most repulsive" place and that the people of his father's generation "killed, … looted, and … defended their country in a valiant, stirring ballet that makes us unfilial descendants who now occupy the land pale by comparison."[181] Here, killing and looting are closely associated with defending their country, blurring the boundary between good and bad. Granddad Yu Zhan'ao is a figure with conflicting attributes, at once a laborer, a murderer, an adulterer, a bandit, and a hero fighting against the Japanese, as previously discussed. This admixture uplifts the unpretentiousness and spontaneity of the narrator's ancestors in contrast to the present-day world, which is contaminated by hypocrisy. At the beginning of the novel, the narrator laments the degeneration of modern humankind: "Surrounded by progress, I feel a nagging sense of our species' regression."[182] By the novel's end, the narrator is disparaging modern life and calling for a return:

> For ten years I had been away from my village. Now I stood before Second Grandma's grave, affecting the hypocritical display of affection I had learned from high society, with a body immersed so long in the filth of urban life that a foul stench oozed from my pores.
>
> …
>
> "Grandson!" [Second Grandma] says magnanimously. "Come home! You're lost if you don't. I know you don't want to, I know you're scared of all the flies, of the clouds of mosquitoes, of snakes slithering across the damp sorghum soil. You revere heroes and loathe bastards, but who among us is not the 'most heroic and most bastardly'?" (Mo Yan, *The Red Sorghum Family*, trans. Howard Goldblatt, 356–357)
>
> 我逃离家乡十年，带着机智的上流社会传染给我的虚情假意，带着被肮脏的都市生活臭水浸泡得每个毛孔都散发着扑鼻恶臭的肉体，又一次站在二奶奶的坟头前……
>
> ……
>
> 二奶奶宽容大度地说：“孙子，回来吧！再不回来你就没救了。我知道你不想回来，你害怕铺天盖地的苍蝇，你害怕乌云一样的蚊虫，你害怕潮湿的高粱地里无腿的爬蛇。你崇尚英雄，但仇恨王八蛋，但谁又不是‘最英雄好汉最王八蛋’呢？”(Mo Yan, *The Red Sorghum Family*, 492–494)

At the same time, the narrator laments the pure red sorghum that he has used as a metaphor for heroic human beings:

> The sorghum around the grave is a variety brought in from Hainan Island, the lush green sorghum now covering the rich black soil of Northeast Gaomi Township is all hybrid. The sorghum that looked like a sea of blood, whose praises I have sung over and

over, has been drowned in a raging flood of revolution and no longer exists....

How I loathe hybrid sorghum.

...They assume the name of sorghum, but are devoid of the dazzling sorghum color. Lacking the soul and bearing of sorghum, they pollute the pure air of Northeast Gaomi Township with their dark, gloomy, ambiguous faces.

Being surrounded by hybrid sorghum instills in me a powerful sense of loss. (Mo Yan, *The Red Sorghum Family*, trans. Howard Goldblatt, 358)

这时，围绕着二奶奶坟墓的已经是从海南岛交配回来的杂种高粱了，这时，郁郁葱葱覆盖着高密东北乡黑色土地的也是杂种高粱了。我反复讴歌赞美的、红得像血海一样的红高粱已被革命的洪水冲激得荡然无存......。

我痛恨杂种高粱。

......它们空有高粱的名称，但没有高粱辉煌的颜色。它们真正缺少的，是高粱的灵魂和风度。它们用它们晦暗不清、模棱两可的狭长脸庞污染着高密东北乡纯净的空气。

在杂种高粱的包围中，我感到失望。

(Mo Yan, *The Red Sorghum Family*, 495)

Obviously, the pure red sorghum, representing the people of his grandparents' generation and their glorious history, is the signified object of his nostalgia. As discussed more fully in chapter 1, the narrator complains about the human "species' regression" and the end of the novel finds him denigrating the disgraceful and cowardly people that he himself represents. The words of his second grandmother, who was raped and killed by Japanese, express his own yearning for a restoration of heroic spirit and manhood. The book's final sentences also show the narrator's determination to grasp the past:

The ghosts of my family are sending me a message to point the way out of this labyrinth:

You pitiable, frail, suspicious, stubbornly biased child, whose soul has been spellbound by poisonous wine, go down to the Black Water River and soak in its waters for three days and three nights—remember, not a day more or a day less—to cleanse yourself, body and soul. Then you can return to your real world. Besides the yang of White Horse Mountain and the yin of the Black Water River, there is also a stalk of pure-red sorghum which you must sacrifice everything, if necessary, to find. When you have found it, wield it high as you re-enter a world of dense brambles and wild predators. It is your talisman, as well as our family's glorious totem and a symbol of the heroic spirit of Northeast Gaomi Township! (Mo Yan, *The Red Sorghum Family*, trans. Howard Goldblatt, 359)

我的整个家族的亡灵，对我发出了指示迷津的启示：
　　可怜的、孱弱的、猜忌的、偏执的、被毒酒迷幻了灵魂的孩子，你到墨水河里去浸泡三天三夜——记住，一天也不能多，一天也不能少，洗净了你的肉体和灵魂，你就回到你的世界里去。在白马山之阳，墨水河之阴，还有一株纯种的红高粱，你要不惜一切努力找到它。你高举着它去闯荡你的荆榛丛生、虎狼横行的世界，它是你的护身符，也是我们家族的光荣的图腾和我们高密东北乡传统精神的象征！
(Mo Yan, *The Red Sorghum Family*, 496)

The last surviving stalk of pure red sorghum symbolizes the root that the writer is searching for and for which he is willing to "sacrifice everything, if necessary."

David Lowenthal stated that "to some people such imaginative returns promise immortality, to others a chance to undo errors or right wrong, to still others an escape from the weight and woes of the present."[183] This last idea applies to Mo Yan, who is dissatisfied with the present because it is dominated by degenerated generations. Harking back to his search for roots, he revisits and re-creates his homeland, a mysterious Northeast Gaomi Township, "a theme park of lost illusions"[184] and a fable of the existential experience of the Chinese people, past and present. In the meantime, this homeland is also a utopia-dystopia that contains Mo Yan's ambivalent sentiment toward the past. Generally speaking, Mo Yan's sweet nostalgic emotion goes back to the remote and fantasized past, where he celebrates the authenticity of human nature that he both finds there and dreams about—the authenticity which to him will be the cure for the modern malady. The bitter element of the author's nostalgia is limited to the near and actual past that he has personally experienced. Although Mo Yan joins the other *xungen* writers in searching for the roots of the Chinese, his own literary creation is rooted in the May Fourth tradition to a certain extent. Mo Yan, however, is distinct from the May Fourth writers, who essentially advocated a total negation of tradition, inasmuch as Mo Yan's work exhibits a dual sense of cultural identification and cultural criticism.

CHAPTER 3

THERE IS NO END TO VIOLENCE

The theme of violence has become more and more pronounced in the work of writers throughout modern Chinese literature from May Fourth literature, to revolutionary writings in Mao's time, to postrevolutionary fiction. In fact, violence as a subject has not simply continued from the May Fourth period into contemporary literature, but it has actually become grimmer in the hands of Chinese writers after the Cultural Revolution. Post-Mao writers write about violence in a much more direct and undisguised tone than their colleagues of earlier times.

In some works of May Fourth literature, such as those by Lu Xun and Shen Congwen, depictions of execution and the like are not uncommon. For Lu Xun, writing about violence is a means to expose the cultural backwardness of traditional China. Examples include "Ah Q zhengzhuan" (阿Q正传) [The true story of Ah Q] and "Yao" (药) [Medicine]. Likewise, his "Zhu jian" (铸剑) [Forging the swords] is a story of revenge that comprises such weird scenes as three human heads floating, playing, and fighting in a large vessel filled with boiling water; the fear evoked by the violent act of beheading is reduced or even replaced by a surreal and playful atmosphere in this legendary narrative. For Shen Congwen, violence is simply a part of the old culture that forms people's everyday lives. His "Xin yu jiu" (新与旧) [New and old] depicts decapitation in detail; it is, after all, a story about a decapitator. Through the story of a professional executioner, Shen shows how society has undergone rapid changes from the time of the late Qing dynasty (1644–1911) to the republican period (1911–1949). Special attention is given to the ritual performances before and after executions, which have become entertainment in the story for the crowd of spectators—and in the story, for the reader as well. The theatrical elements in the story turn a horrible decapitation into a carnival, and tragedy is thus transformed into comedy. Consequently, the horror and uneasiness associated with violence are greatly diminished.

In socialist literature, violence is a device of class struggle that is one of the key guiding principles of Maoist thinking. Socialist fiction, a good example of replacing one violent behavior with another, attributes violence and revolutionary discord to misery and oppression. As one critic indicated, "violence is always justified if it is the most efficient means of throwing off oppression or rectifying some other form of justice."[185] Revolutionary violence, or violence in the name of the people, is described in socialist literature as a proper and legitimate measure in the fight against counterrevolutionary violence, the violence exercised by the oppressing classes before they lost power. As Nancy Armstrong and Leonard Tennenhouse asserted in their introduction to *The Violence of Representation: Literature and the History of Violence*, "a class of people cannot produce themselves as a ruling class without setting themselves off against certain Others."[186] In revolutionary novels, such as *Taiyang zhao zai Sangganhe shang* (太阳照在桑干河上) [The sun shines over the Sanggan River] by Ding Ling, *Lijiazhuang de bianqian* (李家庄的变迁) [Changes in Li Village] by Zhao Shuli (赵树理), and *Baofeng zhouyu* (暴风骤雨) [The hurricane] by Zhou Libo (周立波), this class of people—the proletarians or, to be precise, the poor peasants—has the urge to distinguish the Others from themselves in order to establish and secure their own ruling authority. Then they demonize the Others by naming them, for instance, bloodsuckers or class enemies so as to morally justify class revenge and the collective employment of violence. Even this process of naming, that is, the marking of the linguistic boundary, is violent. There is a paradox in the simultaneous establishment and elimination of difference. On the one hand, as Armstrong and Tennenhouse put it, "the violence of representation is the suppression of difference";[187] but on the other hand, this differentiation or marking of a boundary is inevitable. Furthermore, to set the Others apart is to eradicate the Others eventually.

Violence is a recurring theme in Mo Yan's fiction. Almost from the very beginning of his writing career, Mo Yan's work has included graphic descriptions of violent scenes, some of which rival the violent writing of Yu Hua, for example, who has written several stories that depict chilling cruelty. The earliest and perhaps most unforgettable of Mo Yan's violent images is Uncle Arhat's being flayed alive by Japanese soldiers in *The Red Sorghum Family*. Throughout the past three decades or so, different kinds of violence have been key in the construction of Mo Yan's fictional world, adding a bleak and harsh facet to his work. His 2001 novel *Sandalwood Punishment*—which could be regarded as a masterpiece of violence—reaches an extreme. While Mo Yan is in this sense, too, a successor to his May Fourth ancestors, his representation of violence is in fact also a challenge to Maoist discourse. But Mo Yan's writing about cruelty is not solely a vehicle for cultural, social, and political criticisms, for it has also been observed occasionally to stem from an interest in brutality *per se*. Violence is such an important theme in Mo Yan's works that it deserves a detailed discussion. Therefore this chapter focuses on the author's use of violence, analyzing it from the following perspectives: (1) domestic violence caused by an unlivable life, (2) violence as a challenge to the justification of Mao's theory of class struggle, (3) violence concerning the complex of national hatred, (4) violence between human beings and animals, and (5) the use of color in representations of violence.

VIOLENCE AND HARSH REALITY

A number of individuals in Mo Yan's works choose to end either their own lives or the life of a loved one because of a harsh or unlivable reality. In his discussion of the relationship between human destructiveness and what he calls the "thwarting of life," Erich Fromm argued that the destructive tendencies of human beings are caused by feelings of isolation and powerlessness.[188] The thwarting of life is a situation in which "the isolated and powerless individual is blocked in realizing his sensuous, emotional, and intellectual potentialities."[189] Fromm continued: "Those individual and social conditions that make for suppression of life produce the passion for destruction that forms, so to speak, the reservoir from which the particular hostile tendencies—either against others or against oneself—are nourished." And finally, "the more the drive toward life is thwarted, the stronger is the drive toward destruction; the more life is realized, the less is the strength of destructiveness."[190] Many of Mo Yan's fictional characters are just such "isolated and powerless individuals" who are blocked from realizing even the most basic needs of life. Violence results from this lack of realization and such destructive impulses directed at others or at themselves. The episodes considered here can be categorized according to the object of violence.

Three young people from the countryside commit suicide, the ultimate act of self-destruction: Xiaohu from "Dry River," Fang Jinju (方金菊) from *The Garlic Ballads*, and Qi Wendong (齐文栋) from "Huanle" (欢乐) [Happiness]. All three characters find life unbearably miserable and thus unlivable. In addition, we will also analyze Luo Tong (罗通) from *Forty-One Bombs*, who takes his wife's life.

The first victim is Xiaohu, the younger son in an upper-middle peasant's family. As discussed more fully in the previous chapter, the boy accidentally falls from a tree and hurts the local party secretary's daughter, who is under the tree. The outraged secretary kicks him in the chest, and then his parents and elder brother beat him severely because they believe the boy will ruin their whole family's future. Unable to bear the abuse,

Xiaohu drowns himself in the icy river. The second victim is Fang Jinju, who is in love with the discharged soldier Gao Ma (高马) but forbidden to marry him by her parents. Jinju's parents have already arranged a wife swapping—they sign an agreement with two additional families, and so three men and three women are now bethrothed. With this arrangement, Jinju's handicapped brother will have a chance to get a wife, but she herself will have to marry a sick man twenty-five years older than she. When Gao Ma and Jinju announce their love to her family, they are beaten by her father and brothers. After a long and ineffective struggle, they decide to run away—but are caught. More abuse awaits them. Jinju is so tired of the endless mistreatment that she chooses to end her own life as well as that of her unborn baby. The third victim, Qi Wendong, is a young countryman who attempts to escape his peasant's fate by going to college. He takes the entrance examination each year for five years, during which time his tuition and fees become a heavy burden to his family. Therefore he is frequently abused, mostly verbally, by his brother and especially by his sister-in-law. He kills himself by drinking highly toxic pesticide when he fails the exam a fifth time.

Although Qi's afflictions are perhaps minor compared to the sufferings of Xiaohu and Jinju, his decision to end his life is driven by complete disappointment coupled with extreme detestation for his living environment, a backward rural area populated by ignorant and vulgar people. Xiaohu and Jinju are subject to brutal family violence, which mingles with their undesirable political realities to complicate their tragedies. Both families are among the mass of peasants who

> are still for the most part on the bottom of the social hierarchy, sharing an egalitarianism of backwardness, poverty, and ignorance; but, in the fashion of Orwell's *Animal Farm*, some peasants are more equal than others. Some peasants are rural Communist Party cadres; they support and are supported by the county, provincial, and national Party apparatus. Together these two groups constitute a *tequan jieji* (lit. "a class with special powers") that has been oppressing the mass of the peasants ever since the Great Leap Forward. (Michael S. Duke, "Past, Present, and Future in Mo Yan's Fiction of the 1980s," 48–49)

Xiaohu might possibly ruin the future of his family, especially that of his elder brother who hopes to be enlisted; similarly, Jinju's breaking of the swapped marriage endangers not only her crippled brother's future but also her family's hope of a marriage that would make them related to someone of authority—one party in the arrangement has a cadre uncle. Under these desperate social and political circumstances, both families use violence to vent their anger and disappointment. Xiaohu's parents believe that they are living an unlivable life because of the family's political status, and their brutal punishment of the young boy's unintentional mistake makes his life even more miserable and eventually drives him to commit suicide. Jinju and her family, likewise, are trapped in a vicious circle of thwarting and misfortune that leads to more severe violence.

Whereas some fictional characters choose to end their own lives in protest against their harsh reality, Luo Tong, the father of the child protagonist Luo Xiaotong (罗小通) of *Forty-One Bombs*, originally plans to kill the village leader but changes his mind at the last moment and kills his own wife instead, a switch that adds a level of discomfort to this story, which is carnivalesque in other ways.

The novel, derived from Mo Yan's novella "Ye luozi" (野骡子) [Wild mule], is set during the postrevolutionary era when people in China are competing with one another to get rich under Deng Xiaoping's (邓小平) economic reforms. Luo Tong, a beef-cattle estimation expert who works as a mediator between the cow vendors and the butchers at the local livestock market, runs off with a widow named Wild Mule and has a baby with her; they live together for five years. After the widow dies, he returns to his own home with their five-year-old daughter. During those five years, his own wife Yang Yuzhen (杨玉珍) and son Luo Xiaotong have worked very hard and lived in an extremely thrifty manner. As a result, they have saved enough money to build a new house. Under the leadership of the village head Lao Lan (老兰), or Old Lan, this reunified family joins the villagers to get rich in the wake of the nationwide economic reforms by establishing a butchers' village. But Old Lan leads his villagers to build up their family fortunes using a form of trickery (which is still prevalent in Chinese society today) that is fueled by the lust for money—the villagers inject large amounts of formalin into meat to make it look fresher, ignoring the fact that the chemical will damage consumers' health. Unable to be part of this, the honest and candid Luo Tong is upset by what they have been doing and further disturbed by rumors of an affair between his wife and Old Lan. Eventually he takes hold of an axe in an attempt to attack Old Lan, but changes his mind at the last moment: he instead turns on his own wife and kills her.

This novel is similar to *The Republic of Wine* in that it describes, in an absurd and extravagant way, a postrevolutionary China in which widespread debauchery and dissipation have come into fashion following several decades of stern suppression of human desire during the revolutionary period. Whereas wine is the central metaphor in *The Republic of Wine*, meat plays an extremely important role in *Forty-One Bombs*. Luo Xiaotong, the protagonist as well as the narrator, is revered as the Meat God at the Meat Festival because of his superior ability to eat meat. Paralleled with meat, sex also occupies much space in the novel, adding a dimension of extravagance to the story. On top of its revelation of the uncontrollable human desire in post-Mao capitalist-communist[191] China, the novel also mocks the famous quotation of Gaozi (告子, ca. 420–350 BC), the ancient Chinese philosopher: "To enjoy food and delight in colors is nature" (食色性也。).[192]

Unlike the unbearable situations of the other characters discussed thus far, Luo Tong's life does not seem terrible enough to drive him to murder. But the future that seems so bright for everyone else does not offer any hope to him. Instead, a sense of loneliness isolates him from the majority; he echoes Lu Xun's madman or Kong Yiji (孔乙己) in a way. The fact that Luo Tong climbs a platform built on a huge tree and stays there for hours and later even days at a time demonstrates his intentional isolation from the crowd. He is powerless, especially when he confronts the powerful village head. Moreover, his wife's adoring attitude toward Old Lan indicates her agreement with the latter's policies and also lends credence to the rumor of an affair, a huge humiliation to Luo Tong as a husband. The life that is attractive for everyone else, including his own wife and children, is unbearable for him. As a result, the isolated and powerless Luo Tong chooses to use the only power he has—a weapon and the ability to kill—to fight against his enemy Old Lan in order to defend his dignity as a husband and an honest man. But even with his weapon in hand, Luo Tong is still powerless before the authority of the village head, and in the end he can only vent his resentment and hatred by killing his wife. This is apparently a case of domestic violence; yet it is also the direct result of a new mode of everyday violence in the postrevolutionary society in which people's rights as citizens and consumers are seriously violated. The suppression of human desire during the revolutionary era leads to a morbid yearning for money and sensual enjoyments. Those who suffer and are the victims of this kind of violence in one case may very likely be the perpertrators of violent deeds that victimize other people in another case. In other words, everyone is equally likely to be a victimizer or a victim of violence. Luo Tong's violent behavior is but a concentrated manifestation of the violent society in which he lives, and his self-perception as a loser serves as a sarcastic symbol in Mo Yan's social criticism.

VIOLENCE AND CLASS STRUGGLE

The type of violence that originated from an unfair and cruel society under the rule of the Communist party—for example, the violence experienced by Xiaohu in "Dry River"—is unheard of in revolutionary literature, therefore Mo Yan's questioning of the violence sanctioned in the name of revolution is an explicit challenge to Maoist discourse.

A brief discussion of the writing of violence in socialist literature will facilitate a better understanding of exactly how Mo Yan writes defiantly. First, the three revolutionary novels of Mao Zedong's time previously mentioned—*The Sun Shines over the Sanggan River*, *Changes in Li Village*, and *The hurricane*—filled with scenes of public beating and accusation, are good representatives of the kind of sanctioned violence that is found in "French revolutionary writing," one of the two modes of French revolutionary writing observed by Roland Barthes, which "always proclaimed a right founded on bloodshed or moral justification."[193] These three novels share such a formula: the poor peasants have been subject to the oppression and exploitation of local tyrants or landlords for a long time, then the Communist Party arrives and leads them to overthrow the oppressors. The struggle is long and difficult because at first the peasants are full of worries, but eventually the masses are aroused to denounce the landlords and pour out their grievances. The following is what T. A. Hsia (夏济安) observed in *The Hurricane*: "They [the Communists] revive old memories of hatred, spread gossip, put words into the peasants' mouths, give them a false image of themselves, encourage their hostility and subject them to regimentation."[194] Finally, the peasants become so angry that they beat the landlords—sometimes even to death.

Examples of such public accusation are abundant in the three Mao-era novels. One episode from *The Sun Shines over the Sanggan River* is worth quoting as an example of violence in the name of revolution:

> Peasants surged up to the stage, shouting wildly: "Kill him!" "A life for our lives!"
>
> A group of villagers rushed to beat him. It was not clear who started, but one struck the first blow and others fought to get at him, while those behind who could not reach him shouted: "Throw him down! Throw him down! Let's all beat him!"
>
> One feeling animated them all—vengeance! They wanted vengeance! They wanted to give vent to their hatred, the sufferings of the oppressed since their ancestors' times, the hatred of thousands of years; all this resentment they directed against him. They would have liked to tear him with their teeth.
>
> The cadres could not stop everyone jumping onto the stage. With blows and curses the crowd succeeded in dragging him down from the stage and then more people swarmed towards him. Some crawled over across the heads and shoulders of those in front.
>
> Schemer Chien's [Qian Wengui] silk gown was torn. His shoes had fallen off, the white paper hat had been trampled into pieces underfoot....

Schemer Chien crawled to his feet again and kneeled to kow-tow to the crowd. His right eye was swollen after his beating so that the eye looked even smaller. His lip was split and mud was mixed with the blood. His bedraggled moustaches drooped disconsolately. (Ding Ling, *The Sun Shines over the Sanggan River*, trans. Yang Hsien-yi and Gladys Yang, 289–291)

人们都涌了上来，一阵乱吼："打死他！""打死偿命！"
　　一伙人都冲着他打来，也不知是谁先动的手，有一个人打了，其余的便都往上抢，后面的人群够不着，便大声嚷："拖下来！拖下来！大家打！"
　　人们只有一个感情——报复！他们要报仇！他们要泄恨，从祖宗起就被压迫的苦痛，这几千年来的深仇大恨，他们把所有的怨苦都集中到他一个人身上了。他们恨不能吃了他。
　　虽然两旁有人拦阻，还是禁不住冲上台来的人，他们一边骂一边打，而且真把钱文贵拉下了台，于是人更蜂拥了上来。有些人从人们的肩头上往前爬。
　　钱文贵的绸夹衫被撕烂了，鞋子不知失落在哪里，白纸高帽也被踩烂了，一块一块的踏在脚底下......钱文贵又爬起来了，跪在地下给大家磕头，右眼被打肿了，眼显得更小，嘴唇破了，血又沾上许多泥，两撇胡子稀脏的下垂着......。
(Ding Ling, *The Sun Shines over the Sanggan River*, 265–267)

Although only one episode is quoted here, all the descriptions of this kind of revolutionary violence have something in common: the employment of violent language. The outraged people all "surged" forward and shouted words like "throw him down," "kill him," or "beat him to death," and each scene is gorier than the last. In *The Hurricane*, the landlord Han Number Six (韩老六) is eventually executed, but the scene of execution remains in the background. In *The Sun Shines over the Sanggan River*, cruelty is brought to the fore, and in *Changes in Li Village*, the violence is extreme: the peasants slaughter the landlord Li Ruzhen (李如珍) in public as if they are butchering an animal. The depiction of the bodily mutilation is brutal.

Violence is not the only characteristic these novels share. For one thing, by describing in detail how evil the landlords were and how badly the peasants have been treated, the authors are trying to convince the reader that the violent acts are justified, based on an eye-for-an-eye logic. The landlords have violated the peasants as human beings for years, and now they have to pay for it. In fact, these authors would argue that if the landlords and their ancestors were truly given justice for what they have done to the peasants, they should suffer much more or die ten times over. So going by this logic, the peasants are considered to be quite merciful; violence against them is justified, moralized, and legitimized. "Indeed, since tyranny provides no avenues for peaceful change, violence may well represent the only available recourse for those who reject their continued exploitations."[195] Secondly, the communist cadres always try to stop violence, but they also need to allow the peasants to vent their anger, which stems from bitter suffering and long-nursed hatred. As C. T. Hsia (夏志清) commented, "In all Communist novels about land reform, it is always the people who are after blood and the cadres gratify this desire only to the extent prescribed by legal justice."[196] The third common element in these novels is the fact that the peasants hold a carnival when the landlords' property is to be distributed among them, a festival through which the old world is irreversibly toppled. These characteristics make the novels "revolutionary" and "subversive."

All three novels were very well received by official critics after publication; two of the three, *The Hurricane* and *The Sun Shines over the Sanggan River*, won the Stalin Prize in the early 1950s. In other words, this kind of revolutionary violence was strongly advocated and even institutionalized. This is not surprising given the fact that Mao Zedong, too, endorsed revolutionary violence, telling his people in 1927 that

> revolution is not a dinner party, or writing an essay, or painting a picture, or doing embroidery: it cannot be so refined, so leisurely and gentle, so temperate, kind, courteous, restrained and magnanimous. A revolution is an insurrection, an act of violence by which one class overthrows another. (Translation from Mao Zedong, "Report on an Investigation of the Peasant Movement in Hunan," in *Selected Works of Mao Tse-Tung*, 1:28)

革命不是请客吃饭，不是做文章，不是绘画绣花，不能那样
雅致，那样从容不迫，文质彬彬，那样温良恭俭让。革命是
暴动，是一个阶级推翻一个阶级的暴烈的行动。

(Mao Zedong, "Report on an Investigation of the Peasant
Movement in Hunan," in *Selected Works of Mao Zedong*, 17)

For Mo Yan, this kind of officially sanctioned violence is highly
questionable. He may have shared C. T. Hsia's thoughts regarding Ding
Ling's novel:

> Ting Ling records the fury and the hatred of landlords; but what
> the cadres must have done to generate this fury and hatred, what
> the peasants actually feel while parading their violence, how the
> landlords themselves feel, not so much over their gross physical
> punishment as over its monstrous injustice—with all these deeper
> truths Ting Ling is not concerned, and cannot be concerned.

(C. T. Hsia, *A History of Modern Chinese Fiction*, 487)

It is interesting in this context to note that Mo Yan's lengthy novel
Big Breasts and Wide Hips also features a public accusation. Recounting
the history of a peasant family from the year 1900 up to the post-Mao
period, this novel's central female figure, Mother, gives birth to eight
daughters and a son. Since Mother has sons-in-law with different political backgrounds, her life is heavily imprinted with historical and political complexities. Her second son-in-law, Sima Ku, is a KMT officer as
well as a landlord in his hometown, while her fifth son-in-law, Lu Liren,
serves in the Communist army. The meeting in which the poor peasants
denounce and accuse the landlords is actually a power struggle between
two political forces represented by these two in-laws. When the PLA
troops led by Lu Liren defeat Sima Ku and his KMT army, the Communists decide to have the masses accuse the local landlords, including
Sima himself, although he has already escaped after the battle. A mysterious high-ranking officer, a *darenwu* (大人物) [VIP], is present to
supervise the meeting. A blind man claims that his wife was raped by
Sima Ku and swallowed opium to kill herself afterwards. His mother
was so upset by her daughter-in-law's suicide that she hanged herself.

As a result, the blind man requests that Sima Ku's young son and his even younger twin daughters be shot, in order to die for their father's crime. Lu Liren is reluctant to accede to this request and tries to explain that it would be unfair to kill the innocent young children, so the blind man turns to the VIP for a decision.

> Lu Liren looked at the VIP, pleading with his eyes; the VIP returned his look with an icy stare that was as sharp as a knife. Lu's face was beaded with sweat that dampened his headband, making it look like a wound on his forehead. No longer calm and at ease, he alternated between looking down at his feet and gazing out at the crowd below, the courage to make eye contact with the VIP was long gone.
>
> …
>
> Lu Liren remained standing there, his head bowed, like a piece of petrified wood, for a long moment before snapping out of it. Finally, he headed back, walking as if his legs were made of lead, and stared down at us with madness in his eyes. His eyeballs seemed frozen in their sockets. He looked pathetic up there. Finally, he opened his mouth to speak:
>
> "I hereby sentence Sima Liang, son of Sima Ku, to death, to be carried out immediately! And I sentence Sima Feng and Sima Huang, daughters of Sima Ku, to death, also to be carried out immediately!" (Mo Yan, *Big Breasts and Wide Hips*, trans. Howard Goldblatt, 290–292)
>
> 鲁立人用求援的目光看着大人物，大人物的目光冷酷地盯着他。大人物的目光像剥皮刀一样锋利，鲁立人的脸上冒出了汗水，他失去了从容和潇洒，一会儿低下头注视着自己的脚尖，一会儿抬头望望台下的人群，他再也没有勇气与大人物对视。
>
> ……
>
> 鲁立人站在那儿，低着头，像一根木头。他站在那儿好久，才苏醒过来，拖着两条很沉的腿，无精打采地回到县长应该站立的位置上。他用一种疯狂的目光盯着我们，盯了又是一个好久。他那样子真可怜。好久连接着好久，他终于张开嘴，眼里射出赌徒下大注时的目光，说："我宣布，判处司马库之子司马粮死刑，立即执行！判处司马库之女司马凤、司马凰死刑，立即执行！"
>
> (Mo Yan, *Big Breasts and Wide Hips*, 275–277)

Under the protection of the villagers, Sima Ku's son runs away. His twin sisters, however, are shot on the spot. The reader learns that the blind man who has demanded the deaths of the children is nothing more than a scoundrel who made up the story to frame Sima Ku. Even worse, this fact is made known to the public before the baby girls are killed. While the VIP simply ignores the truth, Lu Liren blocks it from his conscience for the security of his political future. He justifies the death sentences by saying: "On the surface, we'll be executing two children. And yet it's not children we'll be executing, but a reactionary, backward social system. We will be executing two symbols! ... You're either revolutionary or counterrevolutionary, there's no middle ground!" ("我们枪毙的看起来是两个孩子，其实不是孩子，我们枪毙的是一种反动落后的社会制度，枪毙的是两个符号！......不革命就是反革命，没有中间道路可走！["]).[197] By claiming the lives of the innocent children, these executioners demonize themselves. Humanity has succumbed to political needs at best, and to an evil disposition and bloodthirstiness at worst. The children's murder not only directly links this episode to Mo Yan's political allegory, *The Republic of Wine*, in which baby boys are slaughtered and eaten, but also demonstrates the novelist's inheritance of Lu Xun's plea, "Save the children." By exposing the untrustworthiness of the so-called masses and the absurdity of the public accusation, this episode also discloses the novelist's doubt regarding the legitimacy of violence in the name of revolution. Some landlords may indeed have oppressed their tenants and made their lives miserable; nevertheless it is dangerous to make generalizations. As mentioned earlier, the protagonist in Mo Yan's later novel, *Life and Death Are Wearing Me Out*, Ximen Nao, is a good, hardworking, and humane landlord who is wrongly executed during the land-reform movement in the late 1940s. In revolutionary literature, however, cruel scenes such as those in Ding Ling's novel are so common that they have become clichéd and formulaic, imbued with the concept that all rich people are evil, just as crows are black all over the world.

Creating a binary opposition between the rich and the poor is certainly necessary for the theory of class struggle, exactly as Lu Liren claims: you are either revolutionary or counterrevolutionary and there is no middle ground. Mo Yan's description of the meeting involving the accusation in *Big Breasts and Wide Hips* problematizes such an opposition. On the one hand, Mo Yan's picture contains some "deeper truths" that C. T. Hsia would like to see; on the other hand, it alerts the readers to the possibility that the facts have been distorted and that the accusations may be unfair. Mo Yan's treatment leads to the pondering of issues on more profound levels, taking into consideration political and human complexities.

The same novel, for example, includes a scene of physical punishment. Sima Ku is listed as a wanted criminal after the battle, and his mother-in-law and some other family members are arrested because they might know where he is hiding. During the interrogation, they are all hung up by their arms and tortured. The protagonist, Shangguan Jintong, describes his feelings thus:

> My arms hurt, but it was bearable; the pain in my shoulder joints, on the other hand, was excruciating. Our heads slumped forward, our necks stretched out as far as they would go. It was impossible to keep our legs straight, impossible not to straighten out our insteps, and impossible to keep our toes from pointing straight down to the floor. I couldn't stop whimpering ... The weight of Mother's body stretched the rope as taut as a wire; she was the first to start sweating and the one who sweated the most. Nearly colorless steam rose from her scraggly hair.
>
> ...
>
> "Ready to talk?" Inspector Yang asked us. "Come clean, and I'll take you down immediately."
>
> Straining to lift her head and catch her breath, Mother said rasply, "Let the kids down ... I'm the one you want...."
>
> "We'll make them talk!" he announced to the window. "Beat them, and I mean hard!"
>
> (Mo Yan, *Big Breasts and Wide Hips*,
> trans. Howard Goldblatt, 369–370)

我感到手腕刺痛尚可忍受，肩关节的钝痛确实难挨。我们都必然地脑袋前倾，脖子伸长到最大限度，双腿无法不伸直，脚背无法不绷直，脚尖无法不垂直向地。我无法不哀鸣。......母亲肥胖的身体把那根新麻绳子坠得像钢丝一样紧，

> 汗水最多最早地从她身上涌出，她的杂乱的头发里蒸发着雪白的雾气。
> ……
> "你们说不说？"杨公安员道，"只要交待，立即就放下你们。"
> 母亲用力地把头昂起，喘息着说："把我的孩子放下来……一切由我来担承……。"
> 杨公安员对着窗外大叫："用刑，给我狠狠地打！"
> (Mo Yan, *Big Breasts and Wide Hips*, 376–377)

Such a scene is not uncommon in socialist literature, except that the torturers would be exclusively class enemies, whether Chinese who work for the KMT or Japanese invaders who impose punishment on the Communists or other innocent people to force them to reveal secrets. It is unheard-of in revolutionary literature for Communists to torture anyone, let alone the very young and the aged. Being punished for nothing, Mother and her children are merely victims of political struggle, and the bodies being tortured serve to mock the ridiculousness and irrationality of this struggle. As Howard Y. F. Choy claimed, "Insofar as the personal past is concerned, nothing is more immediate than one's own body, the body being both the agent that experiences and desires to know about history, and the medium through which history violently manifests itself."[198] Moreover, when history manifests itself on the body—the most direct, personal, and vulnerable object of infliction—the body is inevitably imprinted with the traumas of the conflict between public and private discourses and becomes the victim of the political, national, and historical grand narratives.

The short story "The Cure," in which the harvesting of human organs will be discussed in detail later in the book, provides another example of Mo Yan's questioning of the violence advocated in the name of revolution. The story is about a country dweller and his son who set out to collect the fresh gall bladders of their fellow villagers immediately after the government has executed them. A man of filial piety whose aged mother suffers from advanced cataracts, the country dweller consults a miracle worker, who advises that a human gall bladder will restore her eyesight.

When the man learns that the armed work detachment's execution will take place the following morning, he goes to the execution ground to wait for the bodies with his own young son (the boy's participation in the organ harvesting arguably represents a negative extension of a cannibalistic culture). The man and his son hide under a bridge. The boy describes what he hears:

> I moved up close to Father and sat down on a clump of weeds. By listening carefully, I could hear a gong in the village, mixed in with a man's raspy voice: "Villagers—go to the southern bridgehead to watch the execution—shoot the tyrannical landlord Ma Kuisan—his wife—puppet village head Luan Fengshan—orders of armed work detachment Chief Zhang—those who don't go will be punished as collaborators."
>
> I heard Father grumble softly, "Why are they doing this to Ma Kuisan? Why shoot him? He's the last person they should shoot."
>
> ...
>
> The arrival of the execution party at the bridgehead was announced by the frantic beating of a gong and muted footsteps. Then a booming voice rang out: "Chief Zhang, Chief Zhang, I've been a good man all my life...."
>
> ...
>
> Another voice, this one flat and cracking with emotion: "Chief Zhang, be merciful ... We drew lots to see who would be village head; I didn't want the job ... We drew lots; I got the short straw—my bad luck ... Chief Zhang, be merciful, and spare my dog life ... I've got an eighty-year-old mother at home I have to take care of...." (Mo Yan, "The Cure," in *Shifu, You'll Do Anything for a Laugh*, trans. Howard Goldblatt, 115–117)
>
> 我偎着爹，坐在一堆乱草上，耸起耳朵，听到村子里响起锣声，锣声的间隙里，有一个粗哑的男人声音传过来：村民们——去南桥头看毙人啦——枪毙恶霸地主马魁三——还有他老婆——枪毙伪村长栾凤山——还有他老婆——武工队张科长有令——不去以通敌论处——
>
> 我听到爹低声嘟哝着："怎么会枪毙马魁三呢？怎么会枪毙马魁三呢？无论枪毙谁也不该枪毙马魁三啊......。"
>
> ......

行刑的队伍逼近了桥头。锣声"咣咣"地响着。"嚓嚓"
的脚步声响着。有一个粗大宏亮的的嗓门哭叫着："张科
长啊张科长，俺可是一辈子没干坏事啊……。"……有一
个扁扁的、干涩的嗓门哀告着："张科长开恩吧……我
这个村长是抓阄抓到的……都不愿干……抓阄，偏我运气
坏，抓上了……开恩饶我一条狗命吧张科长……我家里还
有八十岁的老母没人养老哇……。" (Mo Yan, "The Cure," in
Collected Works of Mo Yan, 5:431–433)

In spite of the intercession of the villagers, the execution is carried
out. Having seen that the brains of the condemned people are splat-
tered all over the place, the executioners are content that their work is
done and proceed to eat their breakfast of jellied bean curd (*doufunao*,
豆腐脑) and deep-fried dough sticks (*youtiao*, 油条). At this point,
the intentional likening of human brains to jellied bean curd—both use
the same Chinese character: *nao* (脑), which literally means *brain*—
has a strong implication of cannibalism, a reference that is deepened
by the chronological placement of the meal immediately after an execution. If the "I" narrator' in Lu Xun's "The New-Year Sacrifice"—
who tries to distract his nagging conscience with delicious shark fin
soup—is indirectly responsible, through his indifference to others' suffering, for the existence of cannibalistic culture, the executioners in Mo
Yan's novel are immediate participants in and creators of this culture.
Even more culpable are those who claim that their mission is liberating
the poor people from the oppressive cannibalistic culture, for they are
actually cannibals on a metaphorical level. I would argue that Mo Yan
not only writes in defiance of the socio-political orthodoxy, but that his
challenging the Maoist legacy develops Lu Xun's cultural and social
criticism into an explicit political criticism, something which requires
great courage from the writer. Mo Yan is even more uncompromising
than Lu Xun in his critique. In Lu Xun's short story "Medicine," the
bun soaked in the blood of the executed revolutionary cannot save the
young man who suffers from tuberculosis—a metaphor for oppressive
and unfair society—yet the flower in front of his grave at the end of
the story at least gives a little bright color, symbolizing hope, to the

otherwise totally gloomy atmosphere. In Mo Yan's "The Cure," however, cannibalistic filial piety does not save the old woman but kills her instead, rendering the adventures and efforts of father and son groundless, fruitless, and thus absurd.

Mo Yan also uses jellied bean curd as a metaphor for human brains in *Big Breasts and Wide Hips*. Shangguan Jintong's school is giving the students a lesson in class struggle: the students are told that during the civil war of 1946–1949, the runaway landlords return and restore their power over peasants, and some of the peasants are buried alive. The landlords dig a pit, make a man or a woman stand in it, and throw sand into the pit up to the person's neck until black blood is seeping out of the victim's nose and ears. The scene is recorded as follows:

> "Little Lion tapped him on the head with his finger and said, 'Say, men, want to try some human brains?' 'Who'd want to eat that stuff?' they said. 'It'd make me puke.' 'Some people have eaten it,' Little Lion said. 'Detachment Leader Chen, for one. Add some soy sauce and strips of ginger, he said, and it tastes like jellied bean curd.'" (Mo Yan, *Big Breasts and Wide Hips*, trans. Howard Goldblatt, 366)

> "......小狮子曲起手指，弹弹进财的头，问那儿个大汉子：'伙计们，吃不吃活人脑子？'大汉子们都说：'谁吃那玩艺儿，恶心死了。'小狮子说：'有吃的，陈支队长就吃。用酱油和姜丝儿一拌，像豆腐脑儿一样。'"
> (Mo Yan, *Big Breasts and Wide Hips*, 372)

In his discussion of Lu Xun's "Medicine," Joseph Lau asserts that in this story, "violence functions as a double-edged metaphor for ignorance and cruelty."[199] By the same token, violence in Mo Yan's story discloses the duality of cannibalism in terms of both its political and cultural significance.

Unlike revolutionary writers such as Ding Ling, Zhou Libo, and Zhao Shuli, Mo Yan shows no enthusiasm for revolutionary violence. On the contrary, whereas the revolutionary writers try to justify the violent acts of the Communists, Mo Yan questions their legitimacy and ridicules their absurdity and irrationality by casting his revolutionaries as remorseless executioners. The examples from his works, especially the execution of Sima Ku's young children, indicate the ambiguity and unreliability of the categorizations "enemy" and "people"; hence it is neither reasonable nor legal for the proletarian dictatorship to suppress its class enemies in the name of the people.

Mo Yan is consistently critical of violence in present-day China. *The Garlic Ballads* is a good example of the author's sympathies for ordinary people who are subject to the tortures of everyday violence. This book is perhaps Mo Yan's most realistic novel, and according to Michael Duke, also his "most overtly ideological text."[200] Based on a historical peasant riot that occurred during the 1980s, the story focuses on garlic-growing peasants who are treated unfairly by the corrupt local government. The angry peasants burn the government building, an act which results in the arrest and imprisonment of some of them. The love story of the unfortunate Jinju and Gao Ma, previously discussed, runs parallel to this main storyline. Violence, again, is a dominant theme of this book—indeed, the novel *per se* is a representation of violence. Earlier in this chapter, Jinju's tragic end was considered; her parents, too, die a miserable death later: her father is hit by a government-owned truck and dies, and the accident is covered up; her mother is imprisoned as one of the rioters and hangs herself in the prison when she learns of the death of her daughter and unborn grandchild. Violence occurs both in the private space of the family circle and in the public spaces of the street, the prison, and the offices of corrupt politicians who cover it up, as shown by the deaths of Jinju's parents.

In the meantime, other peasants in the story are no better off, particularly those who are marginalized as Others by the ruling class. Gao Yang (高羊), another important character in the novel, is a good example. Having been involved in the riot, Gao Yang, a peasant, is sent to prison, where he recalls his miserable life as the son of a landlord. Although his father died a long time ago, he and his mother live on as family members of a landlord and suffer from political discrimination. When his mother passes away, Gao Yang decides not to cremate her body, as the law prescribes; instead he buries her both because he does not have the heart to burn his mother's remains and because he cannot afford a cremation. But this violation of the government's cremation policy is discovered, and Gao Yang is captured by the local militiamen. The scene describing his physical torment is similar to the one in which Mother and her children are tortured in *Big Breasts and Wide Hips*:

> The following morning a squad of militiamen tied Gao Yang to a bench and placed four bricks strung together with hemp around his neck; it felt like a piece of garroting wire that would lop off his head if he so much as moved. Then in the afternoon the police chief tied his thumbs together with a piece of wire and strung him up from a steel overhead beam. He didn't feel much pain, but the moment his feet left the ground, sweat seemed to squirt from every pore in his body.
>   "Now tell us, where's the landlord's wife buried?"
>   (Mo Yan, *The Garlic Ballads*, trans. Howard Goldblatt, 159)

> 第二天上午，他被几个民兵捆在一条长板凳上，脖颈上挂着四块砖头，连结四块砖头的是一根细麻绳，他感到那麻绳像锋利的刀刃一样割着脖子，随时都会把头割下来。下午，治保主任用钢丝拧住他的两个大拇指，把他吊在钢铁的房梁上，他也没感觉到有多么痛，只是在身体脱离地面的一瞬间，汗水咕嘟一声就涌了出来。
>   "说，把地主婆埋到什么地方了？"
>   (Mo Yan, *The Garlic Ballads*, 214)

Whereas revolutionary writers such as Zhou Libo, Ding Ling, and Zhao Shuli defend and promote the accusations and the violent acts of the public as righteous indignation practiced with the blessing of their supreme leader Mao Zedong, Mo Yan repeatedly crafts scenes of violence throughout his different stories in order to condemn such acts. By the end of *The Garlic Ballads*, a young military officer, "an instructor in the Marxist-Leninist Teaching and Research Section at the Artillery Academy" (炮兵学院马列主义教研室正营职教员),[201] is defending the peasants. His defense, according to Michael Duke, is "sadly evocative of grievances against the rural cadres—their economic corruption, local government violations of nation laws, nepotism, and bureaucratism...."[202] Duke observed that this young man is actually the mouthpiece of the author himself.[203] Mo Yan, as discussed in chapter 1, came from a peasant family and served in the military for many years; he was, moreover, a political instructor in the army. His creation of this military officer betrays Mo Yan's intention to produce social criticism and to attack the violent reality in which the basic rights of his peasant brothers and sisters are violated. Interestingly enough, Mo Yan does not choose to follow the mainstream revolutionary tradition, for he serves in the army, which is part of the state apparatus. Mo Yan therefore represents a subversive voice from within; he makes himself an Other in the context of the official discourse.[204] It is therefore not surprising that, as previously mentioned, the publication of *Big Breasts and Wide Hips* drew harsh criticism from the leftist critics on the mainland who believed that Mo Yan had distorted and damaged the image of the Communist Party and of the People's Liberation Army.

VIOLENCE, NATIONALISM, VOYEURISM

It is clear from an examination of the details that Mo Yan's writings are in conflict with Maoist literature almost from the very beginning of his writing career. With respect to the violence represented in times of national crisis, however, Mo Yan's views seem to be politically orthodox. This is particularly true in his denunciation of the crimes committed by the Japanese in *The Red Sorghum Family*. In other words, the Japanese invaders, labeled as cold-blooded killers in revolutionary fiction and movies, are also represented as brutal in Mo Yan's wartime novel. The graphic depiction of Uncle Arhat's dismemberment and his being flayed alive by the Japanese in this novel is chilling and unforgettable, a scene which earned the novelist a reputation for adept writing about violence. A comparison of a scene from the revolutionary novel *Kucaihua* (苦菜花) [The wild bitter flower] by Feng Deying (冯德英) with the scene from *The Red Sorghum Family* illustrates the compatibility on this point of Mo Yan's work with revolutionary literature. In the following excerpt from *The Wild Bitter Flower*, Chinese villagers are forced to "perform" for the Japanese:

> The Japs were looking and laughing wildly, especially the senior officers who sat behind the table to the north. Drinking and having fun, they laughed so hard that one could hardly see their eyes and noses....
>
> The traitor [to China] shouted in a shrill voice again:
> "Look! This one is the greatest: 'Nipple Bell Dance!'"
> A dozen naked, short-haired young women were driven to run round the fire, each of them having a pair of bronze bells on their nipples. Those who were reluctant to run were thrown into the fire.... (My translation)

> 鬼子们看着狂欢大笑。笑得最厉害的是靠北边坐在桌子后面的几位长官。他们一面喝酒一面观赏，笑得鼻子眼睛都没了......。
>
> 那汉奸又尖着嗓子高叫道 :
> "再来看! 这个最精彩啦! 这叫 '奶铃舞'!"
> 十多个留着短发的年青妇女，全身赤露，每人两个奶头上各栓一个铜铃，被逼迫围着火堆跑圈圈。有不愿跑的就被扔进火坑里......。 (Feng Deying, *The Wild Bitter Flower*, 446)

Now consider the scene of Uncle Arhat's skinning from *The Red Sorghum Family*:

> ...Sun Five's knife cut the skin above the ear with a sawing motion. Uncle Arhat screeched in agony as sprays of yellow piss shot out from between his legs ... A Japanese soldier walked up to Sun Five with a white ceramic platter, into which Sun put Uncle Arhat's large, fleshy ear. He cut off the other ear and laid it on the platter alongside the first one.
>
> ...
>
> Sun Five bent over and sliced off Uncle Arhat's genitals with a single stroke, then put them into the platter held by the Japanese soldier, who carried it at eye level as he paraded like a marionette in front of the crowd.
>
> ...

"Skin him, and be quick about it!" the interpreter demanded.
...

Sun Five started at the point on Uncle Arhat's scalp where the scab had formed, zipping the knife blade down, once, twice ... one meticulous cut after another. Uncle Arhat's scalp fell away, revealing two greenish-purple eyes and several misshapen chunks of flesh.... (Mo Yan, *The Red Sorghum Family*, trans. Howard Goldblatt, 37)

......孙五的刀子在大爷的耳朵上像锯木头一样锯着。罗汉大爷狂呼不止，一股焦黄的尿水从两腿间一窜一窜地呲出来。......走过一个端着白瓷盘的日本兵，站在孙五身旁，孙五把罗汉大爷那只肥硕敦厚的耳朵放在瓷盘里。孙五又割掉罗汉大爷另一只耳朵放进瓷盘。

　......
孙五弯下腰，把罗汉大爷的男性器官一刀旋下来，放进日本兵托着的瓷盘里。日本兵两根胳膊僵硬地伸着，两眼平视，像木偶一样从人群前走。

　......
翻译官说："快剥!"

　......
孙五操着刀，从罗汉大爷头顶上外翻着的伤口剥起，一刀刀细索索发响。他剥得非常仔细。罗汉大爷的头皮褪下。露出了青紫的眼珠。露出了一棱棱的肉......。 (Mo Yan, *The Red Sorghum Family*, 44–46)

The juxtaposition of these two excerpts makes it clear that the Japanese soldiers are even more brutal in Mo Yan's novel of the 1980s than in the revolutionary classic that was published in the 1950s. What drives both writers to craft such an inhuman image of the Japanese is a complex national hatred that has become not only the framework but also the core of the Chinese people's collective memory. Mo Yan has developed this mentality and rendered the images of the invaders still more frightening either through his own powers of imagination or through historical facts he has obtained. In *The Wild Bitter Flower*, the Japanese use the women's bodies as entertainment, whereas in *The Red Sorghum Family*, they castrate Uncle Arhat before claiming his life; both scenes have sexual undertones. Indeed, the eroticization of violence makes *The Wild Bitter Flower* more powerful. Raping or humiliating Chinese women, however, had already become a cliché in literary depictions—whether from Mao's time or later—of the violence committed by the Japanese when they invaded China during the two World Wars. Under Mo Yan's pen, the castration of a Chinese man strongly enriches the text, for this violent deed symbolizes the emasculation of a nation with a deeply rooted patriarchal culture. Given the masculine aura of this novel (discussed in chapter 2), the act of castration has significance beyond mere mutilation. Later in the novel, after the ambush, Granddad has his revenge:

> Thirty or more corpses were dragged up onto the bridge, including the old Jap, who had been stripped of his general's uniform by the Leng Detachment soldiers.
> "You women look away," Granddad announced.
> He took out his short sword, split open the crotches of the Jap soldiers' pants, and sliced off their genitalia. Then he ordered a couple of the coarser men to stuff the things into the mouths of their owners. Finally, working in pairs, the men picked up the Japanese soldiers—all in the prime of their youth—and, *one two three*, heaved them over the side: "Jap dogs," they shouted, "go back home!" The Japanese soldiers flew through the air, carrying the family jewels in their mouths, and landed in the river with a splash, a whole school of them caught up in the eastward flow. (Mo Yan, *The Red Sorghum Family*, trans. Howard Goldblatt, 137)

> 三十几具鬼子尸体被乡亲们用铁挠钩拖到桥上，连同那个被冷支队剥走了将军服的老鬼子。
>
> 爷爷说：“女人们回避。”
> 爷爷掏出小剑，逐一豁开鬼子兵的裤裆，把他们的生殖器统统割下来。又叫来两个粗野汉子，把那些玩意儿，是谁的就塞进谁嘴里。然后，十几个汉子，两人一伙，把这些也许是善良的，也许是漂亮的，但基本上都年轻力壮的日本士兵抬起来，悠三悠，喊一声：“东洋狗——回老家——”同时撒手，一个个口衔传家宝的日本兵，展翅滑翔下大桥，落进河水中，鱼贯向东去了。
>
> (Mo Yan, *The Red Sorghum Family*, 173)

An eye for an eye: Granddad, spurred by a similar mentality, also cas-trates the bodies of Japanese soldiers who are "all in the prime of their youth" and sends them "back home" where the patriarchal tradition is equally, if not more deeply, entrenched. Granddad's vengeance is in no way less violent than the behavior of the Japanese on either a philosoph-ical or a cultural dimension.

In 2001 Mo Yan published *Sandalwood Punishment*, a controversial novel that also caught the attention of his readers and critics. Set in the early twentieth century, a time that witnessed the German construction of a railroad in Shandong Province, the Boxer Uprising, and the troops of the Eight Allied Powers attacking Beijing, the story centers on a deadly form of punishment: sandalwood punishment.[205] Sun Bing (孙丙), a Shandong local *maoqiang* (茂 / 猫腔) [*mao*/cat tune] opera singer and the head of a *maoqiang* troupe,[206] kills the German engineer who had sexually assaulted his young wife, resulting in a bloody massacre of the whole village by the Germans. Neither Sun's wife nor their twin babies survive the massacre. The enraged Sun Bing has a narrow escape and joins the Boxers. Sun's oldest daughter from his previous marriage, Sun Meiniang (孙眉娘), has an affair with the county magistrate, who receives an order from the pro-vincial governor Yuan Shikai (袁世凯, 1859–1916) to arrest Sun Bing. Sun is eventually caught, and it is decided that sandalwood punishment will be carried out on him by Meiniang's father-in-law, Zhao Jia (赵甲), a retired court executioner. The instrument of this punishment is a long, straight, smooth sandalwood log, which the executioner inserts in the pris-oner's anus so that the log moves all the way through his body and finally pokes out through one of his shoulders. Because the German governor wants Sun Bing to die on the exact day that the railway opens to traffic (he wishes to use his death as a sacrifice on the day of ceremony), he orders Zhao Jia to keep Sun alive for five days while the log remains in his body. The extremely skillful executioner tries his best to avoid touching Sun's organs when he inserts the log and feeds Sun with ginseng soup every day in order to sustain his life. To console the suffering Sun, the opera troupe performs the cat tune in front of the stage where Sun Bing is exhib-ited to the public, and he joins their singing despite his dire condition;

the whole execution ground is transformed into a carnival scene. But the German troops open fire on the troupe, killing many performers and eventually the county magistrate sticks a dagger into Sun's body the day before the railway is in use, ending his life and his pain—and at the same time intentionally foiling the plans of the smug German.

It is interesting to note the change in the novelist's national complex in this work. Although he takes the mainstream stance vis-à-vis the Japanese invasion and blames the invaders by condemning their inhuman behavior, Mo Yan shifts his focus to his own fellow Chinese citizens, represented primarily by Zhao Jia—who is not only the executioner but also the inventor of the bizarrely cruel punishment. The retired court executioner, who has learned from his master, has carried out much torture himself and is respected and praised by the empress dowager, in fact represents a condensed history of Chinese torture. The essential difference between the torture in *The Red Sorghum Family* and that in *Sandalwood Punishment* is the willingness of the executioners. In the former book, Sun Five is forced by the Japanese to skin Uncle Arhat; his inner psychological torture is no less severe than the physical pain of Arhat, and he goes insane after the execution. In the latter book, on the contrary, though Zhao Jia is ordered by the German through his Chinese superior to invent the punishment, he willingly invests great effort and enthusiasm in it and does his best to finish the task. To some extent, Zhao Jia does what he does not to please the foreigners but to fulfill his own desire. Indeed, he thoroughly enjoys the job, obtains great pleasure from it, and effectively turns the cruel torture into an art form. Although the primary conflict in the novel is still between the Chinese and the foreigners, evil is also inflicted by Chinese on another Chinese. Thus, such a character as Zhao Jia conveys the novelist's strong message and represents Mo Yan's attempt to spearhead the attack on the cannibalism amidst his own people and culture. The author begins with Lu Xun's cultural criticism once more and makes it more remorseless by vividly presenting his readers with the spectacle of execution and torture.[207]

Sandalwood Punishment is controversial mainly because of its intensely violent descriptions. Compared with the graphic scenes in this novel, the brutality in other books by Mo Yan seems somewhat less chilling. First, the sandalwood punishment itself, a development of an incident in an earlier novel, is far more complicated and much crueler than any violence depicted before, so cruel in fact that it challenges the reader's imagination. In *The Garlic Ballads*, "the police chief rammed a thorny branch several inches up [Gao Yang's] ass..." (......治保主任把一根生满硬刺的树棍子戳进他的肛门里约有两拃深......)[208] when he wanted to know where Gao had buried his mother. Perhaps that description is not shocking enough for Mo Yan's purposes: several years later, the author develops this abusive act into a practically unheard-of systematic punishment. Secondly, paired with the atrocious torture, the act of feeding the prisoner nourishing ginseng soup—normally an indication of human affection and care—pushes the cruelty to an extreme. Prolonging a person's life only in order to make him suffer more grossly distorts the sweetness and tenderness of feeding someone soup. Positive human feelings, such as compassion and attentiveness, are perverted in this novel, and the reader consequently experiences a kind of violence as expectations based on past reading are upset and as the reader's psychological fortitude is greatly challenged.

In his analysis of Yu Hua and Shi Zhecun (施蛰存, 1905–2003), Andrew Jones examined both authors' stories about violence through the notion of desire, for which he indicates three levels of inquiry. The third level is "the relation between reading and desire[:] What sorts of desires do we, as readers, bring to the process of reading (and presumably enjoying) these texts?"[209] He admits that he finds himself struggling "to reconcile the violence of these stories with the pleasure [he has] derived from them ... What kind of pleasures do we anticipate as we turn the pages?"[210] Even a reader trained in the works of Mo Yan, Yu Hua, and other contemporary Chinese writers who excel in writing about cruelty may still find it difficult to anticipate any kind of pleasure from reading the violent depictions in *Sandalwood Punishment*. Instead, the process of reading becomes a dilemma: the reader's desire to move on is weakened with each turn of the page even as eagerness to know what happens to the fictional characters heightens. Indeed the story itself, told in a form of folk performance, is enjoyable; only the details of the acts of cruelty become a barrier. The third reason for *Sandalwood Punishment*'s being unprecedentedly cruel and haunting is the graphic detail, filling dozens of pages, with which the violent events are reported. In addition to testing his own nerves, the novelist is measuring his readers' tolerance. Finally, the narrative's emphasis on the spectators, especially the hilarious performance of the cat tune at the end, transforms the process of punishment into a carnival—a narrative move that adds a grotesque yet subversive dimension to the violence.

Spectators in scenes of punishment are significant throughout the book. For example, two occurrences of *lingchi* (凌迟)—death by dismemberment—are especially unforgettable. The attempt of a handsome young official, Qian Xiongfei (钱雄飞), to assassinate Yuan Shikai fails and results in his being sentenced to *lingchi*. Zhao Jia, who has become the best executioner of the court, is to carry out the penalty. According to the rules of the Qing dynasty, the executioner must make exactly five hundred cuts during the process of ending the prisoner's life. Either four hundred and ninety-nine cuts or five hundred and one cuts will render the execution imperfect. Furthermore, the size of each cut and the order of the body parts to be cut are also strictly set.

> ...[Zhao Jia's] right hand held the knife, with which he skillfully peeled off Qian's right nipple, leaving the wound like a blind man's eye socket.
> ...
> "The first cut!"
> ...
> When Zhao Jia finished his fiftieth cut, he was done with Qian's chest muscles on both sides. For now he had done one tenth of his job ... Just as he had planned. Qian never uttered a moan. This made a flaw; otherwise the performance would be much more full of sound and color, vivid and dramatic ... Next should be his genitals. It had to be done in three cuts ... His teacher had said this was the most unbearable part for a male criminal even though he could endure the other parts ... It's a matter of fear and

humiliation. Most men would prefer having their heads chopped off to losing their penises … He grasped that thing and drew it out with his left hand and with his right one he cut it quickly like lightning.

…

At this time, the silent Qian howled in despair. (My translation)

……［赵甲］的右手，操着刀子，灵巧地一转，就把一块铜钱般大小的肉，从钱的右胸脯上旋了下来。这一刀恰好旋掉了钱的乳粒，留下的伤口酷似盲人的眼窝。

……

"第一刀！"

……

赵甲割下第五十片钱肉时，钱的两边胸肌刚好被旋尽。至此，他的工作已经完成了十分之一……正好实现了原定的计划。让他感到美中不足的是，眼前这个汉子，一直不出声号叫。这就使本应有声有色的表演变成了缺乏感染力的哑剧。……接下来就应该旋去裆中之物。这地方要求三刀割尽……师傅说根据他执刑多年的经验，男犯人最怕的不是剥皮抽筋，而是割去裆中的宝贝……是一种心灵上的恐惧和人格上的耻辱。绝大多数的男人，宁愿被砍去脑袋，也不愿被切去男根。……他用左手把那玩意儿从窝里揪出来，右手快如闪电，嚓，一下子，就割了下来。

……

……这时，一直咬住牙关不出声的钱雄飞，发出了绝望［的］嚎叫。(Mo Yan, *Sandalwood Punishment*, 234–242)

Mo Yan spends more than twenty pages on this *lingchi* execution, depicting the facial expressions, psychological activities, and professional experiences of the executioner as well as the reactions of the criminal and the spectators. Obviously, the removal of the male organ is foreshadowed in *The Red Sorghum Family* when Uncle Arhat is flayed, but in *Sandalwood Punishment* the execution scene is more elaborately detailed. Moreover, both the executioner's and the convict's psyches are revealed in a skillful way. First of all, Zhao Jia, the experienced executioner, is not happy about Qian's keeping silent. To him, failure to make Qian scream with pain is a humiliation, for this would greatly disappoint the spectators—this would be akin to coming to watch an opera but getting a mime instead. The executioner and the criminal are like two rival forces competing with each other on the execution ground. The ultimate punishment is not death but pain. If the pain Zhao Jia causes cannot produce the expected result—screaming or crying—then he is proven to be weaker than the lawbreaker and thus is defeated by him. He must find a way to defeat his rival, and the experienced Zhao Jia does it successfully by cutting off Qian's genitals, that critical part of the male body. As for Qian, he knows exactly what would beat his rival and is able to maintain his heroic image until the moment his male organ is destroyed. In other words, his howl betrays his being overpowered by Zhao Jia, whose performance finally wins the applause of the spectators. A comparison of the skinning scene in *The Red Sorghum Family* and the *lingchi* episode in *Sandalwood Punishment* demonstrates at least two things. On the one hand, it is clear that the author's writing skills have become more sophisticated over time, and on the other hand, the disclosure of both the executioner's and the criminal's psychological activities makes the latter novel a more powerful effort at cultural criticism than the former book, in which the execution scene is primarily a description of the invaders' cruelty.

Another *lingchi* scene, interwoven with Qian Xiongfei's execution scene, appears as a flashback in Zhao Jia's memory while he is doing his job—he recalls his teacher's experience dismembering a beautiful prostitute.

> My teacher said that the woman was such a celestial beauty ... that nobody would believe she's a murderer. My teacher said the biggest sympathy an executioner could give to a convict was to do a perfect job. If you respect her, or if you love her, you should make her a model under torture ... There was no skin or flesh left on her body, but her face remained intact. Then came the last cut.
> ...
> ...Zhao Jia recalled, his teacher said when he dismembered the prostitute, the beauty of beauties, he cut her delicate left ear. He was so fond of it that he wished he could keep it. A golden earring with a shiny pearl was still attached to the ear.... (My translation)

师傅说那女子真是天香国色......谁也不会相信她是一个杀人犯。师傅说刽子手对犯人最大的怜悯就是把活儿做好，你如果尊敬她，或者是爱她，就应该让她成为一个受刑的典范。......她的身体已经皮肉无存，但她的脸还丝毫无损。只剩下最后的一刀了。

......

......赵甲想起师傅说过，......凌迟那个绝代名妓时，切下她的玲珑的左耳，真是感到爱不释手，那耳垂上还挂着一只金耳环，环上镶嵌着一粒耀眼的珍珠。

(Mo Yan, *Sandlewood Punishment*, 240–246)

This scene, also foreshadowed in the skinning of Uncle Arhat, especially in the singling out of the ear, again reveals Mo Yan's maturing writing techniques. Dismembering a woman, especially a beautiful one, is different from dismembering a man, inasmuch as a dimension of eroticism is added to the act when her naked body is exhibited in public. Mo Yan does not, however, depict specific parts of the female body (such as her breasts and hips) explicitly, as he has done in other books. Instead he writes about how the city of Beijing turns out to watch the punishment, how Zhao Jia's master mulls over the whole process during many nights after the execution and cuts her body into pieces and then puts it back piece by piece in his mind again and again, and how wonderfully the woman's body smells while it is being tortured, and so on. Eventually, the description comes to rest on her beautiful left ear with the shiny golden pearl earring, which becomes the focal point of all the erotic thoughts of the spectators and the readers alike. The readers, in fact, have been converted into viewers of the execution by the long and detailed description. In this particular context, the ear actually functions as a sex organ: it is erotic in much the same way that Chinese women's bound feet are. This depiction is in fact more sensual and powerful than a direct description of the female genitals would be because the reader's imagination is stimulated and aroused to wild heights. This is somewhat akin to how some view a partially covered body as more sensual than a totally nude one.

These two episodes demonstrate that under Mo Yan's pen, torture has become simply a profession and cruelty is juxtaposed with and even transformed into an art of the aesthetic domain—a completely new reading experience for contemporary Chinese readers. After the publication of the novel, some readers in China accused Mo Yan of "indulging in painful bodily torture, which reveals his eccentric behavior and gloomy psyche" (...... 对肉体被残酷折磨的迷恋，是一种怪癖和阴暗心理).[211] In the opinion of some, "once these kinds of descriptions depart from their critical function, they appear to become a mere enjoyment for the writer" (这样的描写一旦丧失了必要的批判性，就不能不让人怀疑作者是在玩味这些。).[212] But these accusations have not prevented the book from selling well in the market. In an interview with Mo Yan conducted in 2003, the interviewer, Zhang Huimin (张慧敏), mentioned the sale of eighty thousand volumes of *Sandalwood Punishment* as of the interview date, and wondered whether the enthusiastic readership stemmed from an attraction to sex and violence or from a love of folk art. Mo Yan believed that sales should be estimated at least three to five times that number if pirated copies were included and said he did not know why the book had sold so well.[213] According to him, his depiction of torture in *Sandalwood Punishment* is not meant to flaunt violence, as some people have believed, but rather to display the dark side of human nature and reveal a culture of cruelty that exists not only in history but also in modern reality and even in human minds.[214] Although, as mentioned, Mo Yan's superior writing skills make the book an incisive commentary on the evil in society, the writer's propensity to take pleasure in cruelty is nevertheless undeniably visible in this novel. As pointed out in the discussion of Mo Yan's playfulness in *Life and Death Are Wearing Me Out*, sometimes his writing goes beyond his "obsession with China" and falls into the realm of pure enjoyment: his writing of violence in *Sandalwood Punishment* shares the same tendency at times. In this case, enjoyment of writing for the author is to take delight in writing about violence as well as in the imagination of violence. In other words, writing about torture for Mo Yan is arguably tantamount to carrying out the executions himself, and the writer himself has become the executioner on a metaphorical level. This is especially true with respect to the sandalwood punishment, which, as the novelist confessed, mainly comes from his own imagination.[215] The fact that he seems to enjoy the cruelty he invents demonstrates a kind of gratuitous, sensational, and even voyeuristic tendency. Just as writing is in fact a process of execution for the writer, reading may be regarded as an experience of spectatorship for the reader, who may undergo what the novelist's spectators do: the torture "stirs up the hypercritical sympathy of the spectators, and satisfies their evil aesthetic taste at the same time" (既能刺激看客的虚伪的同情心，又能满足看客邪恶的审美心。).[216] The book's rather large and enthusiastic readership may support this argument despite the opprobrium of some readers, especially female ones.[217] If Mo Yan has consciously made himself one of the targets of criticism by assigning some of his fictional characters his own pen name (as previously discussed), in this case he may have unconsciously placed himself among those being attacked by disclosing his enjoyment of cruelty. Turning both the writer and the reader into participants in the cruel punishment is treating them as evidence of the evil features of human nature—proof that a thirst for violence does reside within the human soul. This makes Mo Yan's cultural criticism different from that of Lu Xun: Lu Xun creates a distance between himself and the people or phenomena in question whereas Mo Yan not only includes himself in the criticism, thereby implying that no one will be able to escape, but also sometimes unconsciously provides himself as an example of the evil inherent in human nature.

As far as turning torture into an art of pain is concerned, Foucault's analysis of torture is apt for *Sandalwood Punishment*:

> Torture is a technique … it must produce a certain degree of pain, which may be measured exactly, or at least calculated, compared and hierarchized; death is a torture in so far as it is not simply a withdrawal of the right to live, but is the occasion and the culmination of a calculated gradation of pain … death-torture is the art of maintaining life in pain, by subdividing it into a "thousand deaths," by achieving before life ceases "the most exquisite agonies." … Torture rests on a whole quantitative art of pain. (Michel Foucault, *Discipline and Punish: The Birth of the Prison*, trans. Alan Sheridan, 33–34)

Foucault also noted the nature of rituals of punishment and the importance of spectators, both of which are critical to *Sandalwood Punishment*. Foucault wrote:

> Torture forms part of a ritual. It is an element in the liturgy of punishment ... public torture and execution must be spectacular, it must be seen by all almost as its triumph. The very excess of the violence employed is one of the elements of its glory: the fact that the guilty man should moan and cry out under the blows is not a shameful side-effect, it is the very ceremonial of justice being expressed in all its force. (Michel Foucault, *Discipline and Punish: The Birth of the Prison*, trans. Alan Sheridan, 34)

This applies to the spectacular public punishment and the presence of spectators in Mo Yan's work, in which the notion of *seeing* is a major theme. In Zhao Jia's words:

> On the day that the beautiful prostitute was dismembered, the whole of Beijing city turned out to watch. More than twenty spectators were trampled to death at the Caishikou execution grounds. According to my master, it's sinful to do a bad job on such a beautiful body. You'd be bitten to death by the angry spectators. You know, Beijing's spectators were the hardest to please in the whole world. Fortunately, my master did a wonderful job, and the woman was very cooperative. It was actually a joint performance of the executioner and the condemned. During the process of performance, the condemned ... had better howl in a moderate volume and a distinct rhythm. This way it could stir up the hypercritical sympathy of the spectators, and satisfy their evil aesthetic taste at the same time ... Facing such a beautiful body, people got so excited by their wicked interest, be they men of high morals or virtuous and chaste women. Dismembering a beautiful woman was the greatest tragedy in the human world. My master said those who watched and enjoyed the performance were more fierce and malicious than we executioners. (My translation)
>
> ......凌迟美丽妓女那天，北京城万人空巷，菜市口刑场那儿，被踩死、挤死的看客就有二十多个。师傅说面对着这样美好

的肉体，如果不全心全意地认真工作，就是造孽，就是犯
罪。你如果活儿干得不好，愤怒的看客就会把你活活咬死，
北京的看客那可是世界上最难伺候的看客。那天的活儿，
师傅干得漂亮，那女人配合得也好。这实际上就是一场大
戏，刽子手和犯人联袂演出。在演出的过程中，罪犯......最
好是适度地、节奏分明［地］哀号，既能刺激看客的虚伪
的同情心，又能满足看客邪恶的审美心。......面对着被刀
窝割着的美人身体，前来观刑的无论是正人君子还是节妇
淑女，都被邪恶的趣味激动着。凌迟美女，是人间最惨烈
凄美的表演。师傅说，观赏这表演的，其实比我们执刀的
还要凶狠。(Mo Yan, *Sandlewood Punishment*, 240)

In this case, all spectators are voyeurs. Death has become an entertainment that is consumed by the spectators. "Seen by all" is less a "ceremonial of justice being expressed in all its force," as Foucault postulated, than a routine enjoyment for the masses, offering an element of excitement to their boring everyday lives. Consequently, *seeing* in this book in fact represents Mo Yan's satire on the evil of human nature—that of Chinese people in particular, for the story is set in the historic capital of China. In this respect, Mo Yan is consistent in his goal of turning the deep-rooted weakness of the Chinese people into ridicule, following Lu Xun's tradition of cultural criticism. At the end of his canonized "The True Story of Ah Q," in which the negative side of old traditions and Chinese as a people are remorselessly derided, Lu Xun records the following public execution:

"In twenty years I shall be another...." In his agitation Ah Q uttered half a saying which he had picked up for himself but never used before. "Good!!!" The roar of the crowd sounded like the growl of a wolf. (Lu Xun, "The True Story of Ah Q," in *Lu Xun: Selected Works*, trans. Yang Xianyi and Gladys Yang, 1:153)

　　"过了二十年又是一个......。"
阿Q在百忙中，"无师自通"的说出半句从来不说的话。
　　"好！！！"从人丛里，便发出豺狼的嗥叫一般的声
音来。 (Lu Xun, "The True Story of Ah Q," in *The Collective Works of Lu Xun*, 1:526)

Equating the crowd's voice with the sound of a growling wolf is part of Lu Xun's satirical side. In his famous essay "Nuola zouhou zenyang" (娜拉走后怎样) [What happens after Nora leaves home], he records the following comments about the Chinese masses:

> The masses, especially in China, are always spectators at a drama. If the victim on the stage acts heroically, they are watching a tragedy; if he shivers and shakes they are watching a comedy. Before the mutton shops in Beijing a few people often gather to gape, with evident enjoyment, at the skinning of the sheep. And this is all they get out of it if a man lays down his life. Moreover, after walking a few steps away from the scene they forget even this modicum of enjoyment. (Lu Xun, "What Happens after Nora Leaves Home," in *Lu Xun: Selected Works*, trans. Yang Xianyi and Gladys Yang, 2:91)

> 群众，——尤其是中国的，——永远是戏剧的看客。牺牲上场，如果显得慷慨，他们就看了悲壮剧；如果显得觳觫，他们就看了滑稽剧。北京的羊肉铺前常有几个人张着嘴看剥羊，仿佛颇愉快，人的牺牲能给与他们的益处，也不过如此。而况事后走不几步，他们并这一点愉快也就忘却了。(Lu Xun, "What Happens after Nora Leaves Home," in *The Collective Works of Lu Xun*, 1:163)

Lu Xun mocks the numbness and indifference of the Chinese people toward the fate of others, but Mo Yan carries the ridicule further and reveals the people's sinister nature, depicting them as more morally corrupt than the remorseless executioners. This idea is summarized in a comment made by the German governor in *Sandalwood Punishment*:

> China is undeveloped in all aspects except for punishment. Chinese people are especially talented in punishment, so their methods of torture are the most advanced. Making people suffer the biggest pain before death is an art in China and is the essence of Chinese politics. (My translation)

中国什么都落后，但是刑罚是最先进的，中国人在这方面有特别的天才。让人忍受了最大的痛苦才死去，这是中国的艺术，是中国政治的精髓......。"

(Mo Yan, *Sandlewood Punishment*, 113–114)

It is worth pointing out that the role of Mo Yan's spectators changes when it comes to the final and major punishment at the end of this novel, the sandalwood punishment. Instead of using them as merely a literary means of exposing human evil, Mo Yan depicts them as participants in a Bakhtinian carnival to challenge authority. Sun Bing, the protagonist, also transcends his prototype, Ah Q, to become a true hero of the carnival. The spectators are disappointed by Ah Q, for to them it is ridiculous that he "pass[ed] through so many streets without singing a single line from an opera" (游了那么久的街，竟没有唱一句戏) and "[t]hey had followed him for nothing" (他们白跟一趟了),[218] whereas those in Mo Yan's book join Sun Bing to sing the cat tune, and their act turns the entire execution ground into a performing stage. On his way to the execution ground, Sun Bing saw the following scene and thought to himself:

> The prison van is driving along the streets crowded with spectators. What an actor hopes for the most is a big audience; what is the most moving and tragic in life is riding a prison van to the execution ground. I, Sun Bing, have performed for thirty years; only today is my most glorious day. (My translation)
>
> 囚车行进在大街之上，路边的看客熙熙攘攘。演戏的最盼望人气兴旺；人生悲壮，莫过于乘车赴刑场。俺孙丙演戏三十载，只有今日最辉煌。

(Mo Yan, *Sandlewood Punishment*, 434)

He starts singing and is joined by his fellow villagers, among whom are his troupe members. Then he sees this touching scene:

> After I finished one song, thousands of people on both sides of the street roared in one voice: "Good!" Little Shan, my good disciple, grabbed this opportunity to utter different kinds of meowing that greatly brightened my singing.

...
I saw tears in the eyes of my fellow villagers. At first, kids followed Little Shan to meow, then the adults joined them. Thousands of voices meowed together, as if cats from all over the world were all here. (My translation)

俺一曲唱罢，大街两旁的万千百姓，齐声地喊了一声好。小山子，好徒弟，不失时机地学出了花样繁多的猫叫......使俺的歌唱大大地增添了光彩。

......
俺看到乡亲们一个个热泪盈眶。先是孩子们跟随着小山子学起了猫叫，然后是大人们学起了猫叫。千万人的声音合在了一起，就好似全世界的猫儿都集中在了一起。

(Mo Yan, *Sandlewood Punishment*, 435)

Sun Bing imbues his songs with new meaning, with the power to drive away the foreign forces and defend the Chinese territory. Then he sees that at the sound of his cat tune songs and the meowing of the villagers, both Yuan Shikai and the German governor turn pale, as do the Chinese governmental and foreign soldiers. He sighs: "I will die without regret after such a performance in my life!" (人生能有一次这样的演唱，孙丙死得其所啊！).[219] After the sandalwood punishment has been executed on him and he is tied up to a post to be kept alive for five days, Sun Bing—with the sandalwood log in his body—sings loudly again, while the spectators join him and meow together for a second time. Their utterance is mixed with sad sobbing. The performance is so powerful that the villagers cease to be passive and numb spectators as exemplified in Lu Xun's criticism of Chinese culture. Instead, they are active participants in a carnival challenging the authorities. Moreover, they are transformed by this participation and become a part of Sun Bing, who is a representative of the nationalistic force fighting against foreign powers. In this sense, Mo Yan subverts Lu Xun's notion of the indifferent and submissive crowd represented, for example, by the famous slide-show incident in which strong but unfeeling Chinese men impassively watched their own compatriot being slaughtered by foreigners.

VIOLENCE BETWEEN HUMANS AND NONHUMANS

Violence under Mo Yan's pen serves to reveal how cruelly human beings can treat one another, especially when driven by mortal hatred. However, Mo Yan does not limit his graphic descriptions of violent acts to interactions between human beings; rather, he extends his treatments to include violence inflicted by human on animals. Some good examples can be seen in "Yangmao zhuanyehu" (养猫专业户) [The cat specialist], *The Republic of Wine*, *Forty-One Bombs*, and *Life and Death Are Wearing Me Out*. In some of these works, humans are transformed into animals by their own inhuman behavior.

In the short story "The Cat Specialist," the first-person narrator has been discharged from the army when he runs into his childhood playmate, Daxiang (大响) [Boomer]; the two of them plan to raise and sell cats as their profession. The narrator's uncle and aunt, however, do not want him to get mixed up with Daxiang, who has been labeled a madman and a good-for-nothing by the villagers. The narrator heeds his family's admonitions and finds work elsewhere, leaving Daxiang to become a cat specialist alone. As the story unfolds, progressively more irrational and unreal elements build up a bizarre image of Daxiang, who claims to have the ability to command cats. In the end, Daxiang is proven to be a fraud. Throughout the story, the narrator plays the role of a mere spectator and reporter, one whose brief connection with Daxiang seems nonessential to the story, apart from the fact that it serves to highlight a chilling scene in which cats are killed. The narrator brings home a baby leopard cat, the only survivor of a gratuitous cat butchering by the squad leader who has been informed that he will be discharged from the army. Unwilling to return to his poor hometown after five years of service, the squad leader—who has been taking care of three leopard cat cubs that he and the political commissar have obtained from the mountain—

> began to rant and rave. And then he took a carving knife and chopped off the heads of two of the leopard cat cubs.
> He placed one upon the carving board (the cub still thought it was a game, mew, mew, mew, and scratched at his hand with

its claws), he raised the knife, bellowing, "Company Commander! Up yours!" As he shouted, the knife glanced downwards and the cub's head rolled to the floor. The knife stuck in the carving board, black blood flowed from the cat torso. Its eyes stared out, its tail beat a few times against the block, stood stiffly erect for a moment, and then slowly collapsed. The second cub was placed on the chopping board full of cat blood. Lying next to its sibling's carcass, this cub screamed in a mad frenzy. The squad leader, lip curled, red-eyed, yanked the knife from the chopping block and raised it high, cursing, "Political Commissar! Up yours!" As his voice went up, the knife fell and the cub's head rolled. Cat blood spattered his chest. (Mo Yan, "The Cat Specialist," in *Renditions*, trans. Janice Wickeri, 61)

他又哭又闹。后来，他用菜刀把两只小山猫的头剁下来——他把一只小山猫按在菜板上（小山猫还以为他是开玩笑呢，咪呜咪呜地叫着，用爪子搔他的手），高举起菜刀，吼一声："连长！你娘的！"同时，菜刀闪电般落下，猫头滚到地上，菜刀立在菜板上，猫腔子里流黑血。猫眼眨古，猫尾巴吱吱地响着直竖起来，竖一会儿，慢慢地倒了下去。第二只小山猫又被他按在菜板上，在满板的猫血上，在同胞的尸体旁，这只小山猫发疯地哭叫着。炊事班长歪着嘴，红着眼，从菜板上拔出刀来，高举起，骂一声："指导员，你娘的！"话起刀落，猫头落地，猫血溅了他一胸膛。

(Mo Yan, "The Cat Specialist," in *Collected Works of Mo Yan*, 5:131)

The little mule drawing a wagon in *The Republic of Wine* shares a fate similar to that of the baby cats:

And as the creaky wagon bounded forward, disaster struck: The little black mule lost its footing and crashed to the weedy, seedy, unforgiving ground, like a collapsed greasy black wall. The tip of the driver's whip landed on the animal's rump; it struggled mightily to its feet, shaking uncontrollably and rocking from side to side, piteous brays tearing at the heart of all within earshot. The driver … reached down and lifted out a discolored hoof—green and red and white and black all mixed together—that was wedged between two stone slabs.

…

> The little black mule stood on three legs; its fourth, the maimed rear leg, was thumping against a piece of rotten wood on the ground, like a mallet beating a drum, but with the difference that dark flowing blood stained the wood and the ground around it red. (Mo Yan, *The Republic of Wine*, trans. Howard Goldblatt, 120–121)

> 马车喀嘟嘟往前一跳，不幸的事情发生了：小黑骡子跌倒在杂乱无章的狰狞地面上，好像倒了一堵黑油油的墙壁。车夫对着小黑骡子的屁股打了一鞭，它猛烈挣扎着，站起来，身体剧烈颤抖，摇摇晃晃。小黑骡子痛苦的嘶鸣声撩人心弦。车夫……扑向前，跪在地，从两根石条的夹缝里，捧出一只青红皂白的骡蹄。
>
> ……
>
> 小黑骡三条腿着地，另一条残缺的后腿像鼓槌敲打地面一样频繁地敲打着地上的一根烂木头，暗黑的血咕嘟嘟往外冒，把那根木头和木头周围的其他物质都染红了。
>
> (Mo Yan, *The Republic of Wine*, 146)

Then two women in white uniforms arrive. They are chefs of the guesthouse who are worrying themselves sick about preparing a special dish for the municipal officials who will be in town the next day. Mule hooves are perfect for the leaders, who have become bored with chicken and fish. Therefore, they decide to buy all four hooves from the driver:

> The woman in white raised her hatchet, took aim on the mule's broad forehead, and swung with all her might, burying the ax blade so deeply in its head, she couldn't pull it out, no matter how she tried. And while she was trying to remove her ax, the little black mule's front legs buckled, carrying the rest of the animal slowly to the ground, where it spread out flat on the bumpy, pitted roadway.
>
> …
>
> There was still a bit of life in the little mule, as the shallow, raspy sounds of breathing proved; weak trickles of blood slid down its forehead on either side of the buried hatchet, soaking its eyelashes, nose, and lips.

Once again it was the woman who had buried the hatchet in the mule's forehead who picked up a blue-handled knife, leaped onto the mule's body, grabbed a hoof—a jet-black hoof in a lily-white hand—and described a brisk circle right in the curve where the hoof joined the leg; then another circle, and with a little pressure from the lily-white hand, the mule hoof and mule leg moved away from one another, attached only by a single white tendon. A final flick of the knife, and the hoof and leg parted company once and for all. The lily-white hand rose into the air, and the mule hoof flew into the hand of the other woman in white.

...

The woman in white worked the hatchet until she was finally able to remove it from the forehead of the little black mule, which finally breathed its last: belly up, its legs sticking up stiffly in four directions, like machine-gun barrels. (Mo Yan, *The Republic of Wine*, trans. Howard Goldblatt, 122–123)

白衣女人举起利斧对准骡子宽阔的脑门猝然一击，斧刃儿挤进了骡头，怎么拔也拔不出来，但她还是拔，在她拔斧头的过程中，小黑骡子前腿猛然跪地，然后，缓缓地将整个身躯平摊在凸凸凹凹的地面上。

……

小骡子还没有彻底死亡，粗重的呼吸还在它脖子里响着，柔弱无力的淡薄血液从斧刃的两边洇出来，浸湿了它的睫毛、鼻梁和嘴唇。

还是那个斧劈骡子的白衣女人，操起那柄蓝色的短刀，跳到骡子身边，一手攥住骡蹄——黑色的大骡蹄白色的小嫩手———一手握刀沿着骡蹄与骡腿之间弯曲的接合部，轻快地一转，轻快地又一转——攥蹄的小白手往下一按——骡蹄与骡腿分开，中间只连着一根白色的筋络。短刀一挑，骡蹄与骡腿彻底告别。白手一扬，骡蹄飞到另一个白衣女人手里。

……

白衣女人摇动斧柄，把劈进小黑骡子头颅中的斧头拔出来。

小黑骡子终于死了。它肚皮朝天死了，四条腿僵硬，斜指着大空的四个方向，好像四挺高射机关枪的枪筒。

(Mo Yan, *The Republic of Wine*, 149)

The detailed descriptions of both episodes once again remind the reader of the skinning of Uncle Arhat in *The Red Sorghum Family* and the harvesting of human organs in "The Cure." If the skinning and the harvesting of organs are used in those works to meet some ideological ends, the decapitation and mutilation of the innocent animals, which are depicted as cute and lovely in both cases—in sharp contrast to their miserable fates, which follow immediately—do not seem to have a clear justification. As mentioned above, the narrator of "The Cat Specialist," who witnesses the groundless cat butchering, does not play an important role in the story. It would not make any essential difference if the story—told in the first-person—were told instead in a third-person voice. In other words, if the writer simply intends to tell a story about Daxiang, the cat specialist, removing the first-person narrator would not hurt the story at all because this narrator does not have much connection with Daxiang in the story. Adding a first-person narrator allows the story to include an account of the cat slaughtering that the narrator witnesses while in the army, but it is arguably an instance of Mo Yan's writing about violence simply for the sake of violence. Similarly, the mutilation of the mule does not directly add any overt significance to the novel, which is already hysterical and bizarre in terms of human and animal butchering and cooking. At best, this kind of description makes the narrative clumsy in places; at worst, it creates a centrifugal effect that weakens the effectiveness and power of the story inasmuch as it may distract the attention of the reader from the novel's major theme—in this case, the notion of cannibalism as a political allegory. Although it is not always fair or possible to judge the literary tools a writer should or should not employ in a certain story, in these cases the reader nevertheless senses some kind of sensational pleasure on the part of the writer in the process of composition. The I-narrator in "The Cat Specialist" as well as Ding Gou'er and the truck driver in *The Republic of Wine* can represent the writer as spectators; it is through their eyes that he fulfills his own desire.

This said, the mutation of the mule in *The Republic of Wine* is not entirely superfluous; it discloses the corruption of government officials who enjoy good food every day, to the point that they are tired of chicken and fish. Social commentary is also behind a scene of animal abuse in *Forty-One Bombs*. In order to increase profits, Old Lan and his butchering factory inject formalin solution and water into meat, but they are discovered and warned. Luo Xiaotong, the twelve-year-old meat-addicted boy, has an idea: instead of injecting water into the meat after the animals are butchered, he suggests that they force the animals to drink large amounts of water before killing them. This way they can argue that they are cleansing the animals' organs and meat, not simply injecting water to increase the meat's weight. This is what they do to the animals:

> The workers inserted a soft and transparent plastic hose into a nostril then to the throat and the stomach of an ox....
>
> Then the workers turned on the tap ... Within twelve hours, the flow and volume of water would be about two hundred and fifty kilograms....
>
> ...Some oxen fell on the ground after a few hours, and some coughed loud and threw up the water in their stomach.
>
> ...
>
> After feeding them with water, the beef cattle would be sent to the butchering workshop. But the animals walked with great difficulty. Most of them fell like a heavy wall after a few steps, and could never stand up again. I [Luo Xiaotong] ordered four workers to help an ox get up, but the creature remained on the ground ... showed the whites of his eyes, breathed heavily, and water oozed out from his mouth and nostrils. (My translation)

工人们把柔软的透明塑料管子，插进了牛的鼻孔，从鼻孔进咽喉，一直插到胃里。……

工人们……拧开了……水龙头。十二小时之内，出水量在二百五十斤左右……

……个别牛在注水儿小时后跌倒在地，个别牛大声咳嗽，把胃里的水呕吐出来。

……

肉牛注水完成后，要输送到屠宰车间去。但那些牛……个个步履艰难，大多数的牛走儿步后就像一堵墙壁似的跌翻在地，而且跌翻在地后，绝无自己站起来的可能。我命令四个工人抬一头跌翻在地的牛，但......牛还是四平八稳地躺在地上，翻着白眼，喘着粗气，嘴巴和鼻孔里往外冒水。

(Mo Yan, *Forty-One Bombs*, 290–291)

If this novel can be understood as a fable of postrevolutionary China in which previously suppressed desires for wealth, power, and sensual pleasures surge uncontrollably, this apparently realistic description is an exaggerated but condensed illustration of the evil and remorselessness residing in human souls. As young as Luo Xiaotong is, he surpasses the adults in his creativity for cheating to satisfy the lust for money, totally ignoring the suffering of the animals. Luo Xiaotong joins the boy harvesting organs in "The Cure" and the girl in *The Republic of Wine* wondering whether her parents will cook her little brother for food in a gallery of children's images—signifying a contaminated, if not hopeless, young generation that is the future of the country. In this sense, Mo Yan is even more pessimistic than Lu Xun, who asks in "A Madman's Diary": "Perhaps there are still children who haven't eaten men?" (没有吃过人的孩子，或者还有？).[220] Although Mo Yan's writings tend to be more playful, his criticism never fades—he targets traditional culture and Communist discourse at the ideological level and targets rotten society in the dimension of reality.

Life and Death Are Wearing Me Out includes another scene in which the donkey breaks his hoof, echoing the scene in *The Republic of Wine*. Instead of showing how cruel human beings can be, however, this episode shows how the donkey's master, Lan Lian, who is marginalized as an Other because he refuses to be part of the communist collectivity, is merciful to his donkey. Lan Lian treats all his animals nicely, not only his donkey, even though he has no idea that the animals are actually reincarnations of his former master, Ximen Nao. The marginalized Lan Lian, as a caring and loving person who treats animals nicely, stands in sharp contrast to the cold-bloodedness of the politically correct revolutionaries; this is clear criticism from the novelist. But Lan Lian's kindheartedness to his animals does not redeem all the human cruelty in the book.

Perhaps the most striking and powerful description comes from Book Two, which deals with Ximen Ox. Lan Jiefang, the son of Lan Lian and his wife Yingchun (迎春), who is Ximen Nao's former concubine, abandons his father and joins the People's Commune under pressure from people around him, especially his half brother, Ximen Jinlong—taking the ox with him. Now that the ox is the commune's property, the people have the right to use him as they like. They begin by placing a ring through his nose because he does not seem to be obedient to his new masters. This process turns out to be cruel torture for the animal—they "stuck a hot poker through the septum of [his] nose" (用烧红的铁条捅你鼻孔) and "fitted a brass ring through the burned hole in [his] nose" (将一个 "凸" 字形的铜鼻环穿在你鼻梁上).[221] This is only the beginning of the torture. Ximen Jinlong is greatly annoyed by the ox because the animal has refused to work for him despite the young man's efforts. Later, the grown-up Lan Jiefang tells Big-Headed Lan Qiansui (蓝千岁), the last reincarnation of Ximen Nao,

> as soon as you [the ox] reached the plot of land to be plowed, you lay down on the ground.
>
> …
>
> Jinlong stepped backward, took his whip off his shoulder, and brought it down on the ox's back.
>
> …
>
> Jinlong gave you twenty lashes and only stopped from exhaustion; he was gasping for breath, his forehead was bathed in sweat.
>
> …
>
> You stayed where you were, eyes still shut. Enraged by your defiance, he kicked you in the head and the face and the belly, over and over and over, and from a distance he looked like a shaman in a dance of exorcism.
>
> …
>
> And still you lay there … like a sandbar, as the plowmen stood back and, one after the other, as if it were a competition, expertly swirled their whips in the air and brought them down on your hide, filling the air with a tattoo of loud cracks. The ox's back was crisscrossed with lash marks. Before long, there were traces of blood, and now that the tips of the whips were bloodied, the

cracks were louder and crisper. Harder and harder they came, until your back and your belly looked like cutting boards covered with chunks of bloody flesh.

…

Eventually, they tired. Rubbing their sore arms, they walked up to see if you were dead. You weren't. But your eyes were tightly shut; there were open wounds on the side of your face, staining the ground around your head with blood. You were gasping for breath, and there were violent spasms in your belly, like a female in labor. (Mo Yan, *Life and Death Are Wearing Me Out*, trans. Howard Goldblatt, 210–213)

那天你一到地头，就卧在了地上。

······

金龙撤后几步，将搭在肩头的使牛大鞭扯下，抡圆，猛地抽到牛背上。

······

金龙连抽了你二十鞭，累得气喘吁吁，额头冒汗······。

······

但你紧闭着眼睛，一动不动。金龙狂暴地吼叫着，两脚轮番踢着你的头，你的脸，你的嘴巴，你的肚腹，远远地看起来，他好像一个手舞足蹈的神汉在跳大神。

······

······ 你还是那么静卧着，仿佛一道沙梁。使牛汉子们拉开架势，一个接着一个，比赛似的，炫技般的，挥动长鞭，打在你身上。一鞭接着一鞭，一声追着一声。牛身上，鞭痕纵横交叉，终于渗出血迹。鞭梢沾了血，打出来的声音更加清脆，打下去的力道更加凶狠，你的脊梁、肚腹，犹如剁肉的案板，血肉模糊。

······

他们终于打累了，揉着酸麻的手脖子，上前察看。死了吗？没死。你紧紧地闭着眼睛，腮上有被鞭梢撕裂的血口子，血染红了土地。你大声喘息，嘴巴扎在泥土里。你的肚腹剧烈颤抖，仿佛临产的母牛。

(Mo Yan, *Life and Death Are Wearing Me Out*, 182–184)

Since the ox still refuses to move, Ximen Jinlong is driven insane with a desire to show his power over the animal at any cost. He ties the rope affixed to the Ximen Ox's nose ring to Mongol Ox, the mother of Ximen Ox; he intends to pull Ximen Ox up using his mother's strength.

> The rope grew taut, pulling the nose ring with it ... Ximen Ox's nose was pulled out of shape, like a piece of rubber ... Oh, Ximen Ox, a crisp sound, a pop, marked the splitting of your nose, followed by the thud of your raised head hitting the ground again...
>
> Ximen Jinlong ... ran over to a furrow, scooped up a handful of cornstalks, and piled them behind you ... He lit the stalks, and white smoke carrying a subtle fragrance rose into the air ... Oh, no, Ximen Ox, oh, no, Ximen Ox, who would rather die than stand up and pull a plow for the People's Commune...
>
> The ox's hide was burning, giving off a foul, nauseating odor ... Ximen Ox, your face was burrowing into the ground, your back was like a trapped snake, writhing and popping from the heat. The leather halter caught fire ... Oh, no, Ximen Ox, the charred rear half of your body was too horrible to look at.
>
> "Burn, damn you...," Jinlong was screaming...
>
> Jinlong came back with an armload of cornstalks, stumbling as he walked. My half brother was out of his mind ... something occurred at that moment that stupefied everyone who witnessed it. Ximen Ox, you stood up on shaky legs, minus your harness, your nose ring, and your tether, a free ox, totally liberated from all human control. You began to walk, how hard that must have been, weak in the legs, swaying uncontrollably from side to side; dark blood dripped from your torn nose, slid down to your belly, and from there dripped to the ground like tar ... Step by agonizing step, you walked toward my dad, leaving the land belonging to the People's Commune and entering the one-point-six acres of land belonging to the last independent farmer in the nation, Lan Lian; once there, you collapsed in a heap.
>
> Ximen Ox died on my dad's land.
>
> (Mo Yan, *Life and Death Are Wearing Me Out*, trans. Howard Goldblatt, 214–215)

绳套被抻紧，那鼻环自然被抻紧......西门牛的鼻子被拉得长长的，犹如一块灰白的胶皮。......呜呼，西门牛。然后，西门牛的鼻子，伴随着一声脆响，从中间豁开。昂起的牛头，沉重地砸在地上。......

    西门金龙……跑到沟边，扛来了几捆玉米秸秆，架在了牛的屁股后边……他点着了火，白烟升起，散发出一股清香……呜呼，西门牛。呜呼，宁愿被烧死也不站起来为人民公社拉犁的西门牛。……

    牛的皮肉被烧焦了，臭气发散，令人作呕……西门牛，你的嘴巴拱到土里，你的脊梁骨如同一条头被钉住的蛇，拧着，发出啪啪的声响。套在牛身上的套绳被烧断……呜呼，西门牛，你的后半截，已经被烧得惨不忍睹了。

    "我要烧死你……"金龙嗷叫着……。

    金龙又拖着几捆玉米秸秆跌跌撞撞跑过来，我这重山哥哥，已经半疯了。……就在这时候，令人震惊的事情发生了……西门牛，你抖抖颤颤地站立起来，你肩上没有套索、鼻孔里没有铜环、脖子上没有绳索，你作为一头完全摆脱了人类奴役羁绊的自由之牛站立起来。你艰难地往前走，四肢软弱，支撑不住身体，你的身体摇摇晃晃……黑色的血汇集到你的肚皮上，像凝滞的焦油一样滴到地上。……牛，一步步地向我爹走去。牛走出了人民公社的土地，走进全中国唯一的单干户蓝脸那一亩六分地里，然后，像一堵墙壁，沉重地倒下了。

    西门牛死在我爹的土地上……。

    (Mo Yan, *Life and Death Are Wearing Me Out*, 185–186)

    This lengthy quote comprises different elements—movements, sounds, colors, odors—to form a picture that is as rich as a scene in a film. As readers we hear sounds: that of the whipping, of the human curse, and of the ox's nose splitting. We see colors: the red blood of the ox, turning dark as it drips to the ground, and the white smoke from burning cornstalks. We smell odors: the fragrance of the cornstalks and the nauseating stench from burning the animal's hide. Eventually, all these sensations are mingled with the movements—those of the human beings and those of the ox. While Jinlong and his men are running around the ox beating him with great strength, the animal makes little movement: as soon as he enters the domain of the People's Commune, he refuses to move. No matter how hard the humans try to make him move, he remains still. His motionlessness is a gesture protesting against the collectiveness; the human beings' movements of running, bringing the whips to the animal, kicking and pulling the ox, and lighting a fire to burn him become weak and powerless in front of the motionless Ximen Ox. Instead of making the actors look vigorous, human movement in this scene actually exposes the hysteria of Jinlong and his followers, turning them into clowns. By contrast, the quietness of the animal is a defense of his dignity and sets off the movement he does finally make in the very last moment of his life: he stands up, walks with great pain—step by step—toward the land of Lan Lian and collapses and dies once he is there. He dies a sublime death in the episode's climactic moment—a moment so powerful and shocking, yet touching, that it surpasses all scenes of human death in Mo Yan's oeuvre.

Although this episode is comparable to the *lingchi* scenes in *Sandalwood Punishment* with respect to its details, it conveys a different message and creates a completely different atmosphere. The highly skillful fabrication is enriched by Mo Yan's own sentiment. At times it seems as if the novelist himself is shouting out to condemn the cruelty, albeit through the mouth of the narrator, Lan Jiefang:

> My tears started to flow as soon as they began beating you. I wailed, I begged, I wanted to throw myself on top of you to share your suffering, but my arms were pinned to my sides by the mob that had gathered to watch the spectacle. I kicked and I bit, but the pain I caused had no effect on the people, who refused to let go. How could such decent villagers, young and old, get any enjoyment out of such a bloody tragedy, as if their hearts had turned to stone? (Mo Yan, *Life and Death Are Wearing Me Out*, trans. Howard Goldblatt, 212–213)
>
> 从他们打你时，我的眼泪就开始流淌，我哭喊着，哀求着，想扑上去救你，想伏在你的背上，分担你的痛苦，但我的双臂，被云集在此看热闹的人紧紧拽住，他们忍受着我脚踢、牙啃的痛苦，不放松我，他们要看这流血的悲剧。我不明白，这些善良乡亲，这些叔叔大爷，这些大哥大嫂，这些小孩子们，为什么都变得这样心如铁石......
>
> (Mo Yan, *Life and Death Are Wearing Me Out*, 184)

This complaint recalls the numbed spectators watching their compatriot being slaughtered in Lu Xun's famous slide-show incident. In *Sandalwood Punishment*, Mo Yan surpasses the critique of his predecessor,

Lu Xun, by making his spectators active participants in the anti-imperial protest as well as performers in the subversive carnival. The mob entertained by watching the ox suffer, however, represents a backward movement that expresses Mo Yan's disapproval of people's insensitivity during the revolutionary era that is the setting for *Life and Death Are Wearing Me Out*. The narrator tells the story to the Big-Headed Lan Qiansui in emotional language, using the second-person pronoun. It sounds as if the real author is talking to his reader face to face: "Ximen Ox, please listen to me. I must tell you, because this is what happened in history. I feel obligated to recount history to the one concerned who has forgotten the details" (西门牛，你听我说，我必须说，因为这是发生过的事情，发生过的事情就是历史，复述历史给遗忘了细节的当事者听，是我的责任。).[222] Is this story meant only for Big-Headed Lan Qiansui, who has experienced several reincarnations since living and dying as an ox and has forgotten some details of his previous lives? The text reads as if the author is (re)telling history to all those who have experienced it in order to remind them of tragic historical lessons. This almost sounds like a sermon, a characteristic which is not common in Mo Yan's writings:

> Is this an ox or some sort of god? Maybe it's a Buddha who has borne all this suffering to lead people who have gone astray to enlightenment. People are not to tyrannize other people, or oxen; they must not force other people, or oxen, to do things they do not want to do. (Mo Yan, *Life and Death Are Wearing Me Out*, trans. Howard Goldblatt, 213)
>
> 这还是头牛吗？这也许是一个神，也许是一个佛，它这样忍受着痛苦，是不是要点化身陷迷途的人，让他们觉悟？人们，不要对他人施暴，对牛也不要；不要强迫别人干他不愿意干的事情，对牛也不要。
>
> (Mo Yan, *Life and Death Are Wearing Me Out*, 184)

Indeed, the last sentence of this passage moves beyond the narrator's retelling the events that occurred during his adolescence and shifts into a moralized realm that is rather inconsistent with the overall playful tone of the novel. This obvious and eye-catching inconsistency creates an alienating effect and reveals the heaviness under the veil of playfulness. What appears to be a tale about animal abuse in fact signifies the brutality of human beings: human wickedness, triggered and magnified by ideological fights, has composed the heaviest page in China's recent history.

VIOLENCE AND LANGUAGE: THE USE OF COLOR

One distinctive feature of Mo Yan's works, noted by readers and critics alike, is his unique language, which is characterized by (among other things) its unconstrained flow, unconventional use of diction, and unusually powerful images—including sound images and colors. Mo Yan's exceptionally rich imagination and memories of his past seem to take over when he starts to write; the author is driven forward by his language, as he admits in his autobiographical novella "Bian" (变) [Change]: "My head is crammed full of these assorted memories, and I don't mean to write them down—they just flow out of their own accord" (这些杂七杂八的记忆太多了，不是我要写它们，是它们自己往外冒。).[223] Driven by an impulse to "speak" with his pen, Mo Yan often floods his stories with excessive diction. His style of language might be criticized as exaggerative, superfluous, and distracting, yet it could also be viewed as a parody of the Maoist discourse prevalent during the Cultural Revolution—especially when the writer intentionally employs phrases from revolutionary clichés in a postrevolutionary context. "To write as an ordinary person" (作为老百姓写作), Mo Yan never sets himself above the common people.[224] Instead, he writes about the lives of ordinary people in vivid and unpretentious language that best describes people's everyday lives. This language is often humorous and cynical and even vulgar at times; yet its authenticity, originality, and sincerity enable it to eviscerate the formulaic and empty Maoist discourse. The revolutionary grand narrative pales in comparison to Mo Yan's vigorous and dynamic language, which does not always conform to regular usage. For example, when Grandma in *The Red Sorghum Family* is shot by the Japanese soldiers, the narrator reports that "she cried out in ecstasy." The Chinese adjective is *huankuai* (欢快), a word usually used for joyful occasions. Rarely would people associate death with ecstasy. This untraditional usage of such a word for a death scene greatly contradicts the reader's expectations, formed by habit, and thus alienates the reader. But such a word catches the reader's attention in a way that an adjective conventionally used on such an occasion, such as *tongku* (痛苦) [painful suffering], would not. In this case, moreover, *huankuai* effectively conveys Grandma's unrestrained temperament. Uncommon images like this one that create special artistic effects are abundant in Mo Yan's works, and discussions of them can be found throughout this book. This section analyzes Mo Yan's use of color, especially the pairing of vivid colors with scenes of violence.

Colors play a significant role in Mo Yan's narrative; in his writing of violence, colors develop the stories, strengthening them with an artistic and aesthetic power. Three cases of suicide support this argument and are examined in detail here: (1) Xiaohu in "Dry River," (2) Jinju in *The Garlic Ballads*, and (3) Qi Wendong in "Happiness." In these three cases, Mo Yan's unconventional use of colors creates a unique, sometimes grotesque, but always incomparable fictional aura.

First of all, Mo Yan's special attention to the color red is perhaps his most obvious use of color; red is prominent in many of his fiction titles: *The Red Sorghum Family*, *Red Grove*, "A Transparent Red Radish," "Hong huang" (红蝗) [Red locusts] and "Hong erduo" (红耳朵) [Red ears]. At first glance, Mo Yan's fondness of red is consistent with communist ideology, which regards red as its official color. The idea that the red flag symbolizes the blood of the revolutionary martyrs has become a motto for Chinese people on the mainland.[225] As for literature, the color red appears in the titles of many famous revolutionary works, such as *Hongqi pu* (红旗谱) [Keep the red flag flying] by Liang Bin (梁斌), published in 1957; *Hong ri* (红日) [Red sun] by Wu Qiang (吴强) in 1959; and *Hong yan* (红岩) [Red crag] by Luo Guangbin (罗广斌) and Yang Yiyan (杨益言) in 1961, to list just a few. Cherishing the memory of the martyrs, people are exhorted to carry on the revolutionary cause under the leadership of the Communist Party. Red in Mo Yan's works, however, signifies individuality and a solemn masculine beauty, too; it can also represent a condemnation of violence and serve as a foil to seamy reality. Thus, Mo Yan's use of red can be understood as ironic and parodic to some extent and thus as a "linguistic subversion of Communist discourse."[226]

In Chinese folk culture, colors have long been associated with particular meanings and special occasions. The color red symbolizes happiness and good luck; for instance, a bride wears red on her wedding day and parents give their children money in red envelopes on New Year's Day in the hope that good luck will come to the children. Likewise, black and white are believed to denote something sad and unhappy, so they are commonly used on occasions like funerals. Mo Yan, however, does not follow this tradition. The death scenes of these three young people committing suicide showcase the author's innovative employment of colors.

"Dry River" opens in flashback style with Xiaohu's attempt to kill himself. The color red appears twice in the opening sentence, along with several other colors:

> When the immense watery crimson moon rose over the dusky fields to the east, the smoke and mist enveloping the village grew heavier and appeared to take on the bright melancholy red of the moon. The sun had just set, leaving behind on the horizon a big long swath of purple. A few stunted stars momentarily gave off a pale gleam between the sun and the moon. (Mo Yan, "Dry River," in *Spring Bamboo*, trans. Jeanne Tai, 209)
>
> 一轮巨大的水淋淋的鲜红月亮从村庄东边暮色苍茫的原野上升起来时，村子里弥漫的烟雾愈加厚重，并且似乎都染上了月亮的那种凄艳的红色。这时太阳刚刚落下来，地平线下还残留着一大道长长的紫云。几颗瘦小的星斗在日月之间暂时地放出苍白的光芒。
>
> (Mo Yan, "Dry River," in *Collected Works of Mo Yan*, 5:273)

It is in this "crimson," "red," "purple," and "pale" (white) environment that Xiaohu decides to end his young life. The "watery crimson moon" and its "melancholy red" in Xiaohu's eyes symbolize his own bright red blood. The most unbearable fact is that those who have caused his young body to bleed are his own father and brother. Hopeless, the boy chooses to end this terrible existence. Xia Zhihou's comments on Mo Yan's keen perception of colors, especially the color red, are apt:

> Mo Yan often displays his fine and almost perfect sense of colors in his fiction...
> ...The color red seems to provide Mo Yan's literary talent with an opportunity for expression. When a red image emerges in his mind, it has a mysterious summoning power to him. Mo Yan, who has a keen sense of colors, gets doubly excited under the stimulation of a red signal and creates his best stories in an endless flow. (My translation)
>
> 莫言在他的小说世界里常常表现出对于色彩的近乎完美的良好感觉。……
> ……红色仿佛赋予了莫言的才情以一个集中的宣泄口，当红色意象从他的脑际浮起时，它对莫言便有一种神秘的召唤力，本来就对色彩敏感的莫言，会在红色信号的刺激下加倍地兴奋，常常就在这时源源不断地写下他的最佳文字。
>
> (Xia Zhihou, "The Variability of the Color Red:
From 'A Transparent Red Radish,' 'Red Sorghum,'
to 'Red Locusts,'" in Research Materials about Mo Yan,
ed. He Lihua and Yang Shousen, 221–222)

Nevertheless, this mainland critic does not seem to have noticed Mo Yan's unconventional use of colors, including red. Xiaohu's story ends with the following scene:

> At the very instant when the bright red sun was about to rise, he was awakened by a chorus of an oppressive and barbarous song ... Amidst this silence, the sun emerged slowly from the ground, and all of a sudden burst into warm and tender music, and the music caressed those buttocks striped with gashes and scars and kindled the fires in his head, and at length those tongues of yellowish and reddish flames turned green, grew smaller, flickered fitfully, and died. (Mo Yan, "Dry River," in Spring Bamboo, trans. Jeanne Tai, 227)

鲜红太阳即将升起那一刹那，他被一阵沉重野蛮的歌声
唤醒了。......在这沉默中，太阳冉冉出山，恝然奏起温暖
的音乐，音乐抚摸着他伤痕斑斑的屁股，引燃他脑袋里的火
苗，黄黄的，红红的，终于变绿变小，明明暗暗跳动儿下，
熄灭。(Mo Yan, "Dry River," in *Collected Works of Mo Yan*,
5:285)

Here Mo Yan's diction for death and sadness is surprisingly colorful
and pleasant: "bright red sun," "yellowish," "reddish," "green," "warm
and tender music," and so forth. By Chinese cultural norms, the joyful
colors—especially red—are inappropriate for a heavy occasion like this.
The intentional (mis)use of red and of the cheerful adjectives actually
has the effect of alienating the reader, who must stop to ponder and draw
the conclusion that the little boy is in fact celebrating his departure from
this cruel existence when he finds that death is easier than life. The cause
of such sadness, incongruent with the image of an innocent boy of his
age, is the target of the novelist's condemnation. As a result, this sarcastic/
ironic use of colors and words contributes to the construction of a more
powerful story.

Violence is also mixed with bright colors in *The Garlic Ballads*. For
instance, when Jinju insists on marrying Gao Ma, she is hung up by the
arms and beaten severely by her father and brothers:

> Green sparks flew past her eyes; the sound of crackling flames
> exploded around her ears; jute plants swayed in front of her. The
> chestnut colt was standing beside Gao Ma, licking his face clean
> of dried blood and grime with its purplish tongue as golden lay-
> ers of fog rose from the roadside, from thousands of acres of jute
> plants, and from the pepper crop in Pale Horse County. The colt
> disappeared, then reappeared in the golden fog ... Elder Brother's
> face was ashen, Second Brother's was blue, Father's was green
> and Mother's was black; Elder Brother's eyes were white, Sec-
> ond Brother's were red, Father's were yellow, and Mother's were
> purple. (Mo Yan, *The Garlic Ballads*, trans. Howard Goldblatt,
> 137–138)

她眼前飞舞着绿色的光点，耳边响着火苗燃烧的哗剥声，黄麻的影子在眼前晃动着。那匹枣红色的小马驹站在高马的身旁，伸出紫红色的舌头，舔舐着他脸上的污血和灰尘，一道道金黄的迷雾从路面上升起，从万亩黄麻地里升起，从苍马县的辣椒地里升起，枣红马驹在金黄迷雾里时隐时显......大哥的脸是青的，二哥的脸是蓝的，爹的脸是绿的，娘的脸是黑的，大哥的眼是白的，二哥的眼是红的，爹的眼是黄的，娘的眼是紫的。

(Mo Yan, *The Garlic Ballads*, 189)

That her family members' faces and eyes change colors constantly signifies a demonization of the human world—even those who are most dear to Jinju have become strange and unnatural. Before Jinju hangs herself, she has a conversation with her unborn son, persuading him not to attempt to enter this nasty world. During this conversation, the presence of a friendly purplish red colt represents one last hope. But the animal is eventually driven away by Jinju, who refuses any deliverance or redemption. Jinju dies. Her lover Gao Ma finds her body hanging in his own house:

> In the flickering matchlight, he saw Jinju's purple face as she hung in the opening of the door, bulging eyeballs, lolling tongue, and sagging belly.
> ...
> After clambering unsteadily to his feet, Gao Ma toppled over again, just as seven or eight gaily colored parakeets flew in through the open window, made passes above and below the roof beams, then playfully hugged the walls, brushing past Jinju's hanging corpse.
> ...
> Little green dots played on her face, and he wondered if they were parakeet feathers that had stuck to it. (Mo Yan, *The Garlic Ballads*, trans. Howard Goldblatt, 151, 175, 176)

在动荡不安的小小光明中，他一眼就看到了吊在门框正中的金菊紫红的脸庞，凸出的眼球，耷拉出来的舌头和高高隆着的肚皮。
......

他爬起来，又莫名其妙地，向前栽倒了。七八只花花绿绿
的鹦鹉从敞开的窗户飞进屋里，它们穿过梁头，贴着墙壁，
擦着金菊的尸体，愉快地飞翔着。

……

她的脸上沾着一些绿色的、抖动的斑点。他疑心那是花毛
鹦鹉脱落的羽毛粘到她的脸上。

(Mo Yan, *The Garlic Ballads*, 206, 237, 239)

Then the furious Gao Ma sharpens a saber and heads to the township
compound to cut down sunflowers and chop down trees:

White chips of virgin wood flew, while in the branches above him
swarms of frantic parakeets scattered in the sky, then formed a
cloud of living color that whirled above the township compound,
depositing pale droppings onto the blue roof tiles below until,
wing-weary, they fell like stones, thudding like heavy raindrops.
After felling three pine trees, Gao Ma watched four scarlet moons
climb into the uncommonly expansive sky, one at each point of
the compass, lighting up the land as if it were daytime. Parakeet
feathers shimmered in many colors; birds' eyes sparkled gemlike
in the blinding light. (Mo Yan, *The Garlic Ballads*, trans. Howard
Goldblatt, 178)

白森森的杨树干嘎嘎吱吱地断裂着，树上栖息的数千只鹦鹉
纷纷飞起。起初犹如光芒四射，后来犹如一团彩色的云团，
绕着乡政府大院上空急速飞行，把雨点般的白屎拉在乡政府
蓝色的房瓦上。这些鸟们飞累了，纷纷掉在房顶上——都像
石块一样垂直地掉在房顶上，打得瓦片噼哩啪啦地响。砍倒
了三棵大树，天空变得异乎寻常地宽阔，东西南北四个方向
同时升起了四轮鲜红的月亮，照耀天下如同白昼，鹦鹉们的
羽毛绚丽多彩，它们的眼光华夺目，宛若一颗颗宝石。

(Mo Yan, *The Garlic Ballads*, 241)

Swathed in various beautiful colors, death becomes even more disturbing and grotesque.

Later the reader is informed that

Jinju's body was laid out on the kang, in plain view of Gao Ma.
The sun, directly overhead now, shone down through the red and

yellow jute branches and talon-shaped leaves to light up her face and turn it into a golden chrysanthemum—a *jinju*—whose petals were coaxed open by autumn sunlight. He touched her face. It had the sleek resilience of costly velvet. (Mo Yan, *The Garlic Ballads*, trans. Howard Goldblatt, 180)

金菊的尸体已搬到炕上，高马每时每刻都能看到她。太阳升起很高了，光线透过黄的红的黄麻茎秆和鸡爪形的黄麻叶片，照耀着她的脸，她的脸宛若一朵绽开在秋季艳阳下的金色菊花。他伸出手指去，去触摸她的脸。她的脸光滑有弹性，好像高级的丝绒。 (Mo Yan, *The Garlic Ballads*, 244)

Then Gao Ma asks his neighbors to help him bury Jinju. The dead young woman is dressed in red clothes that the women of the village have made for her. "So the two new rush mats were laid out in the yard and covered with the sheet of pale blue plastic. Then four women carried out Jinju, in her new red satin clothes, and laid her on the plastic" (院子里铺开两张新苇席，新席上展开浅蓝色的塑料布，四个女人把穿着红绸新衣的金菊抬出来，放在塑料布上。).[227] Needless to say, a swollen body in red contrasting with pale blue, and a purple face with a lolling, puffy tongue and bulging eyeballs likened to a golden chrysanthemum with a bewitching smile form an incongruous and even disgusting picture. Bright and happy colors used to describe cruelty and sadness heighten both the tension between the fictional characters and the reader's feelings of uneasiness. In this manner, the evil of violence is ridiculed to an extreme, while the power of the novel is greatly enriched.

In addition to the color red, green in Mo Yan's works is another important color that contributes to a unique aura and artistic effect. As one Chinese critic observed,

> [Mo Yan's] images … enhance not only the poetic sentiment but also deepen the subjectivity of his stories … The images of the color red in *Red Sorghum* and the color green in "Happiness" have been developed into a set of diametrically opposed symbolic systems that demonstrate Mo Yan's greatest success. (My translation)

[莫言的]意象......不仅给作品增添了诗意，而且......加深了
作品的思想性......《红高粱》中的"红"色与《欢乐》中
的"绿"色的意象已形成一个对立的体系，具有最大的象征
意义，写得最为成功。

(Li Wanjun, "An Attempt to Discuss the Use for Reference and
Originality of Mo Yan's Fiction," in *Research Materials about Mo Yan*,
ed. He Luihua and Yang Shousen, 199–200)

In the novella "Happiness," the color green is the dominant color, and the
green images in the story cause great discomfort. In established coding
systems, both Chinese and Western, green is usually related to plants and
therefore interpreted as a metaphor for life and vitality. In "Happiness,"
however, Qi Wendong is so eager to escape from the rural life, which is
largely related to green, that he goes so far as to detest this color: "I will
never sing the praises of the earth—those who do so would be my irrec-
oncilable enemies; I hate the color green—those who eulogize this color
would be ruthless butchers" (我不赞美土地，谁赞美土地谁就是我不
共戴天的仇敌；我厌恶绿色，谁歌颂绿色谁就是杀人不留血痕的屠
棍。).[228] The novella's most unpleasant scene is perhaps one near the end
in which Qi's mother obtains a folk prescription for his father, who has
been diagnosed with cancer, to stew white rice with seven toads, "the older
and bigger the better" (越老越大越好).[229] After some detailed descriptions
of how Qi struggles to overcome his fear and finally catches seven disgust-
ingly ugly toads, of how his mother cooks the creatures with rice, and of
the weird smell the rice emits, the author paints the following picture:

> When the earthen basin was uncovered, you saw those seven
> toads either squatting, crouching, lying or kneeling in the basin as
> if they were still alive; every grain of the white rice was as green
> as jasper—the only rice you could find under heaven... Dad took
> a good bite of a well-cooked toad ... you ran outside and threw
> up. You threw up so hard that your bile was forced out... (My
> translation)

> 揭开瓦盆时，你看到那七只蛤蟆生龙活虎般蹲在卧在仰在
> 跪在瓦盆里，每一粒大米都碧绿碧绿，也是天下难找的米

饭啦......爹夹起一只熟透了的蛤蟆，张嘴就咬......你跑到
门外，把苦胆汁子都吐出来了......
(Mo Yan, "Happiness," in *Collected Works of Mo Yan*, 4:451)

The vivid depiction of the toads, of the rice soaked in the green body
fluid of the animals, and of the indescribable smell form a most bizarre
and undesirable atmosphere, which in combination with the action of
Father's biting a toad, create an extremely disgusting scene.

After drinking the pesticide, Qi Wendong's phobia of green reaches
its peak on the verge of his death:

Happiness, oh happiness! I no longer need to see your green body
covered by green pus, green blood, and green feces, and your soul
filled with green rust and green maggots with my happy eyes! I no
longer need to smell the green stench of your corpse and your
gloomy green filthy money with my happy nose! I no longer need
to listen to your green solemn pledge and the green lies from your
green mouth with my happy ears! I escape from the color green
forever with my happy soul! Now you saw a group of reddish
brown kids playing in the [yellow] muddy river, snow-white foam
splashes onto your golden face; you heard the purplish red mules
and horses chewing the apricot yellow forage; you smelled the
strong fragrance of the bright red blossoms of leafless wild roses
… You were swimming in a river of butterflies, surrounded by
butterfly-like [yellow] jute flowers. Your eyes filled with magnifi-
cence, you were happy! (My translation)

欢乐呵，欢乐！我再也不要看你这遍披着绿脓血和绿粪便的
绿躯体、生满了绿锈和绿蛆虫的灵魂，我欢乐的眼！再也不
要嗅你这个扑鼻的绿尸臭、阴凉的绿铜臭，我欢乐的鼻！再
也不听你绿色的海誓山盟，你绿色嘴巴里喷出的绿色谎言，
我欢乐的耳！永远逃避了绿色我欢乐的灵魂！现在你看到了
一群赭红色的孩子在浑黄的河水中嬉闹，洁白水花飞溅到你
黄金般的脸上；你听到了枣红骡马咀嚼杏黄草料的声音，你
嗅到了不生绿叶的艳红的野蔷薇浓郁的香气......你在蝶的
河里游泳着，蝶一样的黄麻花团团簇簇地包围着你，满眼辉
煌，触目无绿，你欢乐！
(Mo Yan, "Happiness," in *Collected Works of Mo Yan*, 4:452–453)

Like Xiaohu's death scene in "Dry River," this paragraph is replete with color. Here the counterpoint of other colors foils Qi's detestation of green, which again represents his ultimate hatred of the countryside—he not only sees green but also smells it and hears it. Green, representing the backward and uncivilized life of the countryside, surrounds and suffocates him. Going to university is the only way for him to break free from the green net, yet he is unable to fulfill this goal. Therefore, he must choose death as an escape from this trap; it is the only way he can run to the multicolored world. The narrator's description of both green and the other colors makes his choice of destroying himself more convincing. The various colors in the paragraph form a joyful picture that matches the story's title—"Happiness"—and signify a celebration of the character's death and, once again, the writer's unconventional way of writing about death.

To Mo Yan, violence is an external form of human evil that causes suffering and renders reality absurd at best and sinister at worst. Violence is pervasive, unavoidable, and universal, and it resides primarily within the human soul; therefore there is no end to it. When violence as an individual force is approved by society and turned into a collective social force, it becomes a power with the ability to destroy, a power beyond knowledge and reason. Henry James's (1843–1916) comment on evil may summarize what is in the mind of our pessimistic novelist:

> Life is, in fact, a battle. On this point optimists and pessimists agree. Evil is insolent and strong; beauty enchanting but rare; goodness very apt to be weak; folly very apt to be defiant; wickedness to carry the day; imbeciles to be in great places, people of sense in small, and mankind generally, unhappy. (Henry James, "Ivan Turgenieff," in *French Poets and Novelists*, as quoted in J. A. Ward, *The Imagination of Disaster*, 6)

CONCLUSION

Mo Yan is a writer who ponders profoundly, senses sharply, imagines daringly, and writes freely. Readers who immerse themselves in Mo

Yan's fictional world are at risk of exposing themselves to a disturbing exhibition of cruelty, filled with macabre images of torture, mutilation, and death. Not always as consistently sober-minded as some of his contemporaries who are also known for writing about cruelty (such as Yu Hua), Mo Yan's passion can often be detected in his depictions of violence, especially when he is driven by an impulse to speak for his fellow citizens and a commitment to condemn wicked behavior resulting from a cruel reality. First, Mo Yan shows his concern for Chinese people who have suffered from different kinds of violence imposed on them either by their fellow Chinese or by foreign powers in the past. Inspired in part by Lu Xun, these concerns by and large formulate Mo Yan's criticism on the cultural deficiencies of his country. Second, as a writer who was indoctrinated with rosy pictures of socialism as well as the cruelty of enemies in his formative years but confronted obvious discrepancies between what he was told and what he experienced in reality, Mo Yan challenges Maoist discourse by telling stories about the violence that occurred under Mao's rule and by questioning the "legitimate violence" found in revolutionary literature. Thanks to his passionate and sometimes poetic language enriched by extraordinary employment of colors, Mo Yan's writing of violence is artistically appealing and powerful but simultaneously suffocating and disturbing in a way that reminds one of a Van Gogh painting. At the same time, a gratuitous, sensational, and even voyeuristic aspect of his violence is one of the reasons for the controversy surrounding his fictional works. Mo Yan has already been referred to as the Chinese García Márquez or the Chinese Faulkner, and he might also be considered the Chinese Baudelaire, whose descriptions of human evil could be collected in a volume to form the Chinese *Les fleurs du mal*.

Chapter 4

"It Is Hard
Not to Write Satire"

In a World of Vice and Folly

The context in which Mo Yan writes his novels is perhaps best summarized by Dustin Griffin's observations on satire: "The world has always
supplied such an abundance of vice and folly that satirists need only
open their eyes, look about, and begin to speak. Words are drawn or
even forced forth. It is hard *not* to write satire."[230] It is indeed difficult
for Mo Yan, who has experienced the absurdity in specific political circumstances throughout his lifetime and who—more importantly—is
fully aware of the absurdity around him *not* to write satire: he is driven
by an impulse to disclose it. To be sure, the word "absurd" is an appropriate characterization of daily reality in Mainland China, which has
been marked by political struggles since the mid-twentieth century. The
word signifies an existence out of harmony, in which individuals live
an insecure, irrational, and in many ways senseless life. Born into a

middle-peasant family in 1955, Mo Yan has experienced this reality; he is no stranger to all kinds of adversity, including poverty, starvation, and harsh political discrimination.

Mo Yan's literary treatment of the absurd rebels against the beliefs and values of orthodox communist literature in China. In the decades since 1949, the literature sanctioned by the Communist regime painted a rosy picture for the reader: official literature on the mainland has been based on the assumption that under the new government's leadership, people are purified human beings who are physically and mentally healthy and who live in a highly ordered and moralized society that is far removed from all kinds of evil. The people of the rest of the world, however, are living in an abyss of suffering. According to this perspective, any pessimistic or satirical attitude toward the communist reality is hazardous to the nation and is therefore not permitted. In fact, a Chinese writer bears the burden of educating the reader to praise the new society. Reading provides the reader with neither an aesthetic enjoyment nor an understanding of life but with a textbook-type education and with the training necessary for him to adapt to the new society. In short, neither writer nor reader enjoys freedom of choice in terms of literary taste because literature is no more than a practical and controlled instrument of ideology.

Many post-Mao novelists, however, write in defiance of this norm. These writers have lost faith in the so-called new society and the leadership of the ruling party; indeed, they mercilessly deride the state-constructed reality. Mo Yan is one of these writers. He even goes so far as to lay bare a world deprived of all truth, value, reason, and meaning, a world in which people are senseless, helpless, grotesque, and absurd. The targets of his satire are the irrationalities of the present—including the ludicrous political reality—as well as the absurdities of the past. In fact, many of his works heap ridicule on the "everydayness" of reality and culture in China and attack such evils as cultural cannibalism—a critique similar to that leveled by Lu Xun, who used cannibalism as a metaphor to condemn feudalism while writing during the May Fourth period.

Mo Yan has been frequently referred to as an avant-garde writer. Chen Sihe (陈思和), for instance, an important critic in Mainland China, made the following observation:

> The emergence of Ma Yuan, Mo Yan, Can Xue and so on in mid-1980s is an important matter in the history of avant-garde fiction. To a certain extent, we can regard it as the real beginning of avant-garde fiction … Mo Yan has multiple achievements. A personal world of myths and linguistic imagery has taken shape in his writing. Moreover, owing to his unusual sensibility, Mo Yan twists and violates [the rules of] modern Chinese to form a unique personal style. (My translation)
>
> 80年代中期马原、莫言、残雪等人的崛起是先锋小说历史上的大事，某种意义上甚至可以把它当作先锋小说的真正开端。……莫言的成就是多方面的，他的小说形成了个人化的神话世界与语象世界，并由于其感觉方式的独特性而对现代汉语进行了……扭曲与违反，形成了一种独特的个人文体。 (Chen Sihe, *Lectures on Contemporary Chinese Literary History*, 291–292)

Mo Yan has, however, not very often been considered a satirist. Nor has his oeuvre, by and large, been regarded as belonging to the genre of satire. This chapter discusses the ways Mo Yan takes it upon himself to ridicule the follies and vices of society—follies and vices he has both experienced and imagined. Although this analysis refers most frequently to Mo Yan's novels, especially *The Republic of Wine*, other shorter works that are appropriate to the theme are examined as well. The reader may also refer to the earlier discussion of *Life and Death Are Wearing Me Out* and the theme of history (chapter 1), for sarcasm of the absurd is an important element of that book. The present analysis of Mo Yan's satire on the absurd centers on three major and interwoven themes: cannibalism, vulgarity, and the grotesque.

CANNIBALISM

Cannibalism represents a paradox in the history of the human race: on the one hand, it is regarded as "the ultimate secular taboo,"[231] but on the other hand, the act of cannibalism has been recorded in ancient as well as recent history. For instance, cannibalism is said to be practiced by certain tribes in different parts of the world throughout mythology and early history. According to Key Ray Chong's categorization, there are two types of cannibalism: survival cannibalism and learned cannibalism.[232] The first type usually occurs in circumstances of extreme famine caused by natural or man-made disasters, whereas the second "is an institutionalized practice of consuming ... [the] human body; that is to say, it is publicly and culturally sanctioned." The circumstances that might lead to an act of this second type of cannibalism include "hate, love, loyalty, filial piety, desire for the human flesh as a delicacy, punishment, war, belief in the medical benefits of cannibalism, profit, insanity, coercion, religion, and superstition."[233]

China, as a country with one of the longest histories of civilization, is no exception with respect to the practice of eating human beings. Although survival cannibalism has been recorded in China, learned cannibalism seems to be more common there than it is in other parts of the world. Historical records show that Chinese people practice learned cannibalism mostly in circumstances related to filial piety, a desire for human flesh as a delicacy, and a belief in the medical benefits of human parts.

According to John R. Clark, cannibalism is "a topic that normally can be expected to generate in its audience horror and revulsion. For that reason, cannibalism is understandably favored by ... satirists."[234] For instance, Peter Greenaway's controversial movie *The Cook, The Thief, His Wife, and Her Lover* represents cannibalism in "an outrageous, satirical and excessive world about love, sex, food, power, murder, and revenge."[235] The "opulence, decadence, and gluttony" displayed in the movie remind the reader of Mo Yan's *The Republic of Wine*, which is key to this discussion.

The preference among Chinese writers for using cannibalism in their works, however, is for most of them certainly more than an interest in "horror and revulsion." For instance, Liu Zhenyun's (刘震云) "Wengu yijiusier" (温故一九四二) [Reviving 1942] is about a severe drought in Henan (河南) Province which occurred in the year 1942 and in which records of survival cannibalism in Chong's classification indicate the seriousness of the natural disaster.[236] Liu Zhenyun's novella aims to expose the poor administration and the incompetence of the rulers at the time, the KMT government. Another example is Zheng Yi's (郑义) *Hongse jinianbei* (红色纪念碑) [Scarlet memorial], "one of the saddest books ever written about the People's Republic of China and also one of the most important."[237] The non-fiction book describes spine-chilling cases of cannibalism and introduces the reader to an entire cannibal community in Guangxi (广西) Province during the Cultural Revolution of 1966–1976. The revolutionaries ate their so-called class enemies in frenzy, in the name of revolution and class struggle; even ordinary people were driven insane during this extremely irrational time and participated in the cannibalistic activities.

Perhaps Yu Hua could be seen as an exception to the trend of using cannibalism for social commentary. Known for writing fiction filled with disturbing scenes, as an author Yu Hua is somewhat detached from didactic purposes. For instance, the nature of his novella, "Gudian aiqing" (古典爱情) [Classical love], coupled with his dispassionate attitude in describing gory cannibalistic episodes, prevents the story from being seen as an exposé of dark reality. An old story retold, "Classical Love" is a simulation of the cliché *caizi jiaren* (才子佳人) [talented scholars and beautiful ladies], a type of traditional romance fiction, combined with elements of *Liaozhai zhiyi*, a collection of classic Chinese ghost stories. The work is infused with depictions of bloody slaughter, dismemberment, and cannibalism. This gratuitous cruelty serves only to disclose the author's interest in and even obsession with violence rather than social injustice. Nevertheless, in his story "Yijiuba-liu nian" (一九八六年) [1986], the character of the insane man who constantly tortures himself with various ancient punishments is portrayed as a victim of the Cultural Revolution, an element that helps to turn the story into a piece of political criticism.

In this context, Mo Yan is "not only the most imaginative writer to deal with the issue of cannibalism, but is also the novelist who most frequently returns to it."[238] First of all, Mo Yan's frequent return to the topic of cannibalism can be interpreted as one of the thematic continuities of the May Fourth tradition represented by Lu Xun. In his masterwork "A Madman's Diary," one of the earliest short stories of the May Fourth literature, Lu Xun attacks Chinese tradition through the paranoid delusions of a madman, who has read between the lines of Chinese history and discovered nothing but two characters: *chi ren* [eating people], as discussed earlier in this book. The madman becomes convinced that everyone, including himself, is a cannibal; he recalls that his elder brother might have fed him with his little sister's flesh. At the end of his diary, the madman makes a plea to "save the children" (救救孩子) [239]. Although the canon of Chinese history does not lack records of cannibalistic practices, it was not until Lu Xun's "A Madman's Diary," arguably China's first modern vernacular short story, that the concept that Chinese culture was a cannibalistic culture became an important notion in cultural criticism. The father of the new literature, Lu Xun is also a satirist whose

> daring accusation by the Madman is of course quite in line with the prevailing anti-traditionalism of the May Fourth intellectual stance. Other polemicists for the New Culture cause…had popularized the notion of '*lijiao chiren*,' which held that the established rituals and moral tenets had the effect of cannibalizing the Chinese people. (Leo Ou-fan Lee (李欧梵), *Voices from the Iron House*, 54)

The pathological fantasies of a diseased man create an equivocation in "A Madman's Diary," but Lu Xun wrote another piece of fiction that depicts a realistic scene of cannibalism. In "Medicine," the author tells a story in which the father of a diseased boy, driven by a traditional belief in the medical function of human blood, manages to obtain a steamed bun that has been soaked in the blood of an executed revolutionary. The unfortunate son eats the bun, which does not cure him, and he dies soon thereafter. To cite Leo Ou-fan Lee again, this piece is "the most complex symbolic story Lu Xun ever wrote. The story's structure represents an intricate weaving of several symbolic strains which together tell an allegorical story on top of a seemingly realistic plot..."[240] On one symbolic level, the steamed bun soaked in blood ridicules the ignorance and ineffectiveness of the cannibalistic act. It also attacks the absurdity of traditional belief and laments the hopelessness of revolution, although Lu Xun does add a sign of vague hope at the story's end: a wreath of red and white flowers appear on the grave of the revolutionary martyr, adding a touch of brightness to the otherwise totally gloomy picture.

On the surface, Mo Yan adopts Lu Xun's satirical tradition and takes upon himself the mission of social criticism. However, Mo Yan's writing on cannibalism does more than this: it discloses his consistent interest in exposing the hypocrisy of human beings who, he believes, are no more civilized than animals. This belief has qualified Mo Yan as a satirist in terms of Clark's explanation of satire:

> Satire belabors the reader with the dreadful exactly because it does shock; the topic repeatedly serves as a time-honored attention-getting device—capable of breaking down our papier-mâché walls of dignity, aloofness, and high seriousness. Satire insists upon the descent into the bestial, like Circe converting men into swine. (John R. Clark, *The Modern Satiric Grotesque and Its Traditions*, 133)

Northrop Frye, likewise, asserted that

> satire demands at least a token fantasy, a content which the reader recognizes as grotesque, and at least an implicit moral standard, the latter being essential in a militant attitude to experience... The satirist has to select his absurdities... (Northrop Frye, *Anatomy of Criticism*, 224)

Mo Yan selects cannibalism to represent human absurdities. It is worth considering several examples of cannibalism in Mo Yan's short stories before discussing his novel *The Republic of Wine* in detail. In "Qiying"(弃婴) [Abandoned child], Mo Yan describes

> something beautiful that had occurred in a big city... A beautiful, genteel young woman was in the habit of killing and eating young

men. She braised their thighs, steamed their hips, and cooked their shredded hearts and livers in vinegar and garlic. Having devoured quite a few young men, the young woman was the picture of good health. (Mo Yan, "Abandoned Child," in *Shifu, You'll Do Anything for a Laugh*, trans. Howard Goldblatt, 187)

．．．．．．在一个城市里，发生过一个美丽的故事：一个美丽温柔的少妇，杀食年轻男子。股肉红烧，臀肉清蒸，肝和心用白醋生蒜拌之。这个女子吃了许多条男子，吃得红颜永驻。

(Mo Yan, "Abandoned Child,"
in *Collected Works of Mo Yan*, 5:64–65)

Mo Yan also associates this story with the well-known legend of a historical figure, Yi Ya (易牙), who was a favored officer in charge of cooking during the reign of Duke Huan of Qi (齐桓公, ?–643 BC) during the spring and autumn period (770–476 BC). According to the legend, Yi Ya cooked his own young son and presented the dish to the duke so as to please him, for it was believed that a young boy's flesh was especially delicious—better than lamb.[241]

His short story "The Cure," as shown earlier in this book, is about human organ harvesting. In an act of filial piety, a son listens to the miracle worker and attempts to obtain human gall bladder squeezings as a cure for his mother's cataract. With the help of his own son, the man cuts open the bodies of some class enemies who have just been executed (and are still warm and soft) in order to remove their organs. The following is the grotesque scene of harvesting the gall bladder from one body:

Father's jaw set, his eyes bulged. With a sense of determination, he brought his hand down; the knife cut into Ma Kuisan's chest with a slurping sound, all the way to the hilt. He jerked the knife to the side, releasing a stream of blackish blood … I heard a gurgling noise and watched the knife slice through the fatty tissue beneath the skin and release the squirming, yellowish intestines into the opening, like a snake, like a mass of eels; there was a hot, fetid smell.

…

Father cut through the diaphragm and fished around until he had his hand around the heart—still nice and red. ... Finally, alongside the liver, he discovered the egg-sized gall bladder. Very carefully, he separated it from the liver with the tip of his knife, then held it in the palm of his hand to examine it. The thing was moist and slippery and, in the sunlight, had a sheen. Sort of like a piece of fine purple jade. (Mo Yan, "The Cure," in *Shifu, You'll Do Anything for a Laugh*, trans. Howard Goldblatt, 123–124)

爹一咬牙，一瞪眼，一狠心，一抖腕，"噗哧"一声，就把刀子戳进了马魁三的胸膛。刀子吃到了柄，爹把刀往外一提，一股黑血绵绵地渗出来。......

我听到"咕嘟"一声响，先看到刀口两［侧］的白脂油翻出来，又看到那些白里透着鸭蛋青的肠子滋溜溜地窜出来。像一群蛇，像一堆鳝，散发着热烘烘的腥气。

......

爹捅破了马魁三的膈膜，揪出了一颗拳头大的红心。......终于在肝页的背面，发现了那小鸡蛋般大的胆囊。爹小心翼翼地用刀尖把胆囊从肝脏上剥离下来。举着，端详了一会儿，我看到那玩意儿润泽光华映日，宛若一块紫色的美玉。

(Mo Yan, "The Cure," in *Collected Works of Mo Yan*, 5:437–438)

Next, performing like an experienced surgeon, the father deftly removes the gall bladder from another body. Along with his son, the man then rushes home to present the gall bladders to his mother.

This story reminds the reader not only of Lu Xun's "Medicine" but also of the filially pious children of Confucian cultic practices who typically cut flesh from their own bodies in order to feed it to a diseased elder.[242] The notion of filial piety is paradoxically juxtaposed with that of cannibalism in Mo Yan's story. Oddly enough, it seems that before Lu Xun, no one had ever questioned cannibalism when filial piety had been regarded as a virtue. At the point of their intersection in Mo Yan's story, however, the author's minute descriptions of the organ extraction cast this "virtue" in chilling and grotesque light. Unlike the devoted sons in history who fed their parents with their own flesh, this son in Mo Yan's story feeds his mother with other people's organs, an act which reduces the sincerity of his filial piety because his own sacrifice is minimal. Moreover, the comical nature of the miracle worker's prescription adds a ridiculous element to filial piety:

> "Hmm, prescribe something…" Miracle worker Luo told Father to get a pig's gall bladder and have his mother take the squeezings, which should clear her eyes a little.
> "How about a goat's gall bladder?" Father asked.
> "Goats are fine," the physician said; "so are bears. Now if you could get your hands on a human gall bladder … ha, ha … well, I wouldn't be surprised if your mother's eyesight returned to normal." (Mo Yan, "The Cure," in *Shifu, You'll Do Anything for a Laugh*, trans. Howard Goldblatt, 125)
>
> 罗神医说：用个偏方吧——你去弄些猪苦胆，挤出胆汁来让你娘喝，兴许能退出半个瞳仁来。爹问：羊胆行不行？罗神医说：羊胆、熊胆都行——要是能弄到人胆——他哈哈笑着说——你娘定能重见光明。
>
> (Mo Yan, "The Cure," in *Collected Works of Mo Yan*, 5:438)

The most ironic part of the tale, however, is its ending: when the little boy reveals the truth to his grandmother—that she is taking the squeezings of human gall bladders—the old woman dies immediately. In the end, filial piety paired with cannibalism kills the old woman.

As mentioned briefly, the presence of the little boy in this story is carefully planned: the character is a vehicle for Mo Yan's merciless attack on this evil aspect of Chinese culture. Lu Xun's madman made an appeal to save the children, but Mo Yan is more pessimistic: the boy who participates in the whole process of cannibalism will, in all likelihood, carry on this tradition.

Two novels by Mo Yan deserve mention here before discussing *The Republic of Wine*: *The Herbivorous Family* and *Thirteen Steps*. Although cannibalism is not a dominant theme in either of them, the reader cannot miss it, which in *The Herbivorous Family* appears in the form of a historical record—after a plague of locusts, those who survived fed on human corpses—and which in *Thirteen Steps* is hinted at in the custom of eating human placenta.

In *The Republic of Wine*, the theme of preparing human babies to be eaten as a meal may be compared to those in Shen Congwen's *Alisi Zhongguo youji* (阿丽丝中国游记) [Alice in China] or even Jonathan Swift's famous tract, "A Modest Proposal." The multilayered novel is constructed with different narrative voices. The main plot centers on the investigator Ding Gou'er, who is instructed to investigate an astonishing case in a city called Liquorland: it has been reported that the cadres of the city not only eat human babies but also raise infant boys for food. The prime suspect is Diamond Jin, Liquorland's Deputy Head of Propaganda, who was originally a cadre of the mine of Liquorland. The lines of the subplots, which parallel and enrich the main story, comprise correspondence between Li Yidou, "Dr. Liquor," a native of Liquorland and a PhD candidate in liquor studies at Brewer's College, and the fictional character "Mo Yan," a writer in Beijing; nine stories written by Li also appear in tandem with the central story line. An amateur writer, Li writes fantastic stories about the unusual people and events in his hometown in the hope of publishing them in a reputable magazine with the help of "Mo Yan." The correspondence and stories begin as subplots but eventually merge with the main story line to form an organic part of the novel. Moreover, the narrators of the supporting story lines gradually become as equally reliable (or unreliable) as the main story, adding a sense of postmodern playfulness to the novel.

The book begins as a detective story, in which the hero is expected to lead the reader in discovering the truth. Under the guise of the cliché, however, the novel ends up being nothing like a detective story and is antiheroic in nature. If the reader has initially allied Ding with the well-known heroes of the model play *Zhiqu Weihushan* (智取威虎山) [Taking Tiger Mountain by strategy] or of the movie *Zhenchabing* (侦察兵) [The scouts] during the Cultural Revolution, this expectation of heroism will fall short.[243] To be precise, the novel sets itself up as a detective story but gradually fails to conform to the logic of that traditional genre because it signifies an ultimate goal that becomes more and more confusing, unclear, and meaningless as the plot progresses. To a certain extent, the destruction of the detective-story logic originates in the collapse of the heroic image of the protagonist.[244] The hero falls into various snares at the very beginning of his investigation—indulging in the enjoyment of women, wine, and food. Worst of all, he seems to be trapped in a conspiracy by the local cadres to participate in the crime of eating babies. In the end, the detective himself becomes a murder suspect and dies a miserable death.

When Ding Gou'er begins his investigation in Liquorland, he is met with a warm welcome from the mine leaders and Diamond Jin and is treated to a sumptuous banquet, in which the final course is a braised baby. As soon as the detective begins to feel pleased that he has caught the murderers red-handed, he is told that the baby is made of lotus roots, ham, barbecued piglet, and so on. Suspicious, the detective is persuaded to taste this delicious dish and becomes convinced that the baby is a life-like work of art. Nevertheless, when the inebriated detective regains his consciousness after the banquet, he is not sure whether he can believe these people, so he decides to proceed with the investigation. Then he meets the trucker, a married woman, who had given him a ride when he first arrived in Liquorland. They had flirted with each other during their first meeting, and this time, they have sex in the driver's house. Not until Ding is caught in the act by the woman's husband does he learn that she is Diamond Jin's wife. Escaping from Jin's house, the detective flees with the woman to a restaurant owned by a dwarf, only to find that the trucker is one of the dwarf's lovers. The outraged detective shoots the dwarf and the woman, killing them both, and he himself loses his life in a manure pit. Before his death, he has a hallucination in which he sees himself among a group of cannibals enjoying a banquet that includes a braised baby boy as the last course.

Cannibalism, recurring in both the main plot and the "fiction within the fiction" (the letters and the stories), is one of the most important motifs of this novel. In addition, it serves as an agent that complements the main plot and the supplementary stories, and it contributes to the complexity of the novel as a whole. When the reader is informed that the braised baby sitting on the plate ready to be served is not an actual human child but a piece of lifelike artistic work, he must feel a sense of relief, just as the detective does. Two of Dr. Liquor's stories, "Rouhai" (肉孩) [Meat boy] and "Pengren ke" (烹饪课) [Cooking lesson], however, subvert the beautiful image of this work of art in a spine-chilling way.

In "Meat boy," a peasant couple raises their baby boy for the purpose of selling him to the school of gastronomy. In order to compete with other babies for a higher grade—and therefore, more money—the nursing woman eats "a hundred catties of beancakes, ten carp, and four hundred catties of turnips" (一百斤豆饼，十条鲫鱼，四百斤萝卜)[245] to produce better milk for the baby. The parents get up early one morning to bathe the baby in order to make him look cleaner and more tender. The traditional parental love that the reader is expecting does not exist. The mother does not want the baby to be scalded by hot bath water not because she has any affection toward her son, but because she is afraid that a red-skinned boy would get a lower grade. When the baby is finally given the top grade after being weighed and closely examined, the father is ecstatic over the two thousand, one hundred and forty *yuan* (元) he receives from the baby's sale; he exhibits no remorse regarding his son, who is soon to become a meal. Seventy years after Lu Xun's appeal to save the children, Mo Yan draws this picture for the reader:

> Their eldest daughter—a girl of seven or eight clad only in baggy red knee-length shorts, her shoulders hunched, hair a mess, barefoot—walked into the room rubbing her eyes.
> "Die [father], Niang [mother], why are you washing him? You going to cook him and feed him to us?" (Mo Yan, *The Republic of Wine*, trans. Howard Goldblatt, 64)

> 他们最大的女儿——一个七、八岁模样的小姑娘——穿着一条长及膝下的肥大红裤头，光着背，耸着肩胛骨，蓬松着头发，赤着脚，从里屋走出来，搓着眼睛，问：
> "爹，娘，你们洗他干什么？要煮了他给我们吃吗？"
> (Mo Yan, *The Republic of Wine*, 77)

Her question is a further revelation of cannibalism in two ways. First of all, it indicates that the phenomenon of baby eating, or at least the idea that babies are edible, is nothing new to the villagers. Young as this little girl is, she has heard about it before. At this point, the reader may even venture to guess that the child has actually had the experience of eating babies, for this would explain her immediate association of her brother's bath with cooking and eating.[246] Secondly, the little girl's indifference to eating humans—even her own infant brother—implies the strong possibility that the practice of this human evil could continue into the future. Like the cynicism underlying "The Cure," the introduction of this little child reveals Mo Yan's pessimistic, even hopeless, attitude regarding this cannibalistic culture.

It is ironic that the children who are eaten are exclusively boys, while the neglected girls survive. This irony serves as a commentary on the abandonment of baby girls in modern Chinese society, as depicted in Mo Yan's short story "Abandoned Child" and novel *Frog*, alluding to the selective abortion of female fetuses and the infanticide of female newborns that ensued as a result of China's one-child policy. The author criticizes the male-centered culture of the fictional cannibals—girls are not even good enough to eat.[247] On the other hand, I would also suggest that this is a satirical strategy on the part of the novelist through which he points out that after consuming and exhausting its masculine power, the nation will eventually be castrated. This idea is enhanced by another episode in the novel: "Diamond Jin took one of his chopsticks and thrust it into the headless little boy's darling little erect penis. The boy crumbled in the platter and turned into a pile of body parts" (金刚钻操起一根筷子，猛戳到盘中无头男孩秀丽地翘起的小鸡鸡上，男孩立刻解体，变成了一盘杂拌。).[248] Then Jin explains to Ding Gou'er the various materials that have been used to construct what he says is not a real boy so as to clear the detective's mind of doubt. A similar scene of "castration" can be found in one of Dr. Liquor's stories, "Yichi yinghao" (一尺英豪) [Yichi the hero], which is recorded in the fictive *Strange Events in Liquorland* (酒国奇事录).[249] In the legendary account, when the beautiful woman performer serves lunch to the lad who has fallen in love with her, the young man sees a "golden-hued baby boy [sitting] in the center of a platter"

(盘中一金黄男婴).[250] The young man does not dare to touch it with his chopsticks. In order to assure the man that this is no more than a dish, the woman "picked up her chopsticks and stuck them into the baby's penis, which, along with the rest of the body, crumbled under the assault ... [T]he girl said, [t]his boy is not a boy at all, but a boy-shaped fruit" (女举箸猛击男童鸡头，砉然而碎 ...... 女 ...... 曰：此童非童，童形之果尔).[251] Seen in this light, the "boy" must be castrated and deconstructed in order to reveal the truth. One might argue that the creation of Shangguan Jintong, the breast-obsessed character in *Big Breasts and Wide Hips*, is a development of the theme of declining *yang* in present-day China.

The "Cooking Lesson," another of Dr. Liquor's stories, is a lecture teaching the students of the gastronomy college (who are, in fact, still children themselves) how to eat humans (*chi ren*)—to be precise, how to eat children. The most horrifying part is the pedantic lecture. According to the professor who teaches this course,

> rather than being human, the babies we are about to slaughter and cook are small animals in human form that are, based upon strict, mutual agreement, produced to meet the special needs of Liquorland's developing economy and prosperity. In essence, they are no different than the platypuses swimming in the tank waiting to be slaughtered. Please put your minds at ease, and do not let your imagination run wild. You must recite to yourselves a thousand times, ten thousand times: They are not human. They are little animals in human form. (Mo Yan, *The Republic of Wine*, trans. Howard Goldblatt, 222)

> 我们即将宰杀、烹制的婴儿其实并不是人，它们仅仅是一些根据严格的、两厢情愿的合同，为满足发展经济、繁荣酒国的特殊需要而生产出来的人形小兽。它们在本质上与这些游弋在水柜里待宰的鸭嘴兽是一样的，大家请放宽心，不要胡思乱想，你们要在心里一千遍、一万遍地念叨着：它们不是人，它们是人形小兽。(Mo Yan, *The Republic of Wine*, 268)

The first step in preparing the baby boy is to cut an opening on his foot to drain his blood, "which sparkled in the bright lights ... [T]he clear, crisp, ear-pleasing sounds of blood dripping into the jar like a creek flowing through deep ravines" (强光照耀，那线血晶莹极了。...... 血流注到玻璃缸中的声音清脆悦耳，宛若深涧中的溪流。).[252]   The blood being drained here contains rich layers of meaning, and a particular critic's article comes to mind. The author of the article parallels the meat-boy story with Lu Xun's "Medicine" and takes the "allegorical recycling of the human-eating parable ... as a severe social critique."[253] In this critic's opinion, Mo Yan's story reveals a rural-urban antithesis and betrays "trends of commodification and alienation in a developing rural economy. The proposition the fable seems to advance is that 'rural children are ruthlessly eaten by powerful figures in the city.'"[254] I agree with the evocation of a rural-urban binary opposition, and I suggest that the blood is a metaphor for the exploitation of the peasants by the urban "vampires" during the post-Mao reform period.

John R. Clark wrote,

> In fact, increasingly in our century cannibalistic satire becomes more prevalent, more ferocious, more grim. We have witnessed mass slaughter—culminating in the bomb and the gas chamber—what has been designated the Holocaust. Given such an atmosphere, artists are hard put to exceed reality—or even to capture its terrible dimension ... the horrors of the twentieth century have incited satirists to refurbish, to reanimate, older treatments of cannibalism in order to cope with the extravagance of the present scene ... In such a dangerous world, all things are possible—and indeed positively in evidence. (John R. Clark, *The Modern Satiric Grotesque and Its Traditions*, 134)

In the same way, Mo Yan has witnessed tragedies such as the Cultural Revolution, and perhaps for this reason Mo Yan's satire on cannibalism is grimmer than that of Lu Xun: Lu Xun's character uses a human-blood bun to cure his dying son, but Mo Yan's characters sell their son as a product in exchange for money in order to improve their own lives. In other words, while in Lu Xun's story the father is willing to save his son at the expense of his own interests (he gets up at midnight and spends his hard-earned money on the bun), Mo Yan's characters are motivated by selfishness—they sacrifice their son for their own well-being. Parental love and human feelings are totally absent. When they spend money on food, they are symbolically eating their own son. As instructed, the father answers the questions of the staff member of the gastronomy institute:

> "Was this child born specifically for the Special Purchasing Section?"
>
> Yuanbao's [the father] throat was so painfully dry that his affirmative answer sounded forced and strange.
>
> "So, he's not a person, right?" the worker continued.
>
> "Right, he's not a person."
>
> "What you're selling is a special product and not a child, right?"
>
> "Right."
>
> "You give us the merchandise, we pay you. You're a willing seller, we're willing buyers, a fair business transaction. Once the exchange is made, there'll be no quibbling, is that right?"
>
> "Right."
>
> (Mo Yan, *The Republic of Wine*, trans. Howard Goldblatt, 73)

> "这孩子是专门为特购处生的是吗？"
>
> 元宝嗓子干燥痛疼，话出滞怠变音。工作人员继续问：
>
> "所以这孩子不是人是吗？"
>
> "是，他不是人。"元宝回答。
>
> "所以你卖的是一种特殊商品不是卖孩子对吗？"
>
> "对。"
>
> "你交给我们货，我们付给你钱，你愿卖，我们愿买，公平交易，钱货易手永无纠缠对吗？"
>
> "对。" (Mo Yan, *The Republic of Wine*, 88)

In this light, cannibalism is denounced as an extreme in the discourse of a system that is both capitalist and communist (i.e., a capitalist economy with an authoritarian government).[255]

In the book's postscript, Mo Yan admits that the novel is invested with satirical significance:

> Originally I wanted to stay away from politics and write about liquor only… Not until I started writing did I realize that this was impossible. In today's society, drinking has already become

a fight, and banquets have turned into trading rings ... Looking deep into these banquets, one can see all the secrets of this society. As a result, *The Republic of Wine* has a satirical flavor... (My translation)

原想远避了政治，只写酒，......，写起来才知晓这是不可能的。当今社会，喝酒已变成斗争，酒场也变成了交易场。......由酒场深入进去，便可发现这社会的全部奥秘。于是《酒国》便有了一些讽刺意味......。

(Mo Yan, *The Republic of Wine*, 424)

After giving some details of various banquets held at the state's expense, Mo Yan also comments:

I guess if someone were able to put an end to the banquets at public expense, even if for three years only, the money saved would be enough to build another Great Wall... It is easier, however, to blast away the moon than to stop these banquets. So long as this phenomenon exists, people's unspoken criticism will not end. (My translation)

我想中国能够杜绝公费吃喝那怕三年，省下的钱能修一条万里长城。......能把月亮炸掉怕也不能把公费的酒宴取消，而这种现象一日不绝，百姓的腹谤便一日不能止。

(Mo Yan, *The Republic of Wine*, 425)

Having been raised in a peasant's family, Mo Yan feels obligated to reveal the lives of his fellow villagers and be their spokesman; by the same token, as a Chinese, the writer also feels a responsibility to "disclose and criticize" (揭露和批判)[256] the corrupt and destructive nature of this banquet phenomenon in present-day China. It is not surprising, therefore, that he eventually turns his novel into an overt social critique to make "people's unspoken criticism" heard, even though his original intention was to avoid politics altogether.

Kenny K. K. Ng (吴国坤) maintained that "in a metafictional framework," the story of *The Republic of Wine* "can be safely shielded from political accusations since the self-referring text is shown to bear no direct connection with reality."[257] Yet I am inclined to believe that the novel has strong and obvious political implications. Mo Yan conceived the idea for the book in September of 1989, three months after the Tiananmen Square incident of June 4, in which students and workers demanding democracy in Beijing lost their lives; this book can thus easily be seen as a response to the government crackdown against the demonstrators. Therefore I venture to argue that the blood drained from the boy's foot in the story "Cooking Lesson" symbolizes the blood of the Beijing students and workers that spilled from their bodies onto the pavement of Tiananmen Square in the summer of 1989.

Although Mo Yan divulges his intention to attack the banquet phenomenon in the book's postscript, the picture of baby eating is more haunting and disturbing to the reader than that of lavish state banquets. As a matter of fact, the theme of eating children is not absolutely indispensable to the novel *per se* if the novelist intends to attack only the harmfulness of gluttony. Furthermore, Mo Yan lists more cannibals in the last chapter of *The Republic of Wine*, in addition to the historical Yi Ya and Lu Xun's madman. They are Liu Bei (刘备, 161–223) the King of Shu (蜀) in the period of Three Kingdoms (220–280), Li Kui (李逵), an important character in *Shuihu zhuan* (水浒传) [Water margin], and modern people who consume human placenta as a tonic.[258] In compiling this list, the author enriches and reinforces the reader's comprehension of the history of cannibalism in China. It is not, obviously, too venturesome to argue that the novel goes beyond social criticism and enters into the realm of political satire. In a recent interview, Mo Yan has also admitted that "*The Republic of Wine* is a political allegory similar to George Orwell's *Animal Farm* ("《酒国》是一部类似于奥尼尔的《动物庄园》的政治寓言小说。").[259] But whereas George Orwell's *1984* and Aldous Huxley's (1894–1963) *Brave New World* are more like parables foretelling the future of a dictatorial society, Mo Yan's *The Republic of Wine* intends to ridicule the irrationality and absurdity of the present.

Dustin Griffin made the following comments about political satire:

> In fact, the greatest satire was written under the Roman emperors and under kings of England and France who would have resisted any challenge to the "monarchical system." In the late

> twentieth century it has appeared not in the liberal West but in
> Russia and Eastern Europe ... It is difficult, or unnecessary,
> to satirize our political leaders when the newspapers are filled
> with open attacks on their integrity and intelligence. But if open
> challenge is not permitted, writers will turn to irony, indirec-
> tion, innuendo, allegory, fable—to the fictions of satire. (Dustin
> Griffin, *Satire*, 138–139)

This observation is appropriate for the context in which *The Republic of Wine* was written, for it is a context in which people do not enjoy complete freedom of speech and in which important political events, such as the June Fourth Tiananmen Square incident, are still taboo subjects.

The theme of baby killing in *The Republic of Wine* is echoed by another of Mo Yan's tours de force: his eleventh novel, *Frog*, published in 2009. Like many of his stories, *Frog* is set in the novelist's hometown, Northeast Gaomi Township of Shandong Province. Dealing with the controversial one-child policy of the Chinese government, this novel creates a woman protagonist, Aunt, who joins Grandma in *The Red Sorghum Family* and Mother in *Big Breasts and Wide Hips* as another female lead. However, unlike Grandma and Mother, who are established as positive models of women's emancipation, this Aunt is half angel, half devil, in this respect somewhat similar to the dwarf character in *The Republic of Wine*. Hence her character is richer and more complex, lending itself to a multidimensional analysis. On the one hand, as a brilliant gynecologist and a childbirth expert, Aunt brings thousands of healthy babies into the world. On the other hand, as a loyal member of the Communist Party, she faithfully defends party policy and commits countless infanticides. As a result, although she is worshipped as a child-giving goddess, she also conducts many abortions and is therefore condemned as a baby-killing demon. The internal conflicts experienced by Aunt as both a loving woman and a committed party member result in her marriage, later in her life, to an artisan who is known for making clay dolls; Aunt has her husband produce dolls to represent all of the aborted babies who have died in her hands, a gesture which can be interpreted as an act of Aunt's repentance for her former sins.

Frog consists of five chapters. Like *The Republic of Wine*, this book is also composed in an epistolary structure. In *Frog*, each of the five chapters begins with a letter from the first-person narrator, Kedou (蝌蚪) [Tadpole], to a respected Japanese writer, who is thought to be modeled on the prototype of Kenzaburo Oe (大江健三郎). In the first four chapters, the stories of Aunt as narrated by Tadpole are related in his letters; that is, Aunt's stories comprise the major parts of the letters. What makes *Frog* different from *The Republic of Wine* in terms of structure is the last chapter, in which a letter is followed by a nine-act play about an absurd case of a substitute mother in Aunt's remaining years written by Tadpole. The combination of correspondence, narrative, and drama is a successful experiment by Mo Yan that gives the reader a fresh reading experience.

The title, *Wa*, has different dimensions of meanings. First of all, it is a homophone to the *wa* (娲) in the name of *nüwa* (女娲), the legendary goddess who created human beings and patched up the sky. Secondly, this Chinese character (蛙) is very close to *wa* (娃), which means "child" in Chinese: the only difference in pronunciation lies in the tones: the frog character is in the first tone and the child character in the second tone. Thirdly, frogs are known for being fertile and therefore are totemic animals in certain areas of China.

In fact, this is not the first time that Mo Yan touches upon the theme of family planning in China. Similar plots appear in his earlier stories, for example, "Abandoned Child", "Didao" (地道) [Tunnel], and "Explosions." In other words, the motif that is prevalent in the novel *Frog* had existed in Mo Yan's mind for quite a long time. This is another instance of Mo Yan's solicitude for the lives of his fellow Chinese citizens and his eagerness to explore controversial and sensitive topics, such as the one-child policy. Moreover, some subtle details invite the reader to make a daring interpretation. A good example is Tadpole's fifth letter to the Japanese writer. Toward the end of the letter, Tadpole writes the following, a remark followed by two questions: "Every child is unique and irreplaceable. Is it true that blood on one's hands can never be washed away? Is it true that those souls haunted by a sense of guilt can never be freed?" (每个孩子都是唯一的，都是不可替代的。沾到手上的血，是不是永远也洗不净呢？被罪感纠缠的灵魂，是不是永远也得不到解脱呢？").[260] Whose hands and souls is he referring to? Does the blood merely represent the unborn babies? Considering the date of this letter—June 3, 2009—the reader has reason to read the remark and questions as a mournful speech on the eve of the twentieth anniversary of the Tiananmen Square incident. By the same token, the clay dolls that Aunt asks her husband to make to commemorate all the babies she has aborted could be understood as miniature monuments to the young people and students who lost their lives in Beijing twenty years ago. In a conversation with Kenzaburo Oe and Zhang Yimou, Mo Yan directly mentioned the June Fourth incident (this was the first time I had ever heard of a writer from Mainland China discuss the event so directly):

> I don't think it is necessary to avoid talking about 'June Fourth.' When the event was over, it became history, and nobody can change this fact. As a professional writer, I still believe that you'd better speak with your own stories. Only by writing stories would you be able to completely and openly express your opinion of the event. (My translation)
>
> 我觉得对于"六四"，没有必要回避，因为事件过去之后，就是历史，这是谁也不能改变的。对于一个以写小说为职业的作家，我还是觉得，你最好还是用自己的小说说话，只有用小说，你才可能完整地、毫不隐讳地表现出你对事件的看法。 (Mo Yan, "To Write as an Ordinary Person," in *Speak Up, Mo Yan*, 300)

In light of this statement, I argue that both *The Republic of Wine* and *Frog* are the novelist's way of expressing his opinion regarding the Chinese student movement two decades ago.

In conclusion, taking the banquet phenomenon in China today as a point of departure, Mo Yan takes aim at the extravagance of Chinese gastronomy as a symbol of the decadence of Chinese culture.[261] For effect, the writer places this extravagance in an exaggerated framework: the cannibalism of babies. The phenomenon of eating children can easily be read as a metaphor for killing students, who, if not exactly children, are certainly young people who, like children, represent the future. *The Republic of Wine* is a parody of Lu Xun's "A Madman's Diary" in terms of the theme of cannibalism. Xiaobin Yang (杨小滨), one of the critics drawing comparisons between these two fictional works, opined that

> [d]ifferent from Lu Xun's Madman, who is haunted by the paranoid fear of being eaten, Ding Gou'er encounters the cannibalistic community with an inconsistent, schizophrenic attitude. He is, after all, neither an adversary against nor a victim of that community, but a participant in it. (Xiaobin Yang, "*The Republic of Wine*: An Extravaganza of Decline," in *positions*, 22)

In fact, both the madman and Ding Gou'er are participants in cannibalism. What distinguishes these two cannibals is that the madman profoundly resents the sin and wishes to detach himself from it, while Ding Gou'er, whose "putative outrage … is short-lived, perhaps out of a subconscious understanding that, in a pervasive atmosphere of human degradation, eating is better than being eaten. Rather than shoot the cannibals, he joins them."[262] Seen in this light, Mo Yan appears to be more skeptical, satirical, and cynical regarding human nature. Questioning the family planning policy that causes serious social problems, such as infanticide, Mo Yan simultaneously treats a sensitive topic and goes so far as to touch upon one of the greatest taboo subjects in Chinese society. In so doing, his criticism of the cannibalistic features expands to the present-day reality.

VULGARITY

Literary writing in the post-Mao period comprises a completely different landscape than Maoist literature, and one of its most remarkable features is vulgarity—including filthiness, sexual descriptions, and scatological matters—which has been a favored technique among young Chinese writers since the mid-1980s. In fact, this phenomenon is a challenge to the political rhetoric that dominated during Mao's time. David Der-wei Wang commented that:

> One of the most fascinating phenomena in Chinese literature of the late eighties has been the radicalization of traditional realist discourse. Writers in mainland China ... have explored materials hitherto considered untouchable and rendered them in a wide range of forms ... Particularly in mainland China, this rejuvenated creativity has become a powerful critique of Maoist discourse, the formidable literary and political rhetoric that prevailed in China for more than three decades, suppressing all hope of free literary expression. But now, by turning the world into a realm of fantastic and uncanny elements or by identifying normalcy with the grotesque and insane, writers awaken their readers from aesthetic and ideological inertia, initiating them into a new kind of reality. (David Der-wei Wang, "Chinese Fiction for the Nineties," in *Running Wild*, ed. David Der-wei Wang with Jeanne Tai, 243)

An overview of the writing mentality under Mao Zedong's literary policies—the mentality that has been challenged by writers since the eighties—will contextualize the rest of this discussion. As early as 1942, in his famous "Zai Yan'an wenyi zuotanhui shang de jianghua," Mao mandated the Communist literary rules: literature and art should serve the workers, peasants, and soldiers by reflecting their actual lives. In addition, writers should employ the forms with which the working classes are familiar. This is the well-known Chinese socialist realism, which prevailed in Mainland China for about four decades. Popular literature for the first time seemed to attain the greatest ascendancy.

Socialist realism appears to aim at a downward movement, toppling the hierarchy and minimizing the sense of superiority of the literati. What this kind of realism has represented in the postliberation mainland context, however, is completely different from the promotion of popular literature by some men of letters in Chinese history, such as Li Zhi (李贽, 1527–1602) and Feng Menglong (冯梦龙, 1574–1646).[263] In order to celebrate true human nature, these intellectuals highlighted triviality and vulgarity and valued depictions of forbidden topics like physical love and the body. To them, vulgarity was a means of discrediting the orthodoxy, which was by and large dominated by aristocrats; use of vulgarity was also an open subversion of hypocritical value judgments about morality. Obviously, an examination of socialist realism shows that it has embodied only a disguised, distorted, and ideologically shaped reality. The fact is that vulgar matters are ironically put under stricter taboo. The works written during the Cultural Revolution, when the ultraleft trend of thought reached its peak, best showcase the absurdity of this realism: the heroes and heroines without exception are deprived of all basic human needs because these mundane trivialities would only damage the perfection of their images. Consequently, any aspect of daily life that is unrelated to politics is rarely described, and sex is totally prohibited. Interestingly enough, however, excrement is endowed with special political meaning and is frequently depicted in revolutionary writings. On the one hand, it appears to represent the sternest criterion for testing the sincerity and loyalty of intellectuals sent to the countryside, and on the other hand it is used as the most severe punishment for those who refuse to be submissive in class struggles. One of the stock punishments for exiled intellectuals and for the "five bad elements" was to clean toilets and carry night soil.[264] One episode from a revolutionary novel describes the miserable fate of a young woman teacher who unintentionally said something wrong during the Cultural Revolution:

> Teacher Bai Lan [White Orchid] bent down to pour the night soil into the manure pit from the manure buckets. Mao Di [her student, a boy aged eight or nine] rushed onto the earth mound near the pit and pushed a big rock into it while saying: "Make the counterrevolutionary stinky to death!" Teacher Bai Lan was splashed with the muddy and stinking liquid... (My translation)

> 白兰老师弯腰将粪桶里的粪一桶桶倒入粪池，茅弟冲到粪池旁的土堆上，说道："让反革命臭死。"说着，就把一块大石头抛向粪池。浊臭的粪汤溅了白兰老师一身......。
> (Ke Yunlu, "Benighted," in *Huacheng*, 23)

Even worse, if a "bad element" dared to resist the criticism of the revolutionaries, he or she might receive severe castigation. Tie Ning's (铁凝) novel *Da yunü* (大浴女) [Big bathers] contains a scene in which a high school teacher is publicly criticized for having an illegitimate child. The revolutionaries force her to eat human excrement because she refuses to disclose the identity of the child's father.[265] As seen here, excrement is also used to signal those who have lost their political power. The class enemies represented by Liu Shaoqi (刘少奇, 1898–1969), the former president of the People's Republic of China, were labeled "dog's dung" by the Red Guards during the Cultural Revolution.[266]

As a reaction to this kind of unreal "realistic" writings, characters of the Gao Daquan (高大全) type—the protagonist of a model novel during the Cultural Revolution, whose name is homophonous with "tall, big, perfect"—have disappeared, while vulgarity has brimmed over in fiction written since the mid-1980s. Its use has more than one purpose, interestingly: some writers celebrate the resuscitation of suppressed human instincts, whereas others indulge in drawing the most thrilling and grotesque pictures for the reader, even to the extent that the vulgarity, like violence, "stretch[es] the limits of 'taste.'"[267] Scenes of this nature are not unknown to the contemporary Chinese fiction reader; examples include references to abandoned condoms together with the bodies of dead cats floating in the river in Su Tong's "Shu Nong" (舒农) [The brothers Shu]); a man falling into a manure pit in both Yu Hua's "Yige dizhu de si" (一个地主的死) [The death of a landlord] and Mo Yan's *The Republic of Wine*; an old man consuming his daughter-in-law's menstrual blood, and the same old man eating excrement in Liu Heng's (刘恒) *Canghe bairi meng* (苍河白日梦) [Green river daydreams].

These pessimistic writers believe that reality is as dirty and gloomy as anyone could imagine. They are disillusioned with reality, having been presented with a false vision of the world ever since they were born, and they show their absolute distrust of and disappointment with human beings and society. This second attitude contrasts sharply with that of Bakhtin, who believed that

> man is superior to all beings, including the celestial spirits, because he is not only being but also becoming. He is outside all hierarchies, for a hierarchy can determine only that which represents stable, immovable, and unchangeable being, not free becoming. (Mikhail Bakhtin, *Rabelais and His World*, trans. Hélène Iswolsky, 364)

For these Chinese writers, a human being is no more than a biological existence that is host to all kinds of animal instincts. If these authors were to agree with Bakhtin that humanity is outside all hierarchies, it would be only in the sense that humans are by no means superior to any other creatures as traditionally believed. In fact, they may believe that humans are the worst animals of all. In Mo Yan's words:

> Hey, humans, don't have too high an opinion of yourselves, don't give yourselves the air of being the wisest of all species. Essentially human beings are no different from dogs, cats, maggots in manure buckets, or bugs in wall cracks. What best distinguishes humankind from animals is: humans are hypocritical! ... What creatures are humans? When a wolf eats a lamb, it is condemned by humanity as fierce and cruel. Human beings, however, after enjoying a delicious dish of mutton, they belch and tell innocent kids the story of the beautiful and meek lamb. What kind of creature is a human? (My translation)

> 人，不要妄自尊大，以万物的灵长自居，人跟狗跟猫跟粪缸里的蛆虫跟墙缝里的臭虫并没有本质的区别，人类区别于动物界的最根本的标志就是：人类虚伪！……人是些什么东西？狼吃了羊羔被人说成凶残、恶毒，人吃了羊羔肉却打着喷香的嗝给不懂事的孩童讲述美丽温柔的小羊羔羔的故事，人是些什么东西？(Mo Yan, "The Herbivorous Family," in *Collected Works of Mo Yan*, 4:93)

As a result of this pessimistic view of humanity, contemporary Chinese writers have created a downward movement, not in order to elevate humankind's authenticity but in order to strip off its civilized mask. Clark's comment on scatology comes to mind at this point:

> What is satirically grotesque about such a subject [scatology] is obvious: proud, self-delusional man ever aspires to elevate himself and his dignity, whereas the satirist destroys such upward mobility by reducing man to a defecating animal before our eyes. (John R. Clark, *The Modern Satiric Grotesque and Its Traditions*, 117)

Mo Yan is known as an active practitioner of this new authorial fashion; in fact, he is one of the trend's leaders. Analysis of his works indicates that Mo Yan has created something of a paradox inasmuch as he seems to simultaneously agree with and depart from the Bakhtinian reading of Rabelais, which views the lower stratum of the material body and the downward movements in Rabelais' world as positive since they have a subversive significance to the hierarchical norms and values of medieval European culture.[268] Put otherwise, Mo Yan is keenly aware of the binary opposition of civility and vulgarity, so he uses vulgarity as an unorthodox Other, making the Other's voice heard by celebrating the spirit of authenticity and spontaneity, denying the established moral values, and undoing the taboos on obscenity. One literary critic's comment on Jean-Paul Sartre also applies to Mo Yan in this respect: "Vulgarity … represented to Sartre a defiant revolt against bourgeois good taste and 'bad faith.' For this reason, he turned toward vulgarity as a vehicle of authenticity within personal identity."[269] This is certainly true of Mo Yan, but at the same time, Mo Yan's antipathy toward human nature applies to all people regardless of their social or class status.

Mo Yan's enthusiasm for scatology manifests itself in a famous episode of *The Red Sorghum Family*. To show off his uniqueness to Grandma, Granddad (then a brewer) urinates into a wine crock. Granddad is a character with conflicting attributes, as previously discussed in detail. His charisma is enhanced by his crossing the boundary between good and evil. The fact that he copulates with Grandma in the sorghum field and kills the leper to save her from an unfortunate marriage is an impressive defiance of traditional morality; undoubtedly, the overt depiction of his urination adds a shocking effect to the image of this figure. At this point the writer plays a prank on the reader: Granddad's urine unexpectedly produces a crock of exquisite wine with an "unusually rich and mellow fragrance" (更加淳朴浓郁的香气),[270] perhaps due to a chemical reaction. From then on, urine-enhanced wine becomes the secret of this distillery's good business. The reader is amazed to see the integration of this lowly bodily element—urine—and the most important cultural element—food, in this case represented by wine. This is particularly interesting since China is a country with a highly developed food culture, one which has permeated every aspect of life and become extremely complicated and subtle with respect to both politics and human relationships.[271] As Sun Lung-kee maintained,

> To discuss Chinese "harmony," the best point of departure is their renowned cooking skills. Indeed, their excellent cooking skills were born from the harmonization of a great variety of cooking materials with different tastes in a single dish. (My translation)
>
> 谈论中国人的 "和合性" 的最佳起点，莫如中国人驰名世界的烹调术。中国人之所以产生世界上首屈一指的烹调术，是由于他们能够将天下种类繁多而气味各异的食料 "和合" 于同一碟菜肴中。(Sun Lung-kee, *The Deep Structure of Chinese Culture*, 131)

Obviously, the urine-enhanced wine is the result of a "harmony" of urine and alcohol. It is commonly believed that young boys' urine (*tongzi niao*, 童子尿) is a cure for certain diseases; it is therefore medicinal after all. By sublimating the wine, Granddad's urine, paired with his act of urination, adds color to his unconstrained character and challenges the moral hierarchy. In this episode, "the ugly and the negative are … mysteriously transmogrified into the affirmative."[272]

If Granddad's urination in *The Red Sorghum Family* is Mo Yan's celebration of human nature, scatological descriptions elsewhere are more multilayered. In *The Herbivorous Family*, the detailed depictions of defecation and human excrement illustrate Bakhtin's positive point of view on the lower bodily stratum and turn this vulgar bodily activity into a paean on the vitality of humanity:

> After defecating, people of the Northeast Gaomi Township all have a weary but relaxed and happy expression on their faces. In those years, after bowel movements, we all felt that life was as perfect as a flower in full bloom.
> …
> Our stools are as beautiful as trademarked bananas; why can't we eulogize them? When we defecate, we often associate the movement with the ultimate form of love, even elevate it to a religious rite; why can't we eulogize it? (My translation)
>
> 高密东北乡人大便过后脸上都带着轻松疲惫的幸福表情。当年，我们大便后都感到生活美好，宛若鲜花盛开。
> ……
> 我们的大便像贴着商标的香蕉一样美丽为什么不能歌颂，我们大便时往往联想到爱情的最高形式、甚至升华成一种宗教仪式为什么不能歌颂？ (Mo Yan, "Red Locusts," *Collected Works of Mo Yan*, 4:25–29)[273]

In the same novel, however, a tendency to debase the value of human beings is also noticeable. On the night of the Mid-Autumn Festival, the three-year-old character named "Mo Yan" is eating snacks and viewing the moon with his family. After taking a bite of a watermelon, he tells his father that the melon has been contaminated by feces. Tasting it himself but finding nothing wrong with the melon, the father thinks that his son is overly imaginative and tells the little boy to finish the melon to the last bite. The narrator, however, informs the reader that Auntie Nine, then a ten-year-old girl, had cut an opening on the half-grown melon, defecated into it, and then put it back as if it was untouched. When the character "Mo Yan" eats the ripe melon, he actually eats her excrement; so do his father and other members of the family who share the melon with him.

It is interesting that the novelist assigns his own name to this character: no one can escape the debasement of his withering judgment on humanity, not even the author himself. It is therefore not too fanciful to argue that the narrator of "Red Locusts" speaks for the novelist:

> What the hell am I? I know it clearly that I am but excrement wriggling in the rectum of society. Even though I shared a birthday with the world-renowned General Liu Meng, I am unable to change my nature as a piece of shit. (My translation)

> 我他妈的算什么，我清楚地知道我不过是一根在社会的直肠里蠕动的大便，尽管我是和名扬四海的刘猛将军同一天生日，也无法改变大便本质。(Mo Yan, "Red Locusts" *Collected Works of Mo Yan*, 4:2)

Another example of scatology appears in *The Garlic Ballads*, the story about the corrupt local government's unfair treatment of the peasants, who are garlic farmers. The angry peasants burn the government building, and as a result, some of the peasants are arrested and imprisoned. Gao Yang, one of several peasant rioters, recollects the hardships he has experienced throughout his life while in prison. After his mother's death, he buried her, violating the policy of the Communist Party. When his action was made known, the village officials ordered him to exhume the body for cremation. Partly because of his financial difficulties and partly due to filial piety, Gao Yang refused to do so, and his refusal led to his being tortured. After a night in prison, he needs to empty his bladder but finds no appropriate place to do so until he spots an empty wine bottle in a corner of the room; he uses it to relieve himself. When the militiamen discover the bottle, they decide to have some fun by ordering Gao Yang to drink it up.

> Without another word, Gao Yang picked up the bottle and took a mighty swig. It was still warm, and on the salty side, but not bad, all in all. Tipping the bottle back a second time, he gulped about half of the remaining urine, then wiped his mouth with his sleeve as hot tears gushed from his eyes. With a smile frozen on his face,

he said, "Gao Yang, oh Gao Yang, you bastard, how could you be so lucky? Who else could have the good fortune to feast on a delicious onion roll and wash it down with fine wine?" (Mo Yan, *The Garlic Ballads*, trans. Howard Goldblatt, 162)

［高羊］提着酒瓶，仰脖灌了一口，尿液尚温，除了微微咸涩外，并无异味。他咕嘟咕嘟地喝着，一口气喝下去大半瓶。他抬手擦擦嘴巴，眼睛里涌出热泪，脸上带着笑，嘴里说："高羊，高羊，你这个杂种，你说你哪来这么大的福气？吃着葱花馅饼，喝着葡萄美酒，你说你哪来的这么多福气？……"

(Mo Yan, *The Garlic Ballads*, 218)

Throughout his life, Gao Yang drinks his own urine three times. Gao Yang's father is a landlord, one of the "five bad elements" according to the Communist classification, and this leads to Gao Yang and his mother being regarded as enemies of the revolutionaries; therefore what these militiamen do to him is justified by the principles of class struggle. Such political alienation is common in fiction after the close of the Cultural Revolution, but Mo Yan makes his novel more profound by tingeing it with a species alienation of its characters. By imposing and accepting humiliating and inhuman action, both parties are transmogrified into a nonhuman state. Auntie Nine and the character "Mo Yan" in *The Herbivorous Family* have the same tendency toward nonhumanity. The most remarkable feature that distinguishes the militiamen from Auntie Nine is their intentions: the former intentionally humiliate their victim, whereas the latter's deed can be taken as a child's unintentional prank. One may argue, of course, that the little girl's filthy action mirrors the inhuman soul of the people as a whole, a reality which explains the inevitability of the militiamen's nonhumanness.

Mo Yan's *Thirteen Steps* is a complicated novel with shifting narrative levels that create a grotesque and unpleasant aura, an effect which enhances the absurdity of life as depicted in the book. The reader encounters scenes that would conventionally be deemed filthy or indecent—for example, a scene of washing tangled and stinking pork intestines and a scene in which a woman urinates on her male partner's face during sexual intercourse. Perhaps the most striking portrayal, however, is the image of stripping the fat from a dead body. The female protagonist is a beautician who works in a funeral home. She is instructed to strip the fatty deposits from the body of a newly dead senior cadre who had not only been her secret lover but her mother's as well. The purpose of doing this is to ensure that ordinary people will not mistake the cadre for a corrupt official when they watch his funeral on TV. The cold-blooded beautician does as she has been told:

> After cleaning off the fat from Deputy Bureau Chief Wang's face and neck, the beautician stretched herself, swept her eyes over the face of her ex-lover coldly but with deep feeling. Then, using his deep navel as the central line as well as the central point, she made a big cut of half a foot in length. No blood, not even a smell of it. The shining white fat gushed from the cut. A huge white chrysanthemum was blossoming on Chief Wang's belly. (My translation)

> 整容师清理完了王副局长脸上和脖子上的脂肪后，伸展了一下腰肢，冷冷地，感触万千地扫了一眼老情人破碎的脸，然后，以王副局长深陷进去的肚脐为中线、中点，切开了一个半尺长的大口子。一点血也不流，一点血腥味也没有，白花花的脂肪滋滋响着从刀口里冒出来。王副局长的肚子上盛开了一簇庞大的白菊花。 (Mo Yan, *Thirteen Steps*, 103)

Surprised by how much grease a man's belly can contain, the beautician goes on to tear off enough of this white material to make one candle with it. Yet this is not disgusting enough. The beautician has made a deal with a zookeeper, who specializes in beasts of prey and is currently taking care of two ligers (the offspring of a male lion and a female tiger). These rare beasts do not like chicken, beef, or pork, but they have a taste for human flesh. So every week, the caring zookeeper makes an exchange with the beautician, trading the animal meat that his charges will not eat for leftover bits and pieces from the corpses. The system is mutually beneficial: the forty-five catties of grease from Deputy Bureau Chief Wang provide optimal nutrition for the ligers, which will grow up to be true predatory beasts living in the natural environment; and the beautician and her family are better off than their peers because of the meat provided by the zookeeper. Mo Yan here, as elsewhere, ridicules the human race by juxtaposing it with beasts; he pinpoints the absurdity of humans' daily life or what Bakhtin calls "degradation," which is seen in Mo Yan's other works, such as *The Republic of Wine*.

A close examination of *The Republic of Wine* shows that the novel is a good example of the phenomenon of degradation. As mentioned earlier, Ding Gou'er is the hero of what initially appears to be a stereotypical detective story; yet the way Ding's character is shaped is totally anti-traditional. Ding stands in sharp contrast with the revolutionary heroes in works composed under Maoist discourse; a comparison reveals Mo Yan's defiance of Maoist norms. The revolutionary model heroes, who would never be tempted by women or wealth, are invariably the bravest and the most upright of men. No matter how cunning the enemies are, the heroes are always intelligent enough to defeat the evil forces. *The Republic of Wine*, therefore, fails to meet the expectations of the conventional audience or reader; instead, the novelist deliberately degrades his hero by turning him into a clown. The book is an argument that the hero—or heroism—is dead. To quote Clark's words once again:

> The satirist's implication, of course, is quite simple: his cynical vision proposes that in our defective society heroism is tainted or bogus and in our deteriorating era the pious aims, exalted motives, and self-congratulatory claims of artists are at best pompous and misguided, at worst entirely spurious. (John R. Clark, *The Modern Satiric Grotesque and Its Traditions*, 51)

Interestingly, Ding Gou'er's image, or self, is never consistent. When he is in his own city, he is a normal man, an experienced and respected detective who is ready to accept his assignment. Strangely, as soon as he steps into Liquorland, he is no longer a heroic detective—the image to which the reader has become accustomed is perverted as Ding falls into the all-too-typical traps of women and wine from the very beginning of the investigation. He hitches a ride to Liquorland in a truck operated by a pretty but uncouth woman; he is attracted to her and filled with lust, he begins flirting with her. When she claims to be infertile saline-alkali soil, he responds by saying that he is an agronomist who is skilled at applying ammonium sulphate to sterile soil to improve its quality. This barefaced flirtation eventually leads to a sexual encounter at the trucker's place. The pair is caught in the act, however, by the woman's husband, Diamond Jin, who is the prime suspect in the baby-eating case. When the detective and the trucker flee from her house, they take refuge in a restaurant owned by the dwarf Yu Yichi. The situation deteriorates further when the unlucky detective learns that the woman is one of the dwarf's mistresses. Finally this jealous detective shoots both Yu and the woman, thus making himself a murderer. He also becomes a cannibal, for he falls into the trap set by Diamond Jin to intoxicate him. Ding's position as a hero has been overturned: he changes from a detective into a participant in the crime and eventually a criminal suspect.

An element of filthiness adds to the absurdity of this antihero image. Ding's hemorrhoids attack him before he begins his work. At the banquet, the detective gets extremely drunk and finally soaks in his own vomit. After shooting the dwarf and the trucker, he escapes from the restaurant and runs into the street, and he is so dirty and shabby that people mistake him for a madman or a beggar. Finally, he falls into a manure pit, completing his descent into disgrace. Ding's degradation takes him from the wine cup to a manure pit.

THE GROTESQUE

Thomas Mann (1875–1955) once stated his opinions about modern art thus:

> I feel that, broadly and essentially, the striking feature of modern art is that it has ceased to recognize the categories of tragic and comic, or the dramatic classifications, tragedy and comedy. It sees life as tragicomedy, with the result that the grotesque is its most genuine style. (Thomas Mann, "Conrad's 'Secret Agent,'" in *Past Masters and other Papers*, trans. H. T. Lowe-Porter, 240–241)

Mo Yan exemplifies Mann's observation. Many of his works, especially those written more recently, are exactly what Mann called "tragicomedy." Earlier discussions (see chapter 2) have examined how the playfulness in *Life and Death Are Wearing Me Out* turns the recent history of China into a tragicomedy. *The Republic of Wine* is another example; the entire novel is so playful and exaggerated that it is nothing other than a farce. Yet, as discussed earlier, one need not read between the lines to find the two Chinese characters, *chi ren* [eating people], as Lu Xun's madman did. Readers will find the novels more appealing because grief expressed through laughter is sadder and more shocking than grief expressed through conventional channels. As John Clark suggests, "the grotesque mode" has become "more serviceable and more relevant as a means of representing the 'dark side' of human nature,"[274] and "the satirist usually fosters the grotesque as a mirror held up to chaotic and distraught generations..."[275] Instances of the grotesque and of deformity began to appear in fiction written after the Cultural Revolution. One of Mo Yan's contemporaries, Can Xue, is known for writing experimental fiction in which reality is so gloomy and most of her characters so grotesque that some critics attribute her works to madness and hysteria. Can Xue's fiction is on the cutting edge of avant-garde literary trends.[276] Mo Yan, however, surpasses her with his bizarre descriptions, which include a toad with three legs in his novella "Happiness" and a woman with only one breast in his novel *Big Breasts and Wide Hips*. Perhaps the most notable example of deformity in Mo Yan's writing is the character Yu Yichi (余一尺), the dwarf in *The Republic of Wine*.

As indicated by his name, Yu Yichi is only about one foot tall—the word *yichi* (一尺) literally mean "one foot." The character appears both in the main story line and in the novel's subplots. Yu Yichi always looks ageless; his smile is so charming that it wins the sympathy and favorable impressions of people around him, allowing him to lead a life of plenty. In the tide of reform and openness, this small person stands metaphorically head and shoulders above others in spite of his size, for he is a successful businessman. He opens a restaurant and hires other dwarves as waiters and waitresses; he even recruits the twin dwarf daughters of a mysterious high-ranking official of the central government. Needless to say, these miniature girls bring much fame and reputation to Yu's restaurant and to Yu himself, who makes rapid advances in his career overnight.[277] Once Yu has fame and wealth, he vows to sleep with all the beautiful women of Liquorland. For the reader, this figure is unforgettable not so much because he is one of the most wealthy and influential people in Liquorland but because of his disconcerting appearance and behavior. In one odd scene, Dr. Liquor forgets to knock at the door and enters Yu's office at an inopportune moment: Yu is standing on his office desk and kissing a pretty, normal-sized woman. When he jumps down off the desk, he stands only as high as the woman's knees. When she holds him to kiss him good-bye, she resembles a mother holding her baby.

> Not one to shy away from situations like this, the woman bends low, letting her pendulous breasts, which are about to burst out of her dress, drop so heavily on Yu Yichi's face that he winces as she gently picks him up. Judging only by size and weight, it looks like a mother cradling her son…. Almost savagely, she plants a big kiss on his lips, then flings him down basketball-like onto a sofa against the wall. (Mo Yan, *The Republic of Wine*, trans. Howard Goldblatt, 148)
>
> 那女人也是个大方角色，不避嫌疑，弯腰，让两只喷薄欲出的大乳房沉甸甸地砸在余一尺仰起的脸上—砸得余一尺呲牙咧嘴—轻轻地把他抱起来。单纯从体积和重量的角度看，就如同母亲抱着儿了一样......。她几乎是恶狠狠地在他脸上亲了一下，然后，像投掷篮球一样，把他扔到贴着墙壁的长沙发上。(Mo Yan, *The Republic of Wine*, 179)

Several other scenes of the novel are equally weird. When Dr. Liquor makes fun of Yu's size unintentionally, Yu "laughs a sinister laugh, his face swelling up in greens and purples, his eyes emitting a green light, his arms spread like the wings of an aging falcon ready to fly off. He looks absolutely terrifying" (他阴森森地冷笑一声,脸皮胀得青紫,双眼放出绿光,双臂炸开,如同一只振翅欲飞的老雕。这模样委实可怕).[278] In order to show off his special skills to Dr. Liquor, the dwarf flies into the air, looking like "an enormous, disgusting lizard crawling across the ceiling, carefree and relaxed as can be" (像一只庞大的令人恶心的壁虎，在天花板上轻松愉快地爬行着).[279]

When *The Republic of Wine* is read as political satire, this "half angel, half devil" (一半是个天使，一半是个魔鬼)[280] character plays an important role inasmuch as similarities can be found between this image and Deng Xiaoping, the former supreme leader of China. In the novel, Yu "is eighty-five years old this year" (今年已经八十五岁).[281] "He's a dwarf who, born into a literary family, has read all the classics and is well versed in statecraft, yet has endured decades of humiliation. Then, through some magic intervention, he enjoys a meteoric rise, obtaining wealth, fame, and position" (一个出身于书香门 [第]、饱读诗书、满腹经纶的侏儒，忍辱负重几十年，一朝凭借东风力，扶摇直上青云，他得到了金钱、名誉、地位).[282] This description brings to mind the aged Deng, who was small in stature and experienced fluctuations in his political life. His open-door policy and decision to reform China brought prosperity to the country and a better life to its people; nevertheless, some resentment exists because Deng's economic reform led to much greater corruption than had existed under Mao, especially among those who take control of power and abuse it. The Tiananmen Square tragedy he directed in 1989 has also damaged his reputation among those who experienced it, although it is still a strictly forbidden subject of discussion. As a result of all this, Deng has a dual image among Chinese people: half angel, half devil.

Yu Yichi is a character with a complex and uncertain identity. A careful reading of the book reveals that this figure is a tripartite entity: he is the dwarf, the scaly boy, and the red-shirt little demon in one. First, he is Yu Yichi, the owner of the Yichi Restaurant that appears in Dr. Liquor's stories "Lüjie" (驴街) [Donkey avenue] and "Yichi the Hero," as well as in the correspondence between Li and the character "Mo Yan." Eventually, Yu and his restaurant emerge in the novel's main plot when the detective Ding Gou'er kills him and the trucker in Yu's own restaurant. Second, this character represents the scaly boy who also appears in the stories "Meat Boy" and "Donkey Avenue" as well as in the main story line. This boy is "a little hero who, moving through Liquorland like a shadow, performed many good deeds, eliminating evil and eradicating the bad, stealing from the rich to give to the poor" (鱼鳞小子是我们酒国市的一位神出鬼没的少侠，专干锄奸除恶、偷富济贫的好事。).[283] He "has become the embodiment of justice, the enforcer of the people's will, the pressure valve of law and order" (实际上成了正义的化身，成了人民意志的执行者，成了一个维持社会治安的减压阀。).[284] Third, this figure is also the little demon wrapped in a red flag who organizes an uprising among the flesh boys sold to the gastronomy institute and brings a brutal end to an administrator's life in the story "Meat Boy." This little demon becomes one of the dwarf waiters in Yu's restaurant in the story "Donkey Avenue." Are all of these characters one and the same person? In one of Li's stories, "Shentong" (神童) [Child prodigy], the little demon claims that he was the scaly boy, and this is reinforced by one of "Mo Yan's" letters to Li. Moreover, in another story by Li, "Yichi the Hero," Yu Yichi pronounces the following words: "Do you know the identity of that scaly boy who rides a galloping steed up and down Donkey Avenue on moonlit nights? It's me, that's who, me" (你们知道每当月明之夜，在这驴街上纵驴驰骋的鱼鳞小子是谁吗？那就是我，那就是我！).[285] Therefore, we can draw the conclusion that the little demon, the scaly boy, and Yu are the same person—despite the fact that in "Donkey Avenue" Yu and the scaly boy once appear at the same time and despite the fact that the little demon coexists with Yu as he works in Yu's restaurant in the same story. In short, Yu is at once a legendary and a realistic figure in the novel, an ambiguous signifier in Mo Yan's narrative and cross-referential strategies. This "constricted and physically confined"[286] multi-layered character is a grotesque unity that functions to ridicule an abnormal, unnatural, irrational, and absurd Liquorland, itself a miniature of present-day China as the pessimistic novelist perceives it.

According to Mary Russo, contemporary discussion on the grotesque can be divided into two major categories: that of carnival and that of the uncanny. Whereas Bakhtin uses the grotesque bodily image "to conceptualize social formations, social conflict, and the realm of the political," other scholars, such as Wolfgang Kayser, regard it as uncanny, a "particular 'experience' of the 'strange' and 'criminal' variety."[287] What does *grotesque* mean to Mo Yan? I would argue that a duality exists in his works.

Like Yu Yichi in *The Republic of Wine*, Li Yuchan (李玉蝉), the beautician of the funeral home in *Thirteen Steps*, and the deformed girl produced by incestuous parents in the short story "Tuhu de nü'er" (屠户的女儿) [Butcher's daughter], represent absurd reality and human debasement, while the web-fingered people in *The Herbivorous Family* both signify and criticize a hierarchical society.[288] The story of *Thirteen Steps* is full of unimaginable happenings. As mentioned earlier in this chapter, the beautician has made an agreement with the zookeeper to exchange some human parts for meat on a weekly basis; in a detailed scene the reader learns that she strips the fat from her ex-lover's belly. Later this same beautician performs successful plastic surgery to exchange her neighbor's face with that of her own husband, and many problems ensue. She commits adultery when she is a teenager and even shares a lover with her own mother. Not only does the character participate in these unusual and unsavory activities, but she is also physically deformed: over her upper lip is a tuft of emerald (Mo Yan's obsession with the color green drives him to further caricature this character)—a lush, grassy mustache. Needless to say, such a character is certainly "strange," "criminal," and uncanny to the reader. A mustache on the female body complicates the identity of this figure by adding an androgynous quality to it. Furthermore, the character not only blurs the boundary between male and female but also that between human and beast: she is tempted to have sexual intercourse with a monkey in the zoo. Mo Yan is deriding the degradation of human society once again. "The Butcher's Daughter" opens with a peaceful and happy tone: a little girl, the first-person narrator, describes her simple life with her mother and grandfather. Only near the end of the story does the reader realize that as a result of inbreeding, this lovely girl has the grotesque, abnormal body of a mermaid. The most powerful scene of this story is that in which the little girl dreams that her mother is fiercely and resentfully beating her grandfather, who is actually both the girl's grandfather and father. The reader knows that this is not a dream but an actual occurrence. When the disguise of language is torn away, the ugliness of human nature is fully revealed.

The story of the web-fingered people represents the novelist's challenge to the stereotyped notions of normality and human hierarchy. According to legend, the ancestors of the herbivorous family have webbed fingers and toes. In order to prevent the production of web descendants, they are not allowed to practice endogamy—that is, they must not marry another member of the same kinship group. After a young man and a young woman who have defied this law are burned alive, four hundred boys are castrated in order to put an end to the degeneration of their family, since webbed fingers and toes are considered grotesque and abnormal. However, the mass castration only leads to further degeneration and grotesquerie: when those boys grow up, they have neither a beard nor an Adam's apple; instead, they retain the shrill voices of young boys. In short, they are "big, strong, neither male nor female young people" (身高体壮、不男不女的青年人).[289] They finally take revenge by rising up against those who castrated them, but they are defeated. Their failure may signal the novelist's pessimism, but the exchange between the narrator and his daughter at the end of the chapter is profound and inspiring:

> "...Why are we webbed?"
> "Why not?"
> (My translation)

> "......人为什么要生蹼呢？"
> "人为什么不要生蹼呢？"
> (Mo Yan, "The Webbed Ancestors," in *Collected Works of Mo Yan*, 4:238)

The hierarchy and the binary opposition of normal and abnormal are thus questioned.

Mo Yan's desire to invest his works with satire is, to quote Edward and Lillian Bloom, "motivated by ... dissatisfaction with the ways of the world": his "satiric 'intention' ... becomes [his] expression of dismay, disappointment, even revulsion."[290] However, this intention is not shaped by the "moral-didactic impulse" of satire in the traditional sense, nor is Mo Yan misanthropic.[291] Rather, his inclination to eradicate evil and usher in good motivates him to ridicule all sorts of irrational practices that he observes in reality as well as in tradition. Mo Yan diverges from Lu Xun in that he is at times more playful and cynical; his critical voice, however, possesses a revolting quality comparable to Lu Xun's as well as a power that destroys evil.

CONCLUSION

A self-educated peasant who selected the nom de plume Mo Yan, "do not speak," has become one of the most outspoken contemporary Chinese novelists. With his pen, he speaks abundantly, daringly, and successfully. As David Der-wei Wang has remarked,

> from his pen emerges an endless cascade of words. Whatever the subject matter, a torrential flow of rich, unpredictable, often lacerating words remains his trademark. While this claim to silence amid an outpouring of fictional works may signify a contradiction of self-mockery and self-praise, it is precisely why so many literary critics have lent their voices in his support, whether from the perspective of feminism, national discourse, or something else.
> (David Der-wei Wang, "The Literary World of Mo Yan," *World Literature Today*, 487)

The "torrential flow" of words covers a wide range of subject matter. Mo Yan's success starts with his construction of "a family or regional history" that, according to Leo Ou-fan Lee, "is itself the result of an obsession with history … a dominant Chinese cultural trait."[292] The obsession with history leads Mo Yan to ponder the past—both the collective past and the individual past. For the collective past, the three novels, *The Red Sorghum Family*, *Big Breasts and Wide Hips*, and *Life and Death Are Wearing Me Out*, reveal changes in Mo Yan's attitude toward history, moving from tracing history back to a heroic and glorious golden age to questioning, mocking, and even denying history. Yet Mo Yan's denial of history does not serve as an antidote to his obsession; rather, it unveils the author's deeper mania and disappointment. As for the individual past, Mo Yan inspects the psychological path of educated urbanites who have a past directly related to a rural context and who feel dislocated in the city—the prime example of this is the story of an intellectual who encounters his high school sweetheart in his old home town. The result of being unable to return to the past while also feeling uneasy about staying in the present creates a sense of homelessness and a paradoxical nostalgia, leading to a criticism by the intellectual—a critical assessment that approaches cynical self-mockery. These contradictory feelings with respect to the hometown, the symbol of the past, again indicate a vacillation in Mo Yan's perception of history.

Mo Yan is not only skeptical about history but also sardonic about the present. Satire is the most powerful device he employs. As a result, his writings are often marked with ridicule. His sarcasm strongly reminds the reader of Lu Xun, who was known for his relentless attacks on tradition as well as on discontented modern society. In this respect Mo Yan, who shares an "obsession with China" with the May Fourth writers, returns to the May Fourth literary spirit.[293] Mo Yan appears as equally mission driven as Lu Xun and feels obligated to speak on behalf of the Chinese people and to subject evil to strong condemnation. Whereas *The Garlic Ballads* falls into the domain of conventional social criticism, his other works cast blame on ills of every kind, be they historical, traditional, social, or political.

One theme that runs through the past and the present retains Mo Yan's enthusiasm from the beginning is violence. Through writing about violence, Mo Yan remorselessly exposes the dark side of human nature.

It has been observed that his writing on violence has become more and more intense, making him a case study for the critics. Ironically, a major root-seeking writer, Mo Yan is made a rootless and homeless intellectual like Lu Xun by his attack on tradition and his dissatisfaction with the present. Nevertheless, Mo Yan is less prudent in his works, and he is more playful and pessimistic than Lu Xun. Whereas Lu Xun's diction is usually rather terse, which might be attributed in part to the influence of the classical Chinese of which Lu Xun was a master, Mo Yan "speaks" profusely, so much so that he seems to lose control at times. This has become more obvious in his recent works. Furthermore, if Lu Xun was a pioneer in using vernacular language to write fiction and essays, Mo Yan is experimental in both content and form. The more he "speaks," the more clearly his negative opinion on social and human evil is disclosed. At the same time, Mo Yan begins to transcend Lu Xun with respect to the didactic function of literature. In other words, the concept that literature must be educational or at least convey certain messages gradually fades into the background in some of Mo Yan's fictional works, especially those published after the turn of the last century. In this sense, writing for Mo Yan is simply for writing's sake, inasmuch as every now and then his writings seem to be merely a fulfillment of his desire to speak with his pen and have nothing to do with any edifying or moralistic missions. Occasionally, this fulfillment does not even serve the needs of a harmonious and unified writing style.

That being said, most of Mo Yan's stories, as shown in this study, still convey strong messages that serve as cultural, social, or political commentaries. In China, a reader of contemporary Chinese literature will inevitably relate the texts closely to the social and political situation of the country. This is certainly the case in reading Mo Yan's work. Fredric Jameson makes the following observation regarding third-world literature:

> All third-world texts are necessarily ... allegorical, and in a very specific way: they are to be read as what I will call *national allegories*, ... particularly when their forms develop out of predominantly western machineries of representation, such as the novel ... Third-world texts, even those which are seemingly private and

> invested with a properly libidinal dynamic—necessarily project a political dimension in the form of national allegory: *the story of the private individual destiny is always an allegory of the embattled situation of the public third-world culture and society.* (Fredric Jameson, "Third-World Literature in the Era of Multinational Capitalism," in *Social Text*, 69)

This generalization that all third-world texts should be taken as national allegories may be debatable, yet it is appropriate in Mo Yan's case, at least for some of his works. Jameson uses what he calls "the supreme example,"[294] Lu Xun's "A Madman's Diary," to support his argument. He maintains that "Lu Xun's text cannot be appreciated properly without some sense of ... its 'allegorical resonance.' ... [C]annibalism ... is at one and the same time being attributed ... to Chinese society as a whole..."[295] Similarly, Mo Yan's *The Republic of Wine* cannot be fully apprehended without the same allegorical sense that the author's "fellow citizens ... are 'literally cannibals...'"[296] Lu Xun makes his accusation mainly on a cultural dimension, whereas Mo Yan by and large makes his from political, social, and even economical perspectives to fit the post-Mao reality.

In his insightful monograph *The Velvet Prison: Artists Under State Socialism*, Miklós Haraszti, a Hungarian dissident writer, examines the new form of literary censorship by the state in the post-Stalinist era.[297] Geremie Barmé also analyzes the Chinese "velvet prison" of the post-Mao period. He explains the concept as follows:

> The crude, military style of Stalinist (for which we can also read Maoist) rule with its attendant purges, denunciations, and struggles has finally given way to a new dawn of "soft," civilian government. Technocrats reformulate the social contract, one in which ... consensus replaces coercion and complicity subverts criticism. Censorship is no longer the job of a ham-fisted apparat but a partnership involving artists, audiences, and commissars alike. (Geremie R. Barmé, "The Chinese Velvet Prison," in *In the Red*, 7)

The formation of the velvet prison is two-sided. On the one hand, the state authority of the post-Mao era has appeared more tolerant than the Maoist regime, adopting a policy of conciliation; thus "the cacophony of well-known slogans is transformed into a jazz symphony."[298] On the other hand, artists with different opinions have stopped being defiant; instead, they are reconciled to the central power, practicing self-constraint and self-censorship and adjusting their behavior so as to be legitimate, that is, "to maintain their credentials as participants in mainstream intellectual discourse."[299] Based on what Bo Yang (柏杨) and Sun Lung-kee, who have poignantly questioned Chinese culture, regard as the "fatal flaws" of Chinese intellectuals, Barmé believes that Chinese writers seem to have had "a more compliant attitude toward the day-to-day rule of totalitarianism/authoritarianism than did intellectuals in Eastern Europe."[300] And again, "while experimenting with what for China were innovative themes, such as alienation, humanism, absurdity, and sex, state artists were ever careful to conform to the new, expanded state specifications."[301]

After reading such comments, it is tempting to ask whether Mo Yan is one of these state artists, a compromising "prisoner" of the Chinese velvet prison. Or is he rather a true nonconformist, a dissident in a broad sense, one of those branded by Haraszti as a maverick artist? A member of the Chinese Communist Party and a long-time army writer, Mo Yan has for the most part been writing with fetters. Almost from the very beginning of his writing profession, he has been insubordinate in morally and politically forbidden zones, challenging Maoist discourse in terms of both ideology and language. Many other post-Mao writers have also resisted Maoist discourse, and they have achieved much in their experiments. Yet at times Mo Yan seems to be more explicit and writing less "between the lines,"[302] especially in works such as *Big Breasts and Wide Hips*, *The Garlic Ballads*, *The Republic of Wine*, *Life and Death Are Wearing Me Out*, and *Frog*. Moreover, because Mo Yan is the most prolific writer in the domain of serious literature in China today, his achievement and stance are more visible to the readers and critics and therefore more thoroughly subject to their judgment. In the meantime, his playfulness and irony often make his narratives all the more confrontational. His unruly flow of words, mixed with expressions reminiscent of revolutionary clichés and even Maoist terms, can be regarded as a parody of the Maoist style of speaking. It should be noted that this caused difficulties for Mo Yan particularly when he was serving in the army. Furthermore, the literary technique or form he has explored is so sophisticated and unique that it not only "*contains* intellectual and moral implications, ... it [also] *discovers* them," as Mark Schorer (1908–1977) remarked in an article he wrote more than half a century ago.[303] In Mo Yan's works, the word "form" ceases to signify a mere arrangement of materials and story lines, a portrayal of fictional characters, or a categorization of creative methods, such as realism or surrealism. Instead, it has become a direct expression of an artistic state of mind that is inseparable from the content. It does not employ and manipulate images and emotions with rational logic but judges and evaluates life through a direct perception of images that contain rich symbolic significance. The various structures of his novels are particularly successful experiments that enrich the content of the story tremendously. Needless to say, Mo Yan's artistic experiments are a break from the Maoist discourse that allowed very limited creative methods, denounced those who paid more attention to form as "formalists" in a negative sense, and regarded creative methods such as modernism and the absurd in literature as decadent and unhealthy. All in all, Mo Yan's uniqueness and achievements distinguish him from most other contemporary Chinese writers and also place him on a par with his model, Lu Xun, whom he even surpasses in certain respects.

Based on what Mo Yan has accomplished, he is definitely a radical artist with a free spirit. One need not be put in jail or be dragged along the pavement by the police in order to be a dissident. The attacks from the leftists on Mo Yan and *Big Breasts and Wide Hips*, as considered earlier, serve to qualify him as an iconoclast. However, the rapid capitalization and commercialization of post-Mao China must be taken into consideration because these transformational transitions of post-revolutionary China are part of—or help consolidate—the velvet prison. "During the 1980s, it gradually dawned on Chinese artists that if they could not produce popular works that would sell—something that became increasingly worrisome for 'serious' writers—then they must rely on state support..."[304] To a certain extent, it is easier to be ideologically defiant than to stand aloof from material temptations, especially in a society that has been transformed from a planned economy to a market economy in which a worship of wealth prevails. A writer of acclaimed literature who has experimented with various techniques and achieved high quality in his creative works, Mo Yan has also produced, for example, *Red Grove*, a crudely written commercial novel with little artistic value.

Is Mo Yan, then, still a hostage of the velvet prison despite his bravery and novelty? Is there such thing as a pure dissident? Indeed, Mo Yan may not totally qualify as a maverick artist by Haraszti's definition: an artist who "is considered an enemy from the outset, for he rejects state culture at its foundations. He disrupts the smooth operation of the machinery of monopoly and provokes independent activity."[305] In addition, a maverick artist is also an "economic criminal" who "transgresses by willingly sacrificing the privileges of the assimilated," aiming "to be a poor artist in order to remain a free one."[306] Mo Yan may be closer to Haraszti's naïve hero, another type of dissident, yet he deals with the system with the cunning of a state artist. According to Haraszti, a state artist

> recognizes that the only freedom within the socialist system is that of participation. He understands the impossibility of creating art that transcends the system which permits it to exist. He knows the futility of seeking to smuggle messages of freedom between the lines. He could ... cling with cunning, heroic naïveté to this illusion. He could proceed as though censorship were not a law of existence but merely a kind of corruption, a necessary evil, to be endured, or to be circumvented. In other words, he could try to demonstrate his "freedom." (Miklós Haraszti, *The Velvet Prison*, trans. Katalin Landesmann and Stephen Landesmann, 150)

Haraszti believes that the strategy of the state artist is "seriously flawed" because "it isn't just that such 'freedom' is forbidden: it doesn't even exist. It is not, like murder, an act that can be committed. The greatest problem with this freedom is that its existence cannot be demonstrated."[307]

A naïve hero by Haraszti's definition is an artist "who refuse[s] self-censorship" and thus is "rejected by the censors" and "exiled from the world of aesthetics." "The artist's professional license is withdrawn; his privileges are revoked; he is ostracized by the artistic community."[308] Although "with the Naïve Hero there is a chance that he may be excluded only from the realm of aesthetics,"[309] Haraszti asserts that both dissidents "are doomed to irrelevance"[310] because their freedom only exists in theory.[311]

As in the character of Yu Yichi in *The Republic of Wine*, a tripartite entity is also evident in Mo Yan: to some extent he is a combination of these three artists in Haraszti's categorization. At the very least, he possesses some important qualities of each: he is at once a state artist who participates in the socialist system, a naïve hero who refuses self-censorship, and a maverick artist who questions the culture of the state from its root in the context of contemporary China. His own talent, together with the special social circumstances, makes his success possible—willingly or unwillingly, the central government has had less and less control over the market economy that favors a brilliant writer whose popularity among his readers allows him to survive even though his "future holds nothing but endless conflict."[312]

George Konrád, Haraszti's friend, wrote about Haraszti's apprehension in the foreword to Haraszti's book:

> Haraszti's nightmare is simply this: If state socialism keeps expanding and co-opts every kind of criticism, how does a skeptic speak? A clown reveals the circus director's philosophy for taming animals and keeping order under the Big Top. Meanwhile he realizes that he also happens to belong to the troupe. (George Konrád, Foreword, in *The Velvet Prison*, Miklós Haraszti, xii)

Lu Xun does not belong to the troupe. His fictional works basically target the maladies in the culture that constitute the nature of the people—that is, what is called *Chineseness*. His essays also attack the current social and political woes that could have brought menace to his life as they did to the lives of some famous writers of his time, such as Wen Yiduo (闻一多, 1899–1946) and Li Gongpu (李公朴, 1902–1946). Both of them became politically active and outspoken and both were murdered by secret agents of the *Kuomintang*, the nationalist government, in 1946. Lu Xun makes his stance clear by writing as a true objector, protesting against all kinds of evils, ancient and modern. Mo Yan belongs to the troupe; yet a clown working for the troupe differs from a shareholder or a board member of the "corporation" behind the circus in that he is an employee instead of a protector of vested interests. Therefore, his unmasking of the circus director's philosophy is more convincing and powerful. Similarly, an individual in a clown's place is in a better position to betray the "invisible violence"[313] of the velvet prison. Even though in such a prison much of the hardware of a regular prison is not visible, writing from within a velvet prison can still be quite dangerous. Imprisonment and even execution of authors whose writings were considered counterrevolutionary were not uncommon during Mao Zedong's time. One known example is the case of Hu Feng (胡风, 1902–1985) and his followers in the 1950s: Hu was imprisoned for more than twenty years and as many as two thousand people were either arrested or purged. Another example is Yu Luoke (遇罗克, 1942–1970), who was arrested in 1968 and executed in 1970 for writing against the Communist theory of family background, the Communist version of a caste system.

It is true that Mo Yan emerged in the post-Mao period, but the political climate in postrevolutionary China was hard to predict—a dangerous situation for daring writers. For instance, although writers were enjoying, perhaps naively, the relatively free atmosphere after the end of the Cultural Revolution, they were frustrated inasmuch as many of them were criticized in the Anti–Spiritual Pollution Campaign from 1983 to 1984. The campaign was organized by members of the Communist Party who feared that these writers might encourage the spread of Western ideology and liberal ideas to ordinary people. In this sense, Mo Yan is equally as critical and disobedient as Lu Xun—even though he is part of the troupe.

Mo Yan is not, however, a recapitulation of Lu Xun, although his works are marked (as he himself admits) by the earlier writer's influence. When discussion is restricted to the fictional works of both writers, Mo Yan inherits and develops Lu Xun's cultural and social criticism, subjecting himself to the analysis and review of certain features in human nature, but he does not limit himself to this, the trademark of Lu Xun. Rather, Mo Yan willingly turns his works into more direct political critique. His experiments with different writing techniques are fascinating and have helped him achieve great artistic success and make his critical edge even more incisive. As argued throughout this study, signs in Mo Yan's works indicate that he is gradually moving away from the role of the "social conscience" or the "engineer of human souls" that has traditionally been imposed on Chinese writers; likewise, his writings move beyond the ultimate principle in the Chinese literary tradition that literature is a vehicle to convey moral truth or *wen yi zaidao* (文以载道). Mo Yan's unconstrained language and composition in some cases are free from any practical function and in this respect serve the sole purpose of fulfilling his own pleasure in writing. A controversial and widely read author, Mo Yan—the son of a peasant, a self-educated artist—has produced an extremely important body of work that no reader of contemporary Chinese literature can ignore or afford to miss.

NOTES

1. May 4, 1919, was a monumental day in modern Chinese history. On that day, thousands of students demonstrated in Peking (also known as Beijing, 北京), the capital of China, protesting the humiliating foreign policy which the Chinese government had adopted toward Japan. The ensuing strikes by students, workers, and businessmen spread the indignation to the whole country and eventually caused an earth-shaking change in society and ideological thinking in particular. This event was soon named "the May Fourth Movement" by students and has been regarded as a hallmark of the emancipation of people's thoughts. Studies on this important movement are abundant; among them is the pioneering book by Chow Tse-tsung (周策纵, 1916–2007), *The May 4th Movement: Intellectual Revolution in Modern China* (Cambridge, MA: Harvard University Press, 1960).

2. Believing in the theory of "continuing revolution under the proletariat dictatorship," Mao Zedong initiated and directed the Great Proletarian Cultural Revolution in 1966, which brought an entire decade of calamity to China. The whole country was turned upside down and traditional culture was severely damaged. For more details, see Roderick Mac-Farquhar and John K. Fairbank, eds., *The Cambridge History of China,* vol. 15, *The People's Republic, Part II: Revolutions within the Chinese Revolution, 1966–1982* (Cambridge: Cambridge University Press, 1991), 81–435. See also John King Fairbank, *China: A New History* (Cambridge, MA: The Belknap Press of Harvard University Press, 1992), 383–405. An immense number of more specific studies on this significant event in Chinese recent history can be found; see, for example, Joseph W. Esherick, Paul G. Pickowicz, and Andrew G. Walder, eds., *The Chinese Cultural Revolution as History* (Stanford, CA: Stanford University Press, 2006); Paul Clark, *The Chinese Cultural Revolution: A History* (Cambridge: Cambridge University Press, 2008).

3. The invention of revolutionary model plays was the result of the increasing influence of Mao's wife, Jiang Qing (江青, 1914–1991), in literary and artistic circles. The plays were selected as models, examples from which people should learn, because of their revolutionary qualities. Needless to say, although the plays dealt with a variety of subjects, the central theme of each was singing Mao's praises.

4. The Gang of Four, headed by Jiang Qing, was arrested by the central government on October 6, 1976, following Mao's death on September 9, 1976. The other three members were Zhang Chunqiao (张春桥, 1917–2005), Yao Wenyuan (姚文元, 1931–2005), and Wang Hongwen (王洪文, 1935–1992).

5. Mo Yan, ed., *Suokongli de fangjian: yingxiang wo de shibu duanpian xiaoshuo* (锁孔里的房间：影响我的10部短篇小说) [A room seen through the keyhole: Ten short stories that have influenced me], (Beijing: Xinshijie chubanshe, 1999).

6. A mainland scholar, Zhu Binzhong (朱宾忠), published a book entitled *Kuayue shikong de duihua: Fukena yu Mo Yan bijiao yanjiu* (跨越时空的对话：福克纳与莫言比较研究) [A dialogue crossing time and space: A comparison study on Faulkner and Mo Yan]. Conducting a parallel comparison, Zhu presents valuable studies on both Mo Yan and Faulkner. In his conclusion, however, he critiques the quality of the work of both writers and comments that Mo Yan is inferior to Faulkner in certain respects. These comments are open to discussion, especially because such a comparison is complex and problematic when two writers operate in such different circumstances in terms of time, space, language, culture, and social and political systems.

7. Mo Yan's year of birth appears differently in various places and ranges from 1955 to 1957. The confusion stems from a change made to his personal data when he joined the army. To be enlisted, one's age must fall within the span authorized for military service; when Mo Yan enlisted, he had passed the conscription age already. He therefore changed his birth year from 1955 to 1956. As for his name, the writer now uses Mo Yan as his official, legal name. The Chinese characters *mo yan* (莫言) mean "do not speak." According to Mo Yan himself, he chose these two characters as his pen name in order to stop talking because his words had caused trouble to his family. See Mo Yan, "Ji'e he gudu shi wo chuangzuo de caifu" (饥饿和孤独是我创作的财富) [Hunger and loneliness: My muses], preface to *Shifu, You'll Do Anything for a Laugh*, trans. Howard Goldblatt (New York: Arcade Publishing, 2001), xi–xii. In fact, these two characters are a deconstruction of *mo* (谟), the first character of his given name *moye* (谟业), which is composed of a *yan* (言), a word radical that means "word," plus the character *mo* (莫), which means "do not." In other words, the writer played with the character, dividing it up to make a meaningful phrase that would serve as his pen name. Ironically, as a prolific writer, Mo Yan "speaks" with his pen and speaks boldly, as an analysis of his fiction reveals.

8. He Lihua (贺立华), "Honggaoliang gezhe de liyin" (红高粱歌者的履印) [The Footprints of the red sorghum singer], in *Mo Yan yanjiu ziliao* (莫言研究资料) [Research materials about Mo Yan], ed. He Lihua and Yang Shousen (杨守森), (Jinan: Shandong daxue chubanshe, 1992), 13. My translation.

9. Ibid., 14. My translation.

10. Pu Songling, the renowned writer of the early Qing dynasty (1644–1911), authored *Liaozhai zhiyi* (聊斋志异) [Strange stories from the leisure studio], a collection of stories about ghosts, fox-spirits, and other immortal and mortal beings. It has remained popular since its publication, and the term *liaozhai* has become synonymous with fantastic tales.

11. Mao Zedong wrote an article in 1933 entitled "Zenyang fenxi nongcun jieji" (怎样分析农村阶级) [How to differentiate the classes in rural areas], which is collected in *Mao Zedong xuanji* (毛泽东选集) [Selected works of Mao Zedong], one-volume edition (Beijing: Renmin chubanshe, 1967), 113–115 (For the English translation, see Mao Zedong, *Selected Works of Mao Tse-Tung*, vol. 1 [Peking: Foreign Languages Press, 1967], 137–139). This article set the criteria for determining class status in the countryside. The rankings differ slightly in different time periods. For instance, sometimes the category "lower-middle peasants" is omitted, and the group is instead referred to as "hired hands," a category which is considered poorer than poor peasants. For information about the communists' ranking of peasants, see Jonathan D. Spence, *The Search for Modern China* (New York: W.W. Norton, 1990), 480. A table of sample communist classes of households by percentage of the rural population in central China from 1941 to 1945 is included.

12. He Lihua, "The Footprints of the Red Sorghum Singer," 7. My translation.

13. Mo Yan, "Chaoyue guxiang" (超越故乡) [To transcend hometown], in *Hui changge de qiang: Mo Yan sanwen xuan* (会唱歌的墙：莫言散文选) [The wall that can sing: Selected essays of Mo Yan], (Beijing: Renmin wenxue chubanshe, 1998), 234. My translation.

14. John King Fairbank, *The Great Chinese Revolution: 1800–1985* (New York: Harper & Row, 1986), 302.

15. Jonathan D. Spence, *The Search for Modern China*, 583.

16. See Mo Yan, "Hunger and Loneliness: My Muses," xiii.

17. See He Lihua, "The Footprints of the Red Sorghum Singer," 17. My translation.

18. Ibid., 18.

19. Laifong Leung (梁丽芳), *Morning Sun: Interviews with Chinese Writers of the Lost Generation* (Armonk, NY: Sharpe, 1994), 151.

20. The first essay, "Shuoshuo Fukena zhege laotou" (说说福克纳这个老头) [Talk about the old fellow Faulkner], has been collected in Mo Yan, *The Wall that can Sing: Selected Essays of Mo Yan*, 200–203. The speech "Fukena dashu, nihaoma?" (福克纳大叔，你好吗？) [How are you, Uncle Faulkner?] can be found in *Mo Yan sanwen* (莫言散文) [Mo Yan's selected prose], (Hangzhou: Zhejiang wenyi chubanshe, 2000), 292–300. (The original English title is also printed on the book.)

21. Mo Yan, "Talk about the Old Fellow Faulkner," 201. My translation.

22. David Der-wei Wang, "The Literary World of Mo Yan," *World Literature Today* 74, no. 3 (Summer 2000): 488.

23. For the slide-show incident and the famous metaphor of the "iron house," see Lu Xun, "Zixu" (自序) [Preface to *Call to Arms*], in *Lu Xun quanji* (鲁迅全集) [The collected works of Lu Xun], vol. 1 (Beijing: Renmin wenxue chubanshe, 1981), 415–421. Translation from Lu Xun, preface to "Call to Arms," in *Lu Xun: Selected Works*, vol. 1, trans. Yang Xianyi (杨宪益) and Gladys Yang, 2nd ed. (Beijing: Foreign Languages Press, 1980), 33–38.

24. See Lin Yü-sheng, *The Crisis of Chinese Consciousness: Radical Anti-traditionalism in the May Fourth Era* (Madison: University of Wisconsin Press, 1979).

25. A direct by-product of the May Fourth Movement was the establishment of the Chinese Communist Party in 1921. Lu Xun was highly regarded by Mao Zedong, who called him the "chief commander of China's cultural revolution" (中国文化革命的主将); cited in Mao Zedong, "Xin minzhu zhuyi lun" (新民主主义论) [On new democracy], in *Mao Zedong xuanji* (毛泽东选集) [Selected works of Mao Zedong], one-volume edition (Beijing: Renmin chubanshe, 1967), 658. Translation from Mao Zedong, *Selected Works of Mao Tse-Tung*, vol. 2 (Peking: Foreign Languages Press, 1967), 372.

26. See Georg Lukács, *The Historical Novel*, trans. Hannah Mitchell and Stanley Mitchell (Lincoln: University of Nebraska Press, 1983), 283–286.

27. Mo Yan admitted in an interview that *Big Breasts and Wide Hips* is the culmination of all kinds of experiments in his writing career over the decade between his two historical novels. See Lin Zhou (林舟), "Xinling de youli yu guitu: Mo Yan fangtan lu" (心灵的游历与归途：莫言访谈录) [The traveling and returning of the mind: An interview with Mo Yan], *Huacheng* (花城) [Flowery City], no. 3 (1997): 180.

28. Hayden White, *Tropics of Discourse: Essays in Cultural Criticism* (Baltimore: Johns Hopkins University Press, 1978), 122.

29. Georg Lukács, *The Historical Novel*, 283.

30. Luo Guanzhong (罗贯中, ca. 1330–ca. 1400), *Sanguo yanyi* (三国演义) [Romance of the three kingdoms], (Beijing: Renmin wenxue chubanshe, 1972), 1. Translation from Luo Guanzhong, *Three Kingdoms: A Historical Novel*, trans. Moss Roberts (Berkeley: University of California Press, 1999), 3.

31. See Paul Jay, *Being in the Text: Self-Representation from Wordsworth to Roland Barthes* (Ithaca, NY: Cornell University Press, 1984), 35.

32. The film, directed by Zhang Yimou, the celebrated fifth generation director, is based on the first two chapters of the novel: "Honggaoliang" (红高粱) [Red sorghum] and "Gaoliangjiu" (高粱酒) [Sorghum wine].

33. Mo Yan, *Honggaoliang jiazu* (红高粱家族) [The red sorghum family], (Taipei: Hongfan shudian, 1988), 1. Translation from Mo Yan, *Red Sorghum: A Novel of China*, trans. Howard Goldblatt (New York: Viking, 1993), 3.

34. Lu Xun, "Kuangren riji" (狂人日记) [A madman's diary], in *Lu Xun quanji* (鲁迅全集) [The collected works of Lu Xun], vol. 1 (Beijing: Renmin wenxue chubanshe, 1981), 425. Translation from Lu Xun, "A Madman's Diary," in *Lu Xun: Selected Works*, vol. 1, trans. Yang Xianyi & Gladys Yang (Beijing: Foreign Languages Press, 1980), 42 (emphasis added).

35. Linda Hutcheon, *A Poetics of Postmodernism: History, Theory, Fiction* (New York: Routledge, 1988), 97.

36. Mo Yan, *The Red Sorghum Family*, 1. Translation from Mo Yan, *Red Sorghum: A Novel of China*, trans. Howard Goldblatt, 3.

37. Mao Zedong, "Lun lianhe zhengfu" (论联合政府) [On coalition government], in *Mao Zedong xuanji* (毛泽东选集) [Selected works of Mao Zedong], one-volume edition (Beijing: Renmin chubanshe, 1967), 932. Translation from Mao Zedong, *Selected Works of Mao Tse-Tung*, vol. 3 (Peking: Foreign Languages Press, 1967), 207.

38. Mo Yan, *The Red Sorghum Family*, 77. Translation from Mo Yan, *Red Sorghum: A Novel of China*, trans. Howard Goldblatt, 61.

39. Mo Yan, *The Red Sorghum Family*, 83. Translation from Mo Yan, *Red Sorghum: A Novel of China*, trans. Howard Goldblatt, 66.

40. Mo Yan, *The Red Sorghum Family*, 28. Translation from Mo Yan, *Red Sorghum: A Novel of China*, trans. Howard Goldblatt, 24.

41. Howard Y.F. Choy, *Remapping the Past: Fictions of History in Deng's China, 1979–1997* (Leiden: Brill, 2008), 47.

42. Mo Yan, *The Red Sorghum Family*, 2. Translation from Mo Yan, *Red Sorghum: A Novel of China*, trans. Howard Goldblatt, 4.

43. Mo Yan, *The Red Sorghum Family*, 32. Translation from Mo Yan, *Red Sorghum: A Novel of China*, trans. Howard Goldblatt, 27.

44. Here I have adopted Howard F. Y. Choy's translation "liberation of the self" for "个性解放," instead of Goldblatt's translation, "sexual liberation." See Choy, *Remapping the Past: Fictions of History in Deng's China*, 50.

45. Mo Yan, *The Red Sorghum Family*, 492–493. Translation from Mo Yan, *Red Sorghum: A Novel of China*, trans. Howard Goldblatt, 356.

46. Mo Yan, *The Red Sorghum Family*, 53. Translation from Mo Yan, *Red Sorghum: A Novel of China*, trans. Howard Goldblatt, 43.

47. Mo Yan, *The Red Sorghum Family*, 166. Translation from Mo Yan, *Red Sorghum: A Novel of China*, trans. Howard Goldblatt, 132.

48. Mo Yan, *The Red Sorghum Family*, 33. Translation from Mo Yan, *Red Sorghum: A Novel of China*, trans. Howard Goldblatt, 28.

49. Mao Zedong was referred to as "the red, red sun" during the Cultural Revolution.

50. See G. Andrew Stuckey, "Memory or Fantasy? *Honggaoliang*'s Narrator," *Modern Chinese Literature and Culture* 18, no. 2 (Fall 2006): 131–162.

51. Mo Yan, *The Red Sorghum Family*, 288. Translation from Mo Yan, *Red Sorghum: A Novel of China*, trans. Howard Goldblatt, 221.

52. Mo Yan, *The Red Sorghum Family*, 291. Translation from Mo Yan, *Red Sorghum: A Novel of China*, trans. Howard Goldblatt, 223.

53. Mo Yan, *The Red Sorghum Family*, 292. Translation from Mo Yan, *Red Sorghum: A Novel of China*, trans. Howard Goldblatt, 224.

54. Mo Yan, *The Red Sorghum Family*, 496. Translation from Mo Yan, *Red Sorghum: A Novel of China*, trans. Howard Goldblatt, 359.

55. Mo Yan, *The Red Sorghum Family*, 166. My translation.

56. Mo Yan, *The Red Sorghum Family*, 50. Translation from Mo Yan, *Red Sorghum: A Novel of China*, trans. Howard Goldblatt, 40.

57. Mo Yan, *The Red Sorghum Family*, 51. Translation from Mo Yan, *Red Sorghum: A Novel of China*, trans. Howard Goldblatt, 40–41.

58. Mo Yan, *The Red Sorghum Family*, 48. Translation from Mo Yan, *Red Sorghum: A Novel of China*, trans. Howard Goldblatt, 38 (emphasis added).

59. Lu Xun, "Shangshi" (伤逝) [Regret for the past], in *Lu Xun quanji* (鲁迅全集) [The collected works of Lu Xun], vol. 2 (Beijing: Renmin wenxue chubanshe, 1981), 112. Translation from Lu Xun, "Regret for the Past," in *Lu Xun: Selected Works*, vol. 1, trans. Yang Xianyi & Gladys Yang (Beijing: Foreign Languages Press, 1980), 251.

60. Mo Yan, *The Red Sorghum Family*, 5. Translation from Mo Yan, *Red Sorghum: A Novel of China*, trans. Howard Goldblatt, 6.

61. Mo Yan, *Fengru feitun* (丰乳肥臀) [Big breasts and wide hips], (Beijing: Zuojia chubanshe, 1996), 46. Translation from Mo Yan, *Big Breasts and Wide Hips*, trans. Howard Goldblatt (London: Methuen, 2005), 42.

62. Mo Yan, *Big Breasts and Wide Hips*, 612. My translation.

63. Mo Yan, *Big Breasts and Wide Hips*, 626. Translation from Mo Yan, *Big Breasts and Wide Hips*, trans. Howard Goldblatt, 60.

64. Peter Brooks, *Body Work: Objects of Desire in Modern Narrative* (Cambridge, MA.: Harvard University Press, 1993), 1.

65. Mo Yan, *Big Breasts and Wide Hips*, 285. Translation from Mo Yan, *Big Breasts and Wide Hips*, trans. Howard Goldblatt, 299.

66. Mo Yan, *Big Breasts and Wide Hips*, 285. Translation from Mo Yan, *Big Breasts and Wide Hips*, trans. Howard Goldblatt, 299.

67. See Peter Brooks, *Body Work*, 7.

68. Mo Yan, *Big Breasts and Wide Hips*, 180. Translation from Mo Yan, *Big Breasts and Wide Hips*, trans. Howard Goldblatt, 199.

69. Mo Yan, *Big Breasts and Wide Hips*, 181. Translation from Mo Yan, *Big Breasts and Wide Hips*, trans. Howard Goldblatt, 200.

70. Mo Yan, *Big Breasts and Wide Hips*, 192. Translation from Mo Yan, *Big Breasts and Wide Hips*, trans. Howard Goldblatt, 211.

71. Mo Yan, *Big Breasts and Wide Hips*, 327–328. My translation.

72. Mo Yan, *Big Breasts and Wide Hips*, 328. Translation from Mo Yan, *Big Breasts and Wide Hips*, trans. Howard Goldblatt, 329.

73. Mo Yan, *Big Breasts and Wide Hips*, 329. Translation from Mo Yan, *Big Breasts and Wide Hips*, trans. Howard Goldblatt, 330.

74. Mo Yan, *Big Breasts and Wide Hips*, 563. Translation from Mo Yan, *Big Breasts and Wide Hips*, trans. Howard Goldblatt, 513.

75. Mo Yan, *Big Breasts and Wide Hips*, 14. Translation from Mo Yan, *Big Breasts and Wide Hips*, trans. Howard Goldblatt, 9–10.

76. Mo Yan, *Big Breasts and Wide Hips*, 385. Translation from Mo Yan, *Big Breasts and Wide Hips*, trans. Howard Goldblatt, 379.

77. Mo Yan, *Big Breasts and Wide Hips*, 393. Translation from Mo Yan, *Big Breasts and Wide Hips*, trans. Howard Goldblatt, 387.

78. Tao Wan (陶琬), "Waiqu lishi, chouhua xianshi: ping xiaoshuo *Fengru feitun*" (歪曲历史，丑化现实：评小说《丰乳肥臀》) [Distorting history, uglifying reality: On the novel *Big Breasts and Wide Hips*], in *Zhongliu baiqi wencui* (中流百期文萃) [Best essays of the hundred issues of *Zhongliu*] (Beijing: Jincheng chubanshe, 1998), 217. My translation.

79. Ibid., 222. My translation.

80. Ibid., 228. My translation.

81. Wang Derong (汪德荣), "Qiantan *Fengru feitun* guanyu lishi de cuowu miaoxie" (浅谈《丰乳肥臀》关于历史的错误描写) [A simple analysis on the erroneous descriptions about history in *Big Breasts and Wide Hips*], in *Zhongliu baiqi wencui* (中流百期文萃) [Best essays of the hundred issues of *Zhongliu*] (Beijing: Jincheng chubanshe, 1998), 233. My translation.

82. "Wentan de duoluo he beipan: Zai Shandong Gaomi diqu zhandou guo de laohongjun, laobalu kan *Fengru feitun*" (文坛的堕落和背叛——在山东高密地区战斗过的老红军、老八路看《丰乳肥臀》) [The degeneracy and betrayal of the literary arena: A discussion on *Big Breasts and Wide Hips* by veterans of the Red Army and the Eighth Route Army who had fought battles in the Gaomi district of Shandong], in *Zhongliu baiqi wencui* (中流百期文萃) [Best essays of the hundred issues of *Zhongliu*], 243–255.

83. *Mao wenti* is a term coined by Li Tuo (李陀), who argued that the bulk of Mao Zedong's essays, talks, instructions, and other works manifest a special kind of narrative style, a discourse that was dominant in China for decades. All other discourses were suppressed, silenced, forgotten, and eliminated under the absolute hegemony of Maoist discourse. The definition of *Mao wenti* is rather broad, but in general, it refers to the dictatorship of the communist ideology, to the literary policy authorized by Mao, and to a writing style full of lying, boasting, and hollow words. Maoist discourse took over all walks of life—literary and non-literary alike—throughout the entire country. Different types of writings were merely various forms governed by the same discourse. People all over China spoke and wrote in a kind of formulaic, clichéd language that was strange to people of other Chinese-speaking areas, such as Hong Kong and Taiwan. In the late 1970s and early 1980s, literary writers pioneered the challenge to and subversion of this official discourse. Even today, this kind of language is used by many mainlanders without any consciousness, a fact which reveals the strong power and success of Maoist discourse. Li Tuo's articles discussing *Mao wenti* include: "Xuebeng hechu?" (雪崩何处) [Where does the avalanche start?], preface to *Shibasui chumen yuanxing* (十八岁出门远行) [On the road at eighteen], by Yu Hua (Taipei: Yuanliu chuban shiye gufen gongsi, 1990), 5–14; "Xiandai Hanyu yu dangdai wenxue" (现代汉语与当代文学) [Modern Chinese and contemporary literature], *Xindi wenxue* (新地文学) [Literature of a new land] 1, no. 6 (February 1991): 30–43; "Ding Ling bujiandan: Mao tizhi xia zhishifenzi zai huayu shengchan zhong de fuza juese" (丁玲不简单：毛体制下知识分子在话语生产中的复杂角色) [Ding Ling is not simple: The complexity of intellectuals in the production of discourse in Maoist system],

Jintian (今天) [Today], no. 3 (1993): 222–242; "Wang Zengqi yu xiandai Hanyu xiezuo—jiantan Mao wenti" (汪曾祺与现代汉语—兼谈毛文体) [Wang Zengqi and modern Chinese writing—Also on Maoist discourse], *Jintian* (今天) [Today], no. 4 (1997): 1–37.

84. Peter Brooks, *Body Work*, 6.
85. Tao Wan, "Distorting History, Uglifying Reality," 229. My translation.
86. Mo Yan, *Shengsi pilao* (生死疲劳) [Life and death are wearing me out], (Beijing: Zuojia chubanshe, 2006), 8. Translation from Mo Yan, *Life and Death Are Wearing Me Out*, trans. Howard Goldblatt (New York: Arcade Publishing, 2008), 9.
87. Mo Yan, *Life and Death Are Wearing Me Out*, 77. Translation from Mo Yan *Life and Death Are Wearing Me Out*, trans. Howard Goldblatt, 92.
88. Mo Yan, *Life and Death Are Wearing Me Out*, 237. Translation from Mo Yan *Life and Death Are Wearing Me Out*, trans. Howard Goldblatt, 260.
89. Yu Hua, *Huozhe* (活着) [To live], (Hong Kong: Publication [Holdings] Limited, 1994), 150. Translation from Yu Hua, *To Live*, trans. Michael Berry (New York: Anchor Books, 2003), 118–119.
90. Mo Yan, *Life and Death Are Wearing Me Out*, 319. Translation from Mo Yan *Life and Death Are Wearing Me Out*, trans. Howard Goldblatt, 340.
91. Mo Yan, *Life and Death Are Wearing Me Out*, 22. Translation from Mo Yan *Life and Death Are Wearing Me Out*, trans. Howard Goldblatt, 26–27.
92. Robert Segal, ed., *Hero Myths: A Reader* (Oxford: Blackwell Publishers, 2000), 188.
93. Mo Yan, *Life and Death Are Wearing Me Out*, 6. Translation from Mo Yan *Life and Death Are Wearing Me Out,* trans. Howard Goldblatt, 6.
94. Mo Yan, *Life and Death Are Wearing Me Out*, 7. Translation from Mo Yan *Life and Death Are Wearing Me Out,* trans. Howard Goldblatt, 7.
95. Mo Yan, *Life and Death Are Wearing Me Out*, 138. Translation from Mo Yan *Life and Death Are Wearing Me Out,* trans. Howard Goldblatt, 163.
96. Mo Yan, *Life and Death Are Wearing Me Out*, 172. Translation from Mo Yan *Life and Death Are Wearing Me Out,* trans. Howard Goldblatt, 203.
97. Mo Yan, *Life and Death Are Wearing Me Out*, 172. Translation from Mo Yan *Life and Death Are Wearing Me Out,* trans. Howard Goldblatt, 203.
98. Mo Yan, *Life and Death Are Wearing Me Out*, 172. Translation from Mo Yan *Life and Death Are Wearing Me Out,* trans. Howard Goldblatt, 203.
99. Mo Yan, *Life and Death Are Wearing Me Out*, 174. Translation from Mo Yan *Life and Death Are Wearing Me Out,* trans. Howard Goldblatt, 205.
100. Mo Yan, *Life and Death Are Wearing Me Out*, 284. Translation from Mo Yan *Life and Death Are Wearing Me Out,* trans. Howard Goldblatt, 303.

101. Mo Yan, *Life and Death Are Wearing Me Out*, 287. Translation from Mo Yan *Life and Death Are Wearing Me Out,* trans. Howard Goldblatt, 306.
102. In Sun Lung-kee's *Zhongguo wenhua de shenceng jiegou* (中国文化的深层结构) [The deep structure of Chinese culture], which was published in 1983, the author inspires readers with his penetrating analysis of Chinese culture. This book was once banned both in Mainland China and in Taiwan. His 1995 work, *Weiduannai de minzu* [A people not yet weaned], is a continuation of his first book in many ways.
103. This comment is quoted from a conversation between Mo Yan and me in March 2000 in California.
104. In appendix 1 of *A History of Modern Chinese Fiction*, C. T. Hsia advances the now famous argument that modern Chinese literature is burdened by an "obsessive concern with China as a nation afflicted with a spiritual disease and therefore unable to strengthen itself or change its set ways of inhumanity." According to Hsia, all major writers of this genre of literature "are enkindled with this patriotic passion." See C. T. Hsia, appendix 1: "Obsession with China: The Moral Burden of Modern Chinese Literature," in *A History of Modern Chinese Fiction*, 3rd ed. (Bloomington: Indiana University Press, 1999), 533–554.
105. There is no definitive list of *xungen* writers. Mo Yan has been labeled as one of them by many critics. For instance, Li Qingxi (李庆西) regards him as a major *xungen* writer who "has pushed some characteristics of the '*xungen* school' to an extreme" (他将"寻根派"的某些风格特点推向了极致); cited in Li Qingxi, "Xungen: huidao shiwu benshen" (寻根：回到事物本身) [Root seeking: Back to the things per se], *Wenxue pinglun* (文学评论) [Literary review], no. 4 (1988): 22. Li Jiefei (李洁非), however, holds a different opinion. In an article discussing the *xungen* movement and its writers, Li briefly mentions that it would be somewhat strained to categorize Mo Yan as a *xungen* writer, but he does not give any reason for this assessment. See Li Jiefei, "Xungen wenxue: gengxin de kaishi (1984–1985)" (寻根文学：更新的开始 [1984–1985]) [Root-seeking literature: The beginning of renewal (1984–1985)], *Dangdai zuojia pinglun* (当代作家评论) [Contemporary writers review], no. 4 (1995): 106.
106. In late 1984, a group of young writers and critics met at a literary conference in Hangzhou (杭州) to discuss the past and future of Chinese literature. More attention was given to tradition and culture at this conference than had been in previous years (when people focused their attention on more recent history, such as the suffering endured during the Cultural Revolution), as some stories rich in cultural elements or local color

written prior to the meeting had sparked widespread discussion. Such stories included "Qi wang" (棋王) [Chess king] by Ah Cheng (阿城) and "Shangzhou chulu" (商州初录) [The primary records of Shangzhou] by Jia Pingwa (贾平凹). The subsequent year witnessed a spate of manifestos from the *xungen* movement, including "Wenxue de gen" (文学的根) [The roots of literature] by Han Shaogong (韩少功), "Wenhua zhiyue zhe renlei" (文化制约着人类) [Culture restrains mankind] by Ah Cheng, "Liyili wode gen" (理一理我的根) [Sorting out my roots] by Li Hangyu (李杭育), and "Wode gen" (我的根) [My roots] by Zheng Wanlong (郑万隆).

107. Svetlana Boym, introduction to *The Future of Nostalgia* (New York: Basic Books, 2001), xiv.

108. During the Cultural Revolution, a large-scale, forced migration movement took place, in which thousands of students and city youth were sent to rural areas to be "re-educated," as Mao called it, by poor and lower-middle peasants. Not until the end of the Cultural Revolution were these young people allowed to return to the cities. For more information, see Yan Jiaqi (严家其) and Gao Gao (高皋), *Turbulent Decade: A History of the Cultural Revolution*, trans. & ed. D. W. Y. Kwok (Honolulu: University of Hawaii Press, 1996). See especially chapter 15, "Shackling, Attacking, and Oppressing the People."

109. See He Lihua, Yang Shousen, et al., *Guaicai Mo Yan* (怪才莫言) [Mo Yan: An eccentric talent], (Shijiazhuang: Huashan wenyi chubanshe, 1992), 50–52.

110. Ibid., 51.

111. Ibid.

112. David Lowenthal, "Nostalgia Tells It Like It Wasn't," in *The Imagined Past: History and Nostalgia*, ed. Christopher Shaw and Malcolm Chase (Manchester, UK: Manchester University Press, 1989), 19.

113. See Charles A. A. Zwingmann, "'Heimweh' or 'Nostalgic Reaction': A Conceptual Analysis and Interpretation of a Medico-Psychological Phenomenon" (Ph. D. diss., Stanford University, 1959), 251–252.

114. Malcolm Chase and Christopher Shaw, "The Dimensions of Nostalgia," in *The Imagined Past: History and Nostalgia*, ed. Christopher Shaw and Malcolm Chase (Manchester, UK: Manchester University Press, 1989), 1.

115. Dai Jinhua (戴锦华), "Xiangxiang de huaijiu" (想象的怀旧) [Imagined nostalgia], *Tianya* (天涯) [Frontiers], no. 1 (1997): 9. Translated by Judy T. H. Chen as "Imagined Nostalgia," *boundary: 2: an international journal of literature and culture* 24, no. 3 (Fall 1997): 145.

116. See Charles A. A. Zwingmann, 17.

117. Mo Yan, "To Transcend Hometown," 226.

118. Thomas Wolfe, *The Story of a Novel* (New York: Charles Scribner's Sons, 1936), 30.

119. Mo Yan and Wang Yao (王尧), "Cong *Honggaoliang* dao *Tanxiang xing*" (从《红高粱》到《檀香刑》) [From *Red Sorghum* to *Sandalwood Punishment*], in *Mo Yan yanjiu ziliao* (莫言研究资料) [Research materials about Mo Yan], ed. Yang Yang (Tianjin: Tianjin renmin chubanshe, 2005), 106. My translation.

120. Mo Yan, "To Transcend Hometown," 225, 234.

121. Quoted from the 2007–2008 CCTV documentary series *Xiansheng Lu Xun* (先生鲁迅) [Mr. Lu Xun], in which Mo Yan is one of the interviewees to comment on Lu Xun and his works. See www.CCTV-YX.com.

122. Mo Yan, "Baigou qiuqianjia" (白狗秋千架) [White dog and the swings], in *Mo Yan wenji* (莫言文集) [Collected works of Mo Yan], vol. 5 (Beijing: Zuojia chubanshe, 1995), 332. Translation from Mo Yan, "White Dog and the Swings," in *Worlds of Modern Chinese Fiction: Short Stories and Novellas from the People's Republic, Taiwan and Hong Kong*, trans. and ed. Michael S. Duke (Armonk, NY: M.E. Sharpe, 1991), 61.

123. Mo Yan, "White Dog and the Swings," 5:315. Translation from Mo Yan, "White Dog and the Swings," trans. Michael Duke, 47.

124. Lu Xun, "Zhufu" (祝福) [The new-year sacrifice], in *Lu Xun quanji* (鲁迅全集) [The collected works of Lu Xun], vol. 2 (Beijing: Renmin wenxue chubanshe, 1981), 7. Translation from Lu Xun, "The New-Year Sacrifice," in *Lu Xun: Selected Works*, vol. 1, trans. Yang Xianyi and Gladys Yang (Beijing: Foreign Languages Press, 1980), 170.

125. Lu Xun, "Guxiang" (故乡) [My old home], in *Lu Xun quanji* (鲁迅全集) [The collected works of Lu Xun], vol. 1 (Beijing: Renmin wenxue chubanshe, 1981), 476. Translation from Lu Xun, "My Old Home," in *Lu Xun: Selected Works*, vol. 1, trans Yang Xianyi and Gladys Yang (Beijing: Foreign Languages Press, 1980), 90.

126. Lu Xun, "My Old Home," 1:476. Translation from Lu Xun, "My Old Home," trans. Yang Xianyi and Gladys Yang, 1:90.

127. Mo Yan, "White Dog and the Swings," 5:320. Translation from Mo Yan, "White Dog and the Swings," trans. Michael Duke, 51.

128. Mo Yan, "White Dog and the Swings," 5:320. Translation from Mo Yan, "White Dog and the Swings," trans. Michael Duke, 51–52.

129. Jonathan Steinwand, "The Future of Nostalgia in Friedrich Schlegel's Gender Theory: Casting German Aesthetics Beyond Ancient Greece and

Modern Europe," in *Narratives of Nostalgia, Gender, and Nationalism*, ed. Jean Pickering and Suzanne Kehde (New York: New York University Press, 1997), 10.

130. Mo Yan, "White Dog and the Swings," 5:315. Translation from Mo Yan, "White Dog and the Swings," trans. Michael Duke, 47.

131. Lu Xun, "New-Year Sacrifice," 2:21. Translation from Lu Xun, "New-Year Sacrifice," trans. Yang Xianyi and Gladys Yang, 1:187.

132. Yi-tsi Mei Feuerwerker, *Ideology, Power, Text: Self-Representation and the Peasant "Other" in Modern Chinese Literature* (Stanford, CA: Stanford University Press, 1998), 211.

133. Mo Yan, "White Dog and the Swings," 5:323. Translation from Mo Yan, "White Dog and the Swings," trans. Michael Duke, 54.

134. The new government after 1949 advocated narrowing down and eventually eradicating three substantial gaps: that between the city and the countryside, that between workers and peasants, and that between those who are engaged in mental work and those who do manual labor. See, for example, Song Guofan (宋国范), *Shitan sange chabie de xiaomie* (试谈三个差别的消灭) [On the eradication of three substantial gaps], (Changchun: Jilin renmin chubanshe, 1960).

135. Mo Yan, "White Dog and the Swings," 5:324. Translation from Mo Yan, "White Dog and the Swings," trans. Michael Duke, 55.

136. Mo Yan, "White Dog and the Swings," 5:332. Translation from Mo Yan, "White Dog and the Swings," trans. Michael Duke, 61.

137. Mo Yan, "White Dog and the Swings," 5:332. Translation from Mo Yan, "White Dog and the Swings," trans. Michael Duke, 61.

138. Mo Yan, "Kuhe" (枯河) [Dry river], in *Mo Yan wenji* (莫言文集) [Collected works of Mo Yan], vol. 5 (Beijing: Zuojia chubanshe, 1995), 281. Translation from Mo Yan, "Dry River, " in *Spring Bamboo: A Collection of Contemporary Chinese Short Stories*, trans. and comp. Jeanne Tai (New York: Random House, 1989), 220–221.

139. Mo Yan, "Dry River," 5:281. Translation from Mo Yan "Dry River," trans. Jeanne Tai, 211.

140. Mo Yan, "Dry River," 5:284. Translation from Mo Yan "Dry River," trans. Jeanne Tai, 225.

141. Mo Yan, "Dry River," 5:285. Translation from Mo Yan "Dry River," trans. Jeanne Tai, 226.

142. Mo Yan, "Dry River," 5:277. Translation from Mo Yan "Dry River," trans. Jeanne Tai, 215.

143. Mo Yan, "To Transcend Hometown," 236. My translation.

144. Mo Yan, "Dry River," 5:276. Translation from Mo Yan "Dry River," trans. Jeanne Tai, 213.

145. Mo Yan, "Dry River," 5:282. Translation from Mo Yan "Dry River," trans. Jeanne Tai, 223.

146. Mo Yan, "Dry River," 5:282. Translation from Mo Yan "Dry River," trans. Jeanne Tai, 223.

147. Mo Yan, "Dry River," 5:277. Translation from Mo Yan "Dry River," trans. Jeanne Tai, 215.

148. Mo Yan, "Dry River," 5:284. Translation from Mo Yan "Dry River," trans. Jeanne Tai, 225.

149. Mo Yan, "Dry River," 274. Translation from Mo Yan "Dry River, " trans. Jeanne Tai, 210 (emphasis added).

150. According to Mo Yan, he was similarly abused as a young teenager, and the beating scene in "Dry River" is almost an exact reproduction of his own suffering. See Mo Yan, "To Transcend Hometown," 234–236. Although it is not always advantageous—and it is sometimes even risky—to relate the real author's personal experience to the fiction, some knowledge about the author may aid the reader's appreciation of the writing. This is particularly true with a writer like Mo Yan, who relies on his hometown experience. He once stated, "The relationship between hometown and writing may not be especially important for many writers, as they may have undergone things more soul-stirring after escaping their hometowns. But for me, as I have not come across anything special since I left my old home, hometown experience becomes very important. Among my stories, 'Dry River' and 'A Transparent Red Radish' are directly beneficial from my hometown experience" (故乡与写作的关系并不特别重要，因为有许多作家在逃离故乡后，也许经历了惊心动魄的事。但对我个人而言，离开故乡后的经历平淡无奇，所以，就特别看重故乡的经历。我的小说中，直接利用了故乡经历的，是短篇小说《枯河》和中篇小说《透明的红萝卜》。); cited in Mo Yan, "To Transcend Hometown," 234. My translation.

151. One mainland critic points out that Mo Yan has a tendency to write about mutes and that Heihai is one of them. See Cheng Depei (程德培), "Bei jiyi chanrao de shijie: Mo Yan chuangzuo zhong de tongnian shijiao" (被记忆缠绕的世界：莫言创作中的童年视角) [The world haunted by memories: A child's point of view in Mo Yan's writing], in *Mo Yan yanjiu ziliao* (莫言研究资料) [Research materials about Mo Yan], ed. He Lihua and Yang Shousen (Jinan: Shandong daxue chubanshe, 1992), 116. Indeed, deformed and grotesque images, including mute characters,

appear frequently in Mo Yan's works. Nevertheless, Heihai in this story is not a mute. He spoke a lot, as Stonemason tells Chrysanthemum, when he was four or five years old. He gradually spoke less and less over time, but nothing indicates that the boy is unable to speak. This is important because what makes Heihai special is that he is not hindered from speaking by physical limitations; instead, he chooses not to speak with a language used in the ordinary world.

152. Mo Yan, "Toumingde hongluobo" (透明的红萝卜) [A transparent red radish], in *Mo Yan wenji* (莫言文集) [Collected works of Mo Yan], vol. 3 (Beijing: Zuojia chubanshe, 1995), 323. My translation.

153. Mo Yan, "A Transparent Red Radish," 3:328. My translation.

154. Mo Yan, "A Transparent Red Radish," 3:347–348. My translation.

155. Mo Yan, "A Transparent Red Radish," 3:319. My translation.

156. Mo Yan, "A Transparent Red Radish," 3:337. My translation.

157. See Xu Huaizhong, Mo Yan, et al., "You zhuiqiu cai you tese: guanyu 'Toumingde hongluobo' de duihua" (有追求才有特色：关于《透明的红萝卜》的对话) [Seeking brings uniqueness: A conversation about "A Transparent Red Radish"], in *Mo Yan yanjiu ziliao* (莫言研究资料) [Research materials about Mo Yan], ed. He Lihua and Yang Shousen (Jinan: Shandong daxue chubanshe, 1992), 81–82.

158. David Lowenthal, introduction to *The Past Is a Foreign Country* (Cambridge: Cambridge University Press, 1985), xv.

159. Mo Yan, "A Transparent Red Radish," 3:348. My translation.

160. Mo Yan, "A Transparent Red Radish," 3:348. My translation.

161. Mo Yan, "A Transparent Red Radish," 3:349. My translation.

162. "A Transparent Red Radish," 3:349. My translation.

163. Mo Yan, "A Transparent Red Radish," 3:351. My translation.

164. See Xia Zhihou (夏志厚), "Hongsede bianyi: cong 'Toumingde hongluobo,' 'Honggaoliang' dao 'Hong huang'" (红色的变异：从《透明的红萝卜》、《红高粱》到《红蝗》) [The variability of the color red: From "A Transparent Red Radish," "Red Sorghum," to "Red Locusts"], in *Mo Yan yanjiu ziliao* (莫言研究资料) [Research materials about Mo Yan], ed. He Lihua and Yang Shousen (Jinan: Shandong daxue chubanshe, 1992), 223.

165. Ibid., 224.

166. Mo Yan, "A Transparent Red Radish," 3:327. My translation.

167. Mo Yan, "Chishi sanpian" (吃事三篇) [Three essays about eating], in *Hui changge de qiang: Mo Yan sanwen xuan* (会唱歌的墙：莫言散文选)

[The wall that can sing: Selected essays of Mo Yan], (Beijing: Renmin wenxue chubanshe, 1998), 85. My translation.

168. This episode is also recorded in Mo Yan's "Three Essays About Eating" in *The Wall that can Sing: Selected Essays of Mo Yan*, 86–87. Mo Yan once confessed that he was motivated to become a writer by food—he was told a writer was able to have meaty *jiaozi* (饺子) [dumplings] three times a day: "That's when I made up my mind to become a writer someday" (从那时起，我就下定了决心，长大后一定要当一个作家。). See Mo Yan, "Hunger and Loneliness: My Muses," preface to *Shifu, You'll Do Anything for a Laugh*, trans. Howard Goldblatt, xiii.

169. I changed the length of the railway in the translation from twelve miles to twenty-five miles because eighty Chinese *li* is equal to forty kilometers, or approximately 24.85 miles.

170. Mo Yan, "Liangshi" (粮食) [Grain], in *Mo Yan wenji* (莫言文集) [Collected works of Mo Yan], vol. 5 (Beijing: Zuojia chubanshe, 1995), 460. My translation. A similar plot appears in Mo Yan's novel *Big Breasts and Wide Hips*.

171. Mo Yan, "Grain," 5:460. My translation.

172. It is interesting that hunger is the main theme in this piece and that it is often a motif in Mo Yan's fiction from the early stage of his writing career; but in his novel *The Republic of Wine*, he goes to the opposite extreme: an extravagance of gluttony. Whereas in "Grain," the woman is dehumanized inasmuch as she must mimic a cow, with its ruminant stomach, in *The Republic of Wine*, people are alienated to the point of becoming cannibals.

173. Linda Hutcheon, "Irony, Nostalgia, and the Postmodern."

174. Ibid.

175. Jeffrey C. Kinkley, introduction to *The Odyssey of Shen Congwen* (Stanford, CA: Stanford University Press, 1987), 4.

176. Peng Hsiao-yen (彭小妍), *Antithesis Overcome: Shen Congwen's Avant-Gardism and Primitivism* (Taipei: Institute of Chinese Literature and Philosophy Academia Sinica, 1994), 194–195.

177. David Der-wei Wang, "Imaginary Nostalgia: Shen Congwen, Song Zelai, Mo Yan, and Li Yongping," in *From May Fourth to June Fourth: Fiction and Film in Twentieth-Century China*, ed. Ellen Widmer and David Der-wei Wang (Cambridge, MA: Harvard University Press, 1993), 107.

178. Mo Yan, *The Red Sorghum Family*, 1. Translation from Mo Yan, *Red Sorghum: A Novel of China*, trans. Howard Goldblatt, 3.

179. Mo Yan, *The Red Sorghum Family*, 2. Translation from Mo Yan, *Red Sorghum: A Novel of China*, trans. Howard Goldblatt, 3–4.

180. Mo Yan, *The Red Sorghum Family*, 2. Translation from Mo Yan, *Red Sorghum: A Novel of China*, trans. Howard Goldblatt, 4.

181. Mo Yan, *The Red Sorghum Family*, 2. Translation from Mo Yan, *Red Sorghum: A Novel of China*, trans. Howard Goldblatt, 4.

182. Mo Yan, *The Red Sorghum Family*, 2. Translation from Mo Yan, *Red Sorghum: A Novel of China*, trans. Howard Goldblatt, 4.

183. David Lowenthal, introduction to *The Past Is a Foreign Country*, xx.

184. Svetlana Boym, introduction to *The Future of Nostalgia*, xiii.

185. Robert Audi, "Preliminary Theoretical Considerations Concerning the Justification of Violence," in *Violence in Modern Literature*, ed. James A. Gould and John J. Iorio (San Francisco: Boyd & Fraser Publishing, 1972), 66.

186. Nancy Armstrong and Leonard Tennenhouse, "Introduction: Representing Violence, or 'How the West Was Won,'" in *The Violence of Representation: Literature and the History of Violence*, ed. Nancy Armstrong and Leonard Tennenhouse (London: Routledge, 1989), 24.

187. Ibid., 8.

188. See Erich Fromm, *Escape from Freedom* (New York: Holt, Rinehart & Winston, 1941), 181. I am indebted to my friend Birgit Linder, from City University of Hong Kong, for introducing me to the concept of "the unlived life" and Erich Fromm's book.

189. Erich Fromm, *Escape from Freedom*, 181.

190. Ibid., 184.

191. By this term, I mean that China is a capitalist economy with an authoritarian government. For a further explanation, please see "China: Capitalism Doesn't Require Democracy" by Robert B. Reich (http://www.commondreams.org/views06/0110-42.htm).

192. James Legge, trans., *The Chinese Classics*, vol. 2, *The Works of Mencius*, rev. ed. (Taipei: SMC Publishing Inc., 1994), 397. Here the character *se* (色), translated as "delight in colors" by James Legge, actually refers to the beauty of women and thus implies erotic behavior.

193. Roland Barthes, *Writing Degree Zero*, trans. Annette Lavers and Colin Smith (New York: The Noonday Press, 1968), 23.

194. T. A. Hsia, "Heroes and Hero-Worship in Chinese Communist Fiction," in *Chinese Communist Literature*, ed. Cyril Birch (New York: Frederick A. Praeger, 1963), 113.

195. Peter C. Sederberg, *Fires Within: Political Violence and Revolutionary Change* (New York: Harper Collins College Publishers, 1994), 106.

196. C. T. Hsia, *A History of Modern Chinese Fiction*, 3rd ed. (Bloomington: Indiana University Press, 1999), 487.

197. Mo Yan, *Big Breasts and Wide Hips*, 279. Translation from Mo Yan, *Big Breasts and Wide Hips*, trans. Howard Goldblatt, 293–294.

198. Howard Y.F. Choy, *Remapping the Past*, 185.

199. Joseph S.M. Lau, "The 'Little Woman' as Exorcist: Notes on the Fiction of Huang Biyun," *Journal of Modern Literature in Chinese* 2, no. 2 (January 1999):152.

200. Michael S. Duke, "Past, Present, and Future in Mo Yan's Fiction of the 1980s," in *From May Fourth to June Fourth: Fiction and Film in Twentieth-Century China*, ed. Ellen Widmer and David Der-Wei Wang (Cambridge, MA: Harvard University Press, 1993), 52.

201. Mo Yan, *The Garlic Ballads*, 355. Translation from Mo Yan, *The Garlic Ballads*, trans. Howard Goldblatt, 268.

202. Michael S. Duke, "Past, Present, and Future in Mo Yan's Fiction of the 1980s," 69.

203. See ibid.

204. Mo Yan was in active service when he wrote the novels. He was discharged in 1998.

205. The Boxer Uprising, a movement against foreigners waged by peasants and handicraftsmen in north China, occurred in 1900. Troops from eight countries—namely, Britain, the United States, Germany, France, Russia, Japan, Italy, and Austria—were sent to Beijing to suppress the uprising. For more information, see Joseph Esherick, *The Origin of the Boxer Uprising* (Berkeley: University of California Press, 1987); see also Paul Cohen, *History in Three Keys: The Boxers as Event, Experience, and Myth* (New York: Columbia University Press, 1997).

206. Throughout the novel, the character *mao* is most often written in the first tone (猫), meaning "cat"; yet sometimes, it is written in the fourth tone (茂), meaning "luxuriant" and "beautiful." Judging from the context of the story, though, "cat tune" is a more accurate translation than "luxurian and beautiful tune" because the music's origin is related to cats and because the performers usually imitate cats both physically and vocally.

207. In *Big Breasts and Wide Hips*, Mo Yan creates a scene in which a Japanese army doctor saves Mother, Jintong, and his twin sister. I argue that this scene marks the beginning of the the change in Mo Yan's national complex. This episode, although brief, highlights the complexity of human nature; invaders are no longer described as out-and-out evil. Instead, the readers' attention is dragged to the evil features of their own culture.

208. Mo Yan, *The Garlic Ballads*, 215. Translation from Mo Yan, *The Garlic Ballads*, trans. Howard Goldblatt, 159.

209. Andrew F. Jones, "The Violence of the Text: Reading Yu Hua and Shi Zhicun," *positions* 2, no. 3 (Winter 1994): 573.

210. Ibid.

211. See Xie Youshun (谢有顺), "Dang siwang bi huozhe geng kunnan: *Tanxiang xing* zhong de renxing fenxi" (当死亡比活着更困难：《檀香刑》中的人性分析) [When death is harder than life: An analysis of human nature in *Sandalwood Punishment*], in *Mo Yan yanjiu ziliao* (莫言研究资料) [Research materials about Mo Yan], ed. Yang Yang (Tianjin: Tianjin renmin chubanshe, 2005), 275.

212. Ibid.

213. See Mo Yan and Zhang Huimin, "Shi shenme zhicheng zhe *Tanxiang xing*: da Zhang Huimin" (是什么支撑着《檀香刑》：答张慧敏) [What is holding up *Sandalwood Punishment*: To answer Zhang Huimin's questions], in *Mo Yan yanjiu ziliao* (莫言研究资料) [Research materials about Mo Yan], ed. Yang Yang (Tianjin: Tianjin renmin chubanshe, 2005), 70.

214. Ibid.

215. In a personal communication between Mo Yan and me on March 22, 2009, he admitted that although "wood stake punishment" was used in medieval Europe and something similar was practiced among bandits in northeast China in the beginning of the twentieth century, he had actually used his own imagination to create the details of the method of punishment described in his novel.

216. Mo Yan, *Sandalwood Punishment,* 240. My translation.

217. In his article "When Death Is Harder Than Life: An Analysis of Human Nature in *Sandalwood Punishment*," Xie Youshun indicates that mainly female readers dislike Mo Yan's way of writing about punishment and his enjoyment of violence. See Xie Youshun, "When Death Is Harder Than Life," in *Research materials about Mo Yan*, ed. Yang Yang, 275.

218. Lu Xun, "The True Story of Ah Q," 1:527. Lu Xun, "The True Story of Ah Q," in *Lu Xun: Selected Works*, vol. 1, trans. Yang Xianyi and Gladys Yang, 154.

219. Mo Yan, *Sandlewood Punishment*, 435. My translation.

220. Lu Xun, "A Madman's Diary," 1:432. Translation from Lu Xun, "A Madman's Diary," in *Lu Xun: Selected Works*, vol. 1, trans. Yang Xiangyi and Gladys Yang, 51.

221. Mo Yan, *Life and Death Are Wearing Me Out*, 181. Translation from Mo Yan, *Life and Death Are Wearing Me Out*, trans. Howard Goldblatt, 210.

222. Mo Yan, *Life and Death Are Wearing Me Out*, 182. My translation.

223. Mo Yan, "Bian" (变) [Change], in *Ershiyi shiji niandu xiaoshuo xuan: Erlinglingjiu zhongpian xiaoshuo* (21 世纪年度小说选：2009中篇小说)

[The annual selection of fiction of the twenty-first century: Novella of 2009] (Beijing: Renmin wenxue chubanshe, 2010), 589. Translation from Mo Yan, "Change," trans. Howard Goldblatt (London: Seagull Books, 2010), 19.

224. Mo Yan believes that a writer should never consider himself or herself superior to ordinary people and that a writer should not attempt to write for people but as one of them. He revealed this point of view in several interviews and eventually used it as the subtitle of his book *Shuoba Mo Yan: zuowei laobaixing xiezuo—fangtan duihua ji* (说吧莫言：作为老百姓写作访谈对话集) [Speak up, Mo Yan: To write as an ordinary person—A collection of interviews], (Shenzhen: Haitian chubanshe, 2007).

225. In China, the party flag as well as the national flag are both red in color. School children are told, generation after generation, that the flags are dyed with revolutionary martyrs' blood, and so they are the sacred symbols of the revolutionary cause. By the same token, the red scarf worn by the Young Pioneers (an organization of young model students) is a symbolic part of the red flag.

226. See Tonglin Lü (吕彤邻), *Misogyny, Cultural Nihilism, and Oppositional Politics: Contemporary Chinese Experimental Fiction* (Stanford, CA: Stanford University Press, 1995), 63.

227. Mo Yan, *The Garlic Ballads*, 247. Translation from Mo Yan, *The Garlic Ballads*, trans. Howard Goldblatt, 182.

228. Mo Yan, "Huanle" (欢乐) [Happiness], in *Mo Yan wenji* (莫言文集) [Collected works of Mo Yan], vol. 4 (Beijing: Zuojia chubanshe, 1995), 370. My translation.

229. Mo Yan, "Happiness," 4:449. My translation.

230. Dustin Griffin, *Satire: A Critical Reintroduction* (Lexington: Kentucky University Press, 1994), 95. The last sentence of this quotation (i.e., "It's hard *not* to write satire") is taken from a classic work written by the Roman poet Juvenal (ca. 55–ca. 127). See Juvenal, *The Satires*, trans. Niall Rudd (Oxford: Clarendon Press, 1991), 4, Book 1, line 30.

231. Howard Goldblatt, "Forbidden Food: The 'Saturnicon' of Mo Yan," *World Literature Today* 74, no. 3 (Summer 2000): 477.

232. See Key Ray Chong, *Cannibalism in China* (Wakefield, NH: Longwood Academic, 1990), 1.

233. Ibid., 2.

234. John R. Clark, *The Modern Satiric Grotesque and Its Traditions* (Lexington: Kentucky University Press, 1991), 131.

235. Quoted from the introduction of *The Cook, the Thief, His Wife & Her Lover*, VHS, directed by Peter Greenaway (1989; Santa Monica, CA: Vidmark Entertainment, 1990).

236. Liu Zhenyun, "Wengu yijiusier" (温故一九四二) [Reviving 1942], in *Guanren* (官人) [Officials], (Wuhan: Changjiang wenyi chubanshe, 1992).

237. Ross Terrill, foreword to *Scarlet Memorial: Tales of Cannibalism in Modern China*, by Zheng Yi, ed. and trans. T.P. Sym (Boulder, CO: Westview Press, 1996), xi.

238. Howard Goldblatt, "Forbidden Food," 480.

239. Lu Xun, "A Madman's Diary," 1:432. Translation from Lu Xun, "A Madman's Diary, " in *Lu Xun: Selected Works*, vol. 1, trans. Yang Xiangyi and Gladys Yang, 51.

240. Leo Ou-fan Lee, *Voices from the Iron House: A Study of Lu Xun* (Bloomington: Indiana University Press, 1987), 65.

241. This story has been recorded in several historical documents. See, for example, Guanzi (管子) in *Baizi quanshu* (百子全书) [The complete collection of all philosophers], (Hangzhou: Zhejiang renmin chubanshe, 1984), vol. 3, 11.3b.

242. See Tuo Tuo (脱脱, 1313–1355), et al., comps., *Song shi* (宋史) [History of the Song dynasty], vol. 38, *Xiaoyi* (孝义) [Filial piety and righteousness], (Beijing: Zhonghua shuju, 1977), 13387. This volume lists instances of filial sons who fed their sickly parents with their own flesh.

243. *Taking Tiger Mountain by Strategy* is one of the eight model plays that prevailed during the Cultural Revolution. In the play, the hero, Yang Zirong (杨子荣), is a scout in the People's Liberation Army. Disguising himself as a bandit, he slips into the bandit-occupied area and acted successfully from within, in coordination with the PLA force attacking from outside. *The Scouts* has a similar plot, except that the enemies are not bandits but KMT troops. See *Zhenchabing* (侦察兵) [The scouts], motion picture, directed by Li Wenhua (李文化), (Beijing: Beijing dianying zhipianchang, 1974).

244. Critics such as Zhang Hong (张闳), Xiaobin Yang (杨小滨), and Chan Yin-ha (陈燕遐) have pointed out the degeneration of the hero in this novel. See Zhang Hong, "*Jiuguo* sanlun" (酒国散论) [Random discussions on *The Republic of Wine*], *Jintian* (今天) [Today], no. 1 (1996): 88–89; Xiaobin Yang, "*The Republic of Wine*: An extravaganza of decline," *positions* 6, no. 1 (Spring 1998): 14; Chan Yin-ha, "Mo Yan de *Jiu Guo* yu Baheting de xiaoshuo lilun" (莫言的酒国与巴赫汀的小说理论) [Mo Yan's *Republic of Wine* and Mikhail M. Bakhtin's theories of the novel], *Ershiyi shiji*

shuangyuekan (二十一世纪双月刊) [Twenty-first century bimonthly], no. 59 (October 1998): 98.

245. Mo Yan, *Jiuguo* (酒国) [The republic of wine], (Taipei: Hongfan shudian, 1992), 74. Translation from Mo Yan, *The Republic of Wine*, trans. Howard Goldblatt (New York: Arcade Publishing, 2000), 62.

246. In "Shentong" (神童) [Child Prodigy], the third story in Li Yidou's series, the little demon states that all his little brothers were eaten; only his scaly skin saved him.

247. I thank my friend Nicole Barnes, who studies Chinese history and literature, for this inspiring insight.

248. Mo Yan, *The Republic of Wine*, 99. Translation from Mo Yan, *The Republic of Wine*, trans. Howard Goldblatt, 81–82.

249. Mo Yan, *The Republic of Wine*, 227. Translation from Mo Yan, *The Republic of Wine*, trans. Howard Goldblatt, 191.

250. Mo Yan, *The Republic of Wine*, 227. Translation from Mo Yan, *The Republic of Wine*, trans. Howard Goldblatt, 191.

251. Mo Yan, *The Republic of Wine*, 227. Translation from Mo Yan, *The Republic of Wine*, trans. Howard Goldblatt, 191.

252. Mo Yan, *The Republic of Wine*, 272. Translation from Mo Yan, *The Republic of Wine*, trans. Howard Goldblatt, 226.

253. Kenny K. K. Ng, "Metafiction, Cannibalism, and Political Allegory: *Wineland* by Mo Yan," *Journal of Modern Literature in Chinese* 1, no. 2 (January 1998): 134.

254. Ibid., 135.

255. For a further explanation, please see "China: Capitalism Doesn't Require Democracy" by Robert B. Reich (http://www.commondreams.org/views06/0110-42.htm).

256. Mo Yan, *The Republic of Wine*, 425. My translation.

257. Kenny K. K. Ng, "Metafiction, Cannibalism, and Political Allegory," 134.

258. Mo Yan, *The Republic of Wine*, 413. Translation from Mo Yan, *The Republic of Wine*, trans. Howard Goldblatt, 352.

259. Mo Yan, "Haode xiaoshuo yinggai juyou duoyixing: huida Kong Wuchen de wenti" (好的小说应该具有多义性：回答孔舞晨的问题) [A good fiction should have multiple meanings: To answer the questions of Kong Wuchen], in *Shuoba Mo Yan: zuowei laobaixing xiezuo—fangtan duihua ji* (说吧莫言：作为老百姓写作访谈对话集) [Speak up, Mo Yan: To write as an ordinary person—A collection of interviews], (Shenzhen: Haitian chubanshe, 2007), 110.

260. Mo Yan, *Wa* (蛙) [Frog], (Shanghai: Shanghai wenyi chubanshe, 2009), 281–282. My translation.

261. Chan Yin-ha points out that the extravagance of Chinese gastrology signifies a decadence throughout the entire culture. She also differentiates this extravagance from the subversiveness of Bakhtinian carnivalism. See Chan Yin-ha, "Mo Yan's *Republic of Wine* and Mikhail M. Bakhtin's Theories of the Novel," 101–103. Xiaobin Yang also associates the excesses with decline." in his article "*The Republic of Wine*: An extravaganza of decline". Gang Yue (乐刚), however, associates this kind of "gourmet cannibalism" with human carnivorism. See Gang Yue, *The Mouth That Begs: Hunger, Cannibalism, and the Politics of Eating in Modern China* (Durham, NC: Duke University Press, 1999). See especially chapter 3, section 7, pp. 262–287, "From Cannibalism to Carnivorism: Mo Yan's *Liquorland*."

262. Howard Goldblatt, "Forbidden Food," 484.

263. Li Zhi, a controversial intellectual and anti-traditional thinker, highly valued the true and genuine emotion of man, which he said was *tongxin* (童心), or "the heart of a child." He considered literary works of the orthodox tradition to be nonliterature because they did not come from the real nature of man. Instead, he praised popular culture and colloquial language. Feng Menglong was the compiler and editor of three anthologies of vernacular stories: *Yushi mingyan* (喻世明言) [Illustrious words to instruct the world], *Jingshi tongyan* (警世通言) [Comprehensive words to admonish the world], and *Xingshi hengyan* (醒世恒言) [Lasting words to awaken the world]. He also compiled *Shan'ge* (山歌) [The folk songs], *Qingshi* (情史) [History of love], and *Xiaofu* (笑府) [Treasury of jokes].

264. These "five bad elements" are landlords, rich peasants, counterrevolutionaries, evildoers, and rightists.

265. Tie Ning, *Da yunü* (大浴女) [Big bathers], (Shenyang: Chunfeng wenyi chubanshe, 2000), 39–40.

266. It was very common throughout the country during the Cultural Revolution to address class enemies as "filthy and contemptible as dog's dung."

267. Howard Goldblatt, Introduction to *Chairman Mao Would not be Amused: Fiction from Today's China*, ed. Howard Goldblatt (New York: Grove Press, 1995), x.

268. See Mikhail M. Bakhtin, *Rabelais and His World*, trans. Hélène Iswol-sky (Bloomington: Indiana University Press, 1984). See especially chapters 5 and 6.

269. Stuart Zane Charmé, *Vulgarity and Authenticity: Dimensions of Otherness in the World of Jean-Paul Sartre* (Amherst: University of Massachusetts Press, 1991), 7.

270. Mo Yan, *The Red Sorghum Family*, 191. Translation from Mo Yan, *The Red Sorghum Family*, trans. Howard Goldblatt, 150.

271. For the complexity of the Chinese food culture, see Sun Lung-kee, *Zhongguo wenhua de shenceng jiegou* (中国文化的深层结构) [The deep structure of Chinese culture], (Hong Kong: Jixian she, 1983), 39-43.

272. John R. Clark, *The Modern Satiric Grotesque and Its Traditions*, 118.

273. "Hong huang" (红蝗) [Red locusts] is a novella that became the first chapter of the six-chaptered novel *Shicao jiazu* (食草家族) [The herbivorous family], which was later collected in *Mo Yan wenji* (莫言文集) [Collected works of Mo Yan]. Ling Tun Ngai (危令敦) provides a thorough and incisive discussion on defecation activity in his article "Anal Anarchy: A Reading of Mo Yan's 'The Plagues of Red Locusts,'" *Modern Chinese Literature* 10, nos. 1–2 (Spring/Fall 1998): 1–18.

274. See John R. Clark, *The Modern Satiric Grotesque and Its Traditions*, 20.

275. Ibid., 21.

276. For more information about Can Xue's being criticized as paranoid, see Tonglin Lü, "Can Xue: What Is So Paranoid in Her Writings?" in *Misogyny, Cultural Nihilism, and Oppositional Politics: Contemporary Chinese Experimental Fiction* (Stanford, CA: Stanford University Press, 1995), 75-103.

277. Here, the dwarf sisters bear sociological significance: they serve to disclose the social phenomenon that those who are related to government officials in one way or another are more privileged than others. As a result, the novelist's tendency to social criticism is made explicit.

278. Mo Yan, *The Republic of Wine*, 179. Translation from Mo Yan, *The Republic of Wine*, trans. Howard Goldblatt, 149.

279. Mo Yan, *The Republic of Wine*, 217. Translation from Mo Yan, *The Republic of Wine*, trans. Howard Goldblatt, 180–181.

280. Mo Yan, *The Republic of Wine*, 213. Translation from Mo Yan, *The Republic of Wine*, trans. Howard Goldblatt, 177.

281. Mo Yan, *The Republic of Wine*, 217. Translation from Mo Yan, *The Republic of Wine*, trans. Howard Goldblatt, 180.

282. Mo Yan, *The Republic of Wine*, 165. Translation from Mo Yan, *The Republic of Wine*, trans. Howard Goldblatt, 135.

283. Mo Yan, *The Republic of Wine*, 190. Translation from Mo Yan, *The Republic of Wine*, trans. Howard Goldblatt, 157.

284. Mo Yan, *The Republic of Wine*, 190–191. Translation from Mo Yan, *The Republic of Wine*, trans. Howard Goldblatt, 158.

285. Mo Yan, *The Republic of Wine*, 217. Translation from Mo Yan, *The Republic of Wine*, trans. Howard Goldblatt, 180.

286. John R. Clark, *The Modern Satiric Grotesque and Its Traditions*, 24.

287. Mary Russo, *The Female Grotesque: Risk, Excess and Modernity* (New York: Routledge, 1994), 7–8.

288. Originally Mo Yan wrote a novella "Shengpu de zuxian" (生蹼的祖先) [The webbed ancestors]. This story, like "Red Locusts," later became a chapter of the novel *The Herbivorous Family* collected in *Mo Yan wenji* (莫言文集) [Collected works of Mo Yan], vol. 4 (Beijing: Zuojia chubanshe, 1995).

289. Mo Yan, "The Webbed Ancestors," 4:229. My translation.

290. Edward A. Bloom and Lillian D. Bloom, *Satire's Persuasive Voice* (Ithaca, NY: Cornell University Press, 1979), 21.

291. The words "moral-didactic impulse" and "misanthropy" are used by Edward and Lillian Bloom to discuss satire and the satiric intension of satirists. See Edward A. Bloom and Lillian D. Bloom, *Satire's Persuasive Voice*, 21.

292. Leo Ou-fan Lee, "Reflections on Change and Continuity in Modern Chinese Fiction," in *From May Fourth to June Fourth: Fiction and Film in Twentieth-Century China*, ed. Ellen Widmer and David Der-wei Wang (Cambridge, MA: Harvard University Press, 1993), 378.

293. See C. T. Hsia, appendix 1: "Obsession with China," 533–554.

294. Fredric Jameson, "Third-World Literature in the Era of Multinational Capitalism," *Social Text: Theory, Culture, Ideology* 15 (Fall 1986): 69.

295. Ibid., 71.

296. Ibid.

297. See Miklós Haraszti, *The Velvet Prison: Artists Under State Socialism*, trans. Katalin Landesmann and Stephen Landesmann (New York: The Noonday Press, 1987).

298. Ibid., 114.

299. Geremie R. Barmé, "The Chinese Velvet Prison," in *In the Red: On Contemporary Chinese Culture* (New York: Columbia University Press, 1999), 6–7.

300. Ibid., 6.
301. Ibid., 9.
302. Miklós Haraszti, *The Velvet Prison*, 144.
303. Mark Schorer, "Technique as Discovery," in *Essentials of the Theory of Fiction*, ed. Michael Hoffman and Patrick Murphy (Durham, NC: Duke University Press, 1988), 108.
304. Geremie Barmé, "The Chinese Velvet Prison," 17.
305. Miklós Haraszti, *The Velvet Prison*, 152.
306. Ibid., 153.
307. Ibid., 150.
308. Ibid., 151.
309. Ibid., 152.
310. Ibid., 150.
311. Ibid., 152.
312. Ibid.
313. "Invisible violence" is a term used by the Czech dissident Václav Havel. Haraszti later dubbed it "the velvet prison." See Geremie Barmé, "The Chinese Velvet Prison," 7.

BIBLIOGRAPHY

PRIMARY TEXTS

Feng, Deying （冯德英）. *Kucaihua* (苦菜花) [The wild bitter flower]. Beijing: Renmin wenxue chubanshe, 1959.

Ke, Yunlu (柯云路). "Mengmei" (蒙昧) [Benighted]. *Huacheng* (花城) [Flowery city], no. 4 (2000): 4–85.

Liu, Zhenyun (刘震云). *Guanren* (官人) [Officials]. Wuhan: Changjiang wenyi chubanshe, 1992.

Lu Xun (鲁迅). *Lu Xun quanji* (鲁迅全集) [The collected works of Lu Xun], 16 vols. Beijing: Renmin wenxue chubanshe, 1981.

Luo, Guanzhong (罗贯中). *Sanguo yanyi* (三国演义) [Romance of the three kingdoms]. Beijing: Renmin wenxue chubanshe, 1972.

Mo Yan (莫言). "Bian" (变) [Change]. In *Ershiyi shiji niandu xiaoshuo xuan: Erlinglingjiu zhongpian xiaoshuo* (21 世纪年度小说选：2009 中篇小说) [The annual selection of fiction of the twenty-first century: novella of 2009]. Beijing: Renmin wenxue chubanshe, 2010.

———. *Fengru feitun* (丰乳肥臀) [Big breasts and wide hips]. Beijing: Zuojia chubanshe, 1996.

———. *Honggaoliang jiazu* (红高粱家族) [The red sorghum family]. Taipei: Hongfan shudian, 1988.

———. *Jiuguo* (酒国) [The republic of wine]. Taipei: Hongfan shudian, 1992.

———. *Mo Yan wenji* (莫言文集) [Collected works of Mo Yan]. 5 vols. Beijing: Zuojia chubanshe, 1995.

———. *Shengsi pilao* (生死疲劳) [Life and death are wearing me out]. Beijing: Zuojia chubanshe, 2006.

———. *Shisan bu* (十三步) [Thirteen steps]. Taipei: Hongfan shudian, 1990.

———. *Sishiyi pao* (四十一炮) [Forty-one bombs]. Shenyang: Chunfeng wenyi chubanshe, 2003.

———. *Tanxiang xing* (檀香刑) [Sandalwood punishment]. Beijing: Zuojia chubanshe, 2001.

———. *Tiantang suantai zhi ge* (天堂蒜薹之歌) [The garlic ballads]. Taipei: Hongfan shudian, 1989.

———. *Wa* (蛙) [Frog]. Shanghai: Shanghai wenyi chubanshe, 2009.

Tie, Ning (铁凝). *Da yunü* (大浴女) [Big bathers]. Shenyang: Chunfeng wenyi chubanshe, 2000.

Yu, Hua (余华). *Huozhe* (活着) [To live]. Hong Kong: Publication (Holdings) Limited, 1994.

TRANSLATIONS

Ding, Ling (丁玲). *The Sun Shines over the Sangkan River.* Translated by Yang Xianyi (杨宪益) and Gladys Yang. Beijing: Foreign Languages Press, 1954.

Duke, Michael S., ed. *Worlds of Modern Chinese Fiction: Short Stories and Novellas from the People's Republic, Taiwan and Hong Kong.* Armonk, NY: M. E. Sharpe, 1991.

Lu Xun. *Lu Xun: Selected Works.* 4 vols. 2nd ed. Translated by Yang Xianyi (杨宪益) and Gladys Yang. Beijing: Foreign Languages Press, 1980.

Luo, Guanzhong. *Three Kingdoms: A Historical Novel.* Translated by Moss Roberts. Berkeley: University of California Press, 1999.

Mao Zedong (毛泽东). *Selected Works of Mao Tse-Tung.* 4 vols. Peking: Foreign Languages Press, 1967.

Mo Yan. *Big Breasts and Wide Hips.* Translated by Howard Goldblatt. London: Methuen, 2005.

———."The Cat Specialist." Translated by Janice Wickeri. *Renditions* (Autumn 1989): 59–68.

———. *Change*. Translated by Howard Goldblatt. London: Seagull Books, 2010.

———. *The Garlic Ballads*. Translated by Howard Goldblatt. New York: Viking, 1995.

———. *Life and Death Are Wearing Me Out*. Translated by Howard Goldblatt. New York: Arcade Publishing, 2008.

———. *Red Sorghum: A Novel of China*. Translated by Howard Goldblatt. New York: Viking, 1993.

———. *The Republic of Wine*. Translated by Howard Goldblatt. New York: Arcade Publishing, 2000.

———. *Shifu, You'll Do Anything for a Laugh*. Translated by Howard Goldblatt. New York: Arcade Publishing, 2001.

Tai, Jeanne, trans. *Spring Bamboo: A Collection of Contemporary Chinese Short Stories*. New York: Random House, 1989.

Yu Hua. *To Live*. Translated by Michael Berry. New York: Anchor Books, 2003.

Secondary Sources

Armstrong, Nancy, and Leonard Tennenhouse. "Introduction: Representing Violence, or 'How the West Was Won.'" In *The Violence of Representation: Literature and the History of Violence*, edited by Nancy Armstrong and Leonard Tennenhouse. London: Routledge, 1989.

Audi, Robert. "Preliminary Theoretical Considerations Concerning the Justification of Violence." In *Violence in Modern Literature*, edited by James A. Gould and John J. Iorio, 62–74. San Francisco: Boyd & Fraser, 1972.

Baizi quanshu (百子全书) [The complete collection of all philosophers]. Hangzhou: Zhejiang renmin chubanshe, 1984.

Bakhtin, Mikhail. *Rabelais and His World*. Translated by Hélène Iswolsky. Bloomington: Indiana University Press, 1984.

Barmé, Geremie R. *In the Red: On Contemporary Chinese Culture*. New York: Columbia University Press, 1999.

Barthes, Roland. *Writing Degree Zero*. Translated by Annette Lavers and Colin Smith. New York: Noonday Press, 1968.

Bloom, Edward A., and Lillian D. Bloom. *Satire's Persuasive Voice*. Ithaca, NY: Cornell University Press, 1979.

Boym, Svetlana. *The Future of Nostalgia*. New York: Basic Books, 2001.

Brooks, Peter. *Body Work: Objects of Desire in Modern Narration*. Cambridge, MA: Harvard University Press, 1993.

Chan, Yin-ha (陈燕遐). "Mo Yan de *Jiu Guo* yu Baheting de xiaoshuo lilun" (莫言的《酒国》与巴赫汀的小说理论) [Mo Yan's *Jiu Guo* and Mikhail M. Bakhtin's theories of the novel]. *Ershiyi shiji shuangyuekan* (二十一世纪双月刊) [Twenty-first century bimonthly], no. 59 (October 1998): 94–104.

Charmé, Stuart Zane. *Vulgarity and Authenticity: Dimensions of Otherness in the World of Jean-Paul Sartre*. Amherst: University of Massachusetts Press, 1991.

Chase, Malcolm, and Christopher Shaw. "The Dimensions of Nostalgia." In *The Imagined Past: History and Nostalgia*, edited by Christopher Shaw and Malcolm Chase. Manchester, UK: Manchester University Press, 1989.

Chen, Sihe (陈思和). *Zhongguo dangdai wenxueshi jiaocheng* (中国当代文学史教程) [Lectures on contemporary Chinese literary history]. Shanghai: Fudan daxue chubanshe, 1999.

Cheng, Depei (程德培). "Bei jiyi chanrao de shijie: Mo Yan chuangzuo zhong de tongnian shijiao" (被记忆缠绕的世界：莫言创作中的童年视角) [The world haunted by memories: A child's point of view in

Mo Yan's writing]. In *Mo Yan yanjiu ziliao* (莫言研究资料) [Research materials about Mo Yan], edited by He Lihua and Yang Shousen, 110–121. Jinan: Shandong daxue chubanshe, 1992.

Chong, Key Ray. *Cannibalism in China*. Wakefield, NH: Longwood Academic, 1990.

Chow, Tse-tsung (周策纵). *The May 4th Movement: Intellectual Revolution in Modern China*. Cambridge, MA: Harvard University Press, 1960.

Choy, Howard Y. F. (蔡元丰). *Remapping the Past: Fictions of History in Deng's China, 1979–1997*. Leiden: Brill, 2008.

Clark, John R. *The Modern Satiric Grotesque and Its Traditions*. Lexington: Kentucky University Press, 1991.

Clark, Paul. *The Chinese Cultural Revolution: A History*. Cambridge: Cambridge University Press, 2008.

Cohen, Paul. *History in Three Keys: The Boxers as Event, Experience, and Myth*. New York: Columbia University Press, 1997.

Dai, Jinhua (戴锦华). "Xiangxiang de huaijiu" (想象的怀旧) [Imagined nostalgia]. *Tianya* (天涯) [Frontiers], no. 1 (1997): 8–15. Translated by Judy T. H. Chen as "Imagined Nostalgia." *boundary 2: an international journal of literature and culture* 24, no. 3 (Fall 1997): 143–161.

Ding, Ling. *Taiyang zhao zai Sangganhe shang* (太阳照在桑干河上) [The sun shines over the Sanggan river]. Beijing: Renmin wenxue chubanshe, 1952.

Duke, Michael S. *Blooming and Contending: Chinese Literature in the Post-Mao Era*. Bloomington: Indiana University Press, 1985.

———. "Past, Present, and Future in Mo Yan's Fiction of the 1980s." In *From May Fourth to June Fourth*, edited by Ellen Widmer and David Der-wei Wang, 43–70. Cambridge, MA: Harvard University Press, 1993.

Esherick, Joseph. *The Origin of the Boxer Uprising*. Berkeley: University of California Press, 1987.

Esherick, Joseph, Paul G. Pickowicz, and Andrew G. Walder, eds. *The Chinese Cultural Revolution as History*. Stanford, CA: Stanford University Press, 2006.

Fairbank, John King. *China: A New History*. Cambridge, MA: Belknap Press of Harvard University Press, 1992.

———. *The Great Chinese Revolution: 1800–1985*. New York: Harper & Row, 1986.

Feuerwerker, Yi-tsi Mei. *Ideology, Power, Text: Self-Representation and the Peasant "Other" in Modern Chinese Literature*. Stanford, CA: Stanford University Press, 1998.

Foucault, Michel. *Discipline and Punish: The Birth of the Prison*. Translated by Alan Sheridan. New York: Vintage Books, 1977.

Fromm, Erich. *Escape from Freedom*. New York: Holt, Rinehart and Winston, 1941.

Frye, Northrop. *Anatomy of Criticism: Four Essays*. Princeton, NJ: Princeton University Press, 1957.

Goldblatt, Howard, ed. *Chairman Mao Would Not Be Amused: Fiction from Today's China*. New York: Grove Press, 1995.

———. "Forbidden Food: The 'Saturnicon' of Mo Yan." *World Literature Today* 74, no. 3 (Summer 2000): 477–486.

Griffin, Dustin. *Satire: A Critical Reintroduction*. Lexington: Kentucky University Press, 1994.

Haraszti, Miklós. *The Velvet Prison: Artists Under State Socialism*. Translated by Katalin Landesmann and Stephen Landesmann. New York: A New Republic Book, 1983.

He Lihua (贺立华). "Honggaoliang gezhe de liyin" (红高粱歌者的履印) [The footprints of the red sorghum singer]. In *Mo Yan yanjiu ziliao* (莫言研究资料) [Research materials about Mo Yan], edited by He Lihua and Yang Shousen, 1–21. Jinan: Shandong daxue chubanshe, 1992.

He, Lihua, and Yang Shousen (杨守森), eds. *Mo Yan yanjiu ziliao* (莫言研究资料) [Research materials about Mo Yan]. Jinan: Shandong daxue chubanshe, 1992.

He, Lihua, Yang Shousen, et al. *Guaicai Mo Yan* (怪才莫言) [Mo Yan: An eccentric talent]. Shijiazhuang: Huashan wenyi chubanshe, 1992.

Hsia, C. T. (夏志清). *A History of Modern Chinese Fiction*. 3rd ed. Bloomington: Indiana University Press, 1999.

Hsia, T. A. (夏济安). "Heroes and Hero-Worship in Chinese Communist Fiction." In *Chinese Communist Literature*, edited by Cyril Birch, 113–138. New York: Frederick A. Praeger, 1963.

Hutcheon, Linda. *A Poetics of Postmodernism: History, Theory, Fiction*. New York: Routledge, 1988.

———. "Irony, Nostalgia, and the Postmodern." Toronto: University of Toronto English Library, 1997. Listed under "Literary Criticism." www.library.utoronto.ca/utel

James, Henry. "Ivan Turgenieff." In *French Poets and Novelists*. Quoted by J. A. Ward, *The Imagination of Disaster: Evil in the fiction of Henry James*. Lincoln: University of Nebraska Press, 1961.

Jameson, Fredric. "Third World Literature in the Era of Multinational Capitalism." *Social Text: Theory, Culture, Ideology* 15 (Fall 1986): 65–88.

Jay, Paul. *Being in the Text: Self-Representation from Wordsworth to Roland Barthes*. Ithaca, NY: Cornell University Press, 1984.

Jones, Andrew F. "The Violence of the Text: Reading Yu Hua and Shi Zhicun." *positions* 2, no. 3 (Winter 1994): 570–602.

Juvenal. *The Satires*. Translated by Niall Rudd. Oxford: Clarendon Press, 1991.

Kayser, Wolfgang. *The Grotesque in Art and Literature*. Translated by Ulrich Weisstein. Bloomington: Indiana University Press, 1963.

Kinkley, Jeffrey C. *The Odyssey of Shen Congwen*. Stanford, CA: Stanford University Press, 1987.

Lau, Joseph S. M. (刘绍铭). "The 'Little Woman' as Exorcist: Notes on the Fiction of Huang Biyun." *Journal of Modern Literature in Chinese* 2, no. 2 (January 1999): 149–163.

Lee, Leo Ou-fan (李欧梵). "Reflections on Change and Continuity in Modern Chinese Fiction." In *From May Fourth to June Fourth*, edited by Ellen Widmer and David Der-Wei Wang, 361–383. Cambridge, MA: Harvard University Press, 1993.

———. *Voices from the Iron House: A Study of Lu Xun*. Bloomington: Indiana University Press, 1987.

Legge, James, trans. *The Chinese Classics*. Vol. 2, *The Works of Mencius*. Revised edition. Taipei: SMC Publishing, 1994.

Leung, Laifong (梁丽芳). *Morning Sun: Interviews with Chinese Writers of the Lost Generation*. Armonk, NY: M. E. Sharpe, 1994.

Li, Jiefei (李洁非). "Xungen wenxue: gengxin de kaishi, 1984–1985" (寻根文学：更新的开始 1984–1985) [Root-seeking literature: The beginning of renewal, 1984–1985]. *Dangdai zuojia pinglun* (当代作家评论) [Contemporary writers review], no. 4 (1995): 101–113.

Li, Qingxi (李庆西). "Xungen: huidao shiwu benshen" (寻根：回到事物本身) [Root seeking: Back to the things per se]. *Wenxue pinglun* (文学评论) [Literary review], no. 4 (1988): 14–23.

Li, Tuo (李陀). "Ding Ling bujiandan: Mao tizhi xia zhishifenzi zai huayu shengchan zhong de fuza juese" (丁玲不简单：毛体制下知识分子在话语生产中的复杂角色) [Ding Ling is not simple: The complexity of intellectuals in the production of discourse in the Maoist system]. *Jintian* (今天) [Today], no. 3 (1993): 222–242.

———. "Wang Zengqi yu xiandai Hanyu xiezuo—jiantan Mao wenti" (汪曾祺与现代汉语写作——兼谈毛文体) [Wang Zengqi and modern Chinese writing—Also on Maoist discourse]. *Jintian* (今天) [Today], no. 4 (1997): 1–37.

———. "Xiandai Hanyu yu dangdai wenxue" (现代汉语与当代文学) [Modern Chinese and contemporary literature]. *Xindi wenxue* (新地文学) [Literature of a new land] 1, no. 6 (February 1991): 30–43.

———. "Xuebeng hechu?" (雪崩何处) [Where does the avalanche start?]. Preface to *Shibasui chumen yuanxing* (十八岁出门远行) [On the road at eighteen], by Yu Hua, 5–14. Taipei: Yuanliu chuban shiye gufen gongsi, 1990.

Li, Wanjun (李万钧). "Shilun Mo Yan xiaoshuo de jiejian tese he duchuangxing" (试论莫言小说的借鉴特色和独创性) [An attempt to discuss the use for reference and originality of Mo Yan's fiction]. In *Mo Yan yanjiu ziliao* (莫言研究资料) [Research materials about Mo Yan], edited by He Lihua and Yang Shousen, 189–203. Jinan: Shandong daxue chubanshe, 1992.

Lin, Yü-sheng (林毓生). *The Crisis of Chinese Consciousness: Radical Antitraditionalism in the May Fourth Era.* Madison: University of Wisconsin Press, 1979.

Lin Zhou (林舟). "Xinling de youli yu guitu: Mo Yan fangtan lu" (心灵的游历与归途：莫言访谈录) [The traveling and returning of the mind: An interview with Mo Yan]. *Huacheng* (花城) [Flowery city], no. 3 (1997): 177–184.

Lowenthal, David. "Nostalgia Tells It Like It Wasn't." In *The Imagined Past: History and Nostalgia,* edited by Christopher Shaw and Malcolm Chase, 18–32. Manchester, UK: Manchester University Press, 1989.

———. *The Past Is a Foreign Country.* Cambridge: Cambridge University Press, 1985.

Lü, Tonglin (吕彤邻). *Misogyny, Cultural Nihilism, and Oppositional Politics: Contemporary Chinese Experimental Fiction.* Stanford, CA: Stanford University Press, 1995.

Lukács, Georg. *The Historical Novel*. Translated by Hannah Mitchell and Stanley Mitchell. Lincoln: University of Nebraska Press, 1983.

MacFarquhar, Roderick, and John K. Fairbank, eds. *The Cambridge History of China*. Vol. 15, *The People's Republic, Part II: Revolutions within the Chinese Revolution, 1966–1982*. Cambridge: Cambridge University Press, 1991.

Mann, Thomas. *Past Masters and Other Papers*. Translated by H. T. Lowe-Porter. Freeport, NY: Books for Libraries Press, 1968.

Mao Zedong. *Mao Zedong xuanji*（毛泽东选集）[Selected works of Mao Zedong]. One-volume edition. Beijing: Renmin chubanshe, 1967.

Mo Yan. *Hui changge de qiang: Mo Yan sanwen xuan* (会唱歌的墙：莫言散文选) [The wall that can sing: Selected essays of Mo Yan]. Beijing: Renmin wenxue chubanshe, 1998.

———. "Ji'e he gudu shi wo chuangzuo de caifu" (饥饿和孤独是我创作的财富) [Hunger and loneliness: My muses]. Preface to *Shifu, You'll Do Anything for a Laugh*, translated by Howard Goldblatt. New York: Arcade Publishing, 2001.

———. *Mo Yan sanwen* (莫言散文) [Mo Yan's selected prose]. Hangzhou: Zhejiang wenyi chubanshe, 2000.

———. *Shuoba Mo Yan: zuowei laobaixing xiezuo—fangtan duihua ji* (说吧莫言：作为老百姓写作访谈对话集) [Speak up, Mo Yan: To write as an ordinary person; A collection of interviews]. Shenzhen: Haitian chubanshe, 2007.

———. "Shuoshuo Fukena zhege laotou" (说说福克纳这个老头) [Talk about the old fellow Faulkner]. In *Hui changge de qiang: Mo Yan sanwen xuan* (会唱歌的墙：莫言散文选) [The wall that can sing: Selected essays of Mo Yan]. Beijing: Renmin wenxue chubanshe, 1998.

———, ed. *Suokongli de fangjian: yingxiang wo de shibu duanpian xiaoshuo* (锁孔里的房间：影响我的10部短篇小说) [A room seen through the keyhole: Ten short stories that have influenced me]. Beijing: Xinshijie chubanshe, 1999.

Mo Yan, and Wang Yao (王尧). "*Cong Honggaoliang dao Tanxiang xing*" (从《红高粱》到《檀香刑》) [From *Red Sorghum to Sandalwood Punishment*]. In *Mo Yan yanjiu ziliao* (莫言研究资料) [Research materials about Mo Yan], edited by Yang Yang, 86–110. Tianjin: Tianjin renmin chubanshe, 2005.

Mo Yan, and Zhang Huimin (张慧敏). "Shi shenme zhicheng zhe *Tanxiang xing*: da Zhang Huimin" (是什么支撑着《檀香刑》：答 张慧敏) [What is holding up *Sandalwood Punishment*: To answer Zhang Huimin's questions]. In *Mo Yan yanjiu ziliao* (莫言研究资 料) [Research materials about Mo Yan], edited by Yang Yang 70–76. Tianjin: Tianjin renmin chubanshe, 2005.

Ng, Kenny K. K. (吴国坤). "Metafiction, Cannibalism, and Political Allegory: *Wineland* by Mo Yan." *Journal of Modern Literature in Chinese* 1, no. 2 (January 1998): 121–148.

Ngai, Ling Tun (危令敦). "Anal Anarchy: A Reading of Mo Yan's 'The Plagues of Red Locusts.'" *Modern Chinese Literature* 10, nos. 1–2 (Spring/Fall 1998): 1–18.

Nietzsche, Friedrich. *The Birth of Tragedy and the Genealogy of Morals*. Translated by Francis Golffing. New York: Doubleday, 1956.

Peng Hsiao-yen (彭小妍). *Antithesis Overcome: Shen Congwen's Avant-Gardism and Primitivism*. Taipei: Institute of Chinese Literature & Philosophy Academia Sinica, 1994.

Pusey, James Reeve. *Lu Xun and Evolution*. Albany: State University of New York Press, 1998.

Reich, Robert B. "China: Capitalism Doesn't Require Democracy." *CommonDreams.org* (January 10, 2006). http://www.commondreams. org/views06/0110-42.htm (accessed December 3, 2010).

Russo, Mary. *The Female Grotesque: Risk, Excess and Modernity*. New York: Routledge, 1994.

Schorer, Mark. "Technique as Discovery." In *Essentials of the Theory of Fiction*, edited by Michael Hoffman and Patrick Murphy, 101–114. Durham, NC: Duke University Press, 1988.

Sederberg, Peter C. *Fires Within: Political Violence and Revolutionary Change*. New York: HarperCollins College Publishers, 1994.

Segal, Robert, ed. *Hero Myths: A Reader*. Oxford: Blackwell Publishers, 2000.

Shaw, Christopher, and Malcolm Chase, eds. *The Imagined Past: History and Nostalgia*. Manchester, UK: Manchester University Press, 1989.

Song, Guofan (宋国范). *Shitan sange chabie de xiaomie* (试谈三个差别的消灭) [On the eradication of three substantial gaps]. Changchun: Jilin renmin chubanshe, 1960.

Spence, Jonathan D. *The Search for Modern China*. New York: W. W. Norton, 1990.

Steinwand, Jonathan. "The Future of Nostalgia in Friedrich Schlegel's Gender Theory: Casting German Aesthetics Beyond Ancient Greece and Modern Europe." In *Narratives of Nostalgia, Gender, and Nationalism*, edited by Jean Pickering and Suzanne Kehde, 9–29. New York: New York University Press, 1997.

Stuckey, G. Andrew. "Memory or Fantasy? *Honggaoliang*'s Narrator." *Modern Chinese Literature and Culture* 18, no. 2 (Fall 2006): 131–162.

Sun, Lung-kee (孙隆基). *Weiduannai de minzu* (未断奶的民族) [A people not yet weaned]. Taipei: Juliu tushu gongsi, 1995.

———. *Zhongguo wenhua de shenceng jiegou* (中国文化的深层结构) [The deep structure of Chinese culture]. Hong Kong: Jixian she, 1983.

Tao Wan (陶琬). "Waiqu lishi, chouhua xianshi: ping xiaoshuo *Fengru feitun*" (歪曲历史，丑化现实：评小说《丰乳肥臀》) [Distorting history, uglifying reality: On the novel *Big Breasts and Wide Hips*]. In *Zhongliu baiqi wencui* (中流百期文萃) [Best essays of the one hundred issues of *Zhongliu*], 215–230. Beijing: Jincheng chubanshe, 1998.

Terrill, Ross. Foreword to *Scarlet Memorial: Tales of Cannibalism in Modern China*, by Zheng Yi (郑义). Edited and translated by T. P. Sym. Boulder, CO: Westview Press, 1996.

Tuo Tuo (脱脱), et al., comps. *Song shi* (宋史) [History of the Song dynasty]. Beijing: Zhonghua shuju, 1977.

Wang, David Der-wei (王德威). "Imaginary Nostalgia: Shen Congwen, Song Zelai, Mo Yan, and Li Yongping." In *From May Fourth to June Fourth*, edited by Ellen Widmer and David Der-wei Wang, 107–132. Cambridge, MA: Harvard University Press, 1993.

———. "The Literary World of Mo Yan." *World Literature Today* 74, no. 3 (Summer 2000): 487–494.

———, ed. *Running Wild: New Chinese Writers*. New York: Columbia University Press, 1994.

Wang, Derong (汪德荣). "Qiantan *Fengru feitun* guanyu lishi de cuowu miaoxie" (浅谈《丰乳肥臀》关于历史的错误描写) [A simple analysis on the erroneous descriptions about history in *Big Breasts and Wide Hips*]. In *Zhongliu baiqi wencui* (中流百期文萃) [Best essays of the one hundred issues of *Zhongliu*], 231–235. Beijing: Jincheng chubanshe, 1998.

Ward, J. A. *The Imagination of Disaster: Evil in the fiction of Henry James*. Lincoln: University of Nebraska Press, 1961.

"Wentan de duoluo he beipan: Zai Shandong Gaomi diqu zhandou guo de laohongjun, laobalu kan *Fengru feitun*" (文坛的堕落和背叛——在山东高密地区战斗过的老红军、老八路看《丰乳肥臀》) [The degeneracy and betrayal of the literary arena: A discussion on *Big Breasts and Wide Hips* by veterans of the Red Army and the Eighth Route Army who had fought battles in the Gaomi district of Shandong]. In *Zhongliu baiqi wencui* (中流百期文萃) [Best essays of the one hundred issues of *Zhongliu*], 243–255. Beijing: Jincheng chubanshe, 1998.

White, Hayden. *The Content of the Form: Narrative Discourse and Historical Representation*. Baltimore: Johns Hopkins University Press, 1987.

———. *Topics of Discourse: Essays in Cultural Criticism*. Baltimore: Johns Hopkins University Press, 1978.

Widmer, Ellen, and David Der-wei Wang, eds. *From May Fourth to June Fourth: Fiction and Film in Twentieth-Century China*. Cambridge, MA: Harvard University Press, 1993.

Wolfe, Thomas. *The Story of a Novel*. New York: Charles Scribner's Sons, 1936.

Xia, Zhihou (夏志厚). "Hongsede bianyi: cong '*Toumingde hongluobo*,' '*Honggaoliang*' dao '*Honghuang*'" (红色的变异：从《透明的红萝卜》、《红高粱》到《红蝗》) [The variability of the color red: From "A Transparent Red Radish," "Red Sorghum," to "Red Locusts"]. In *Mo Yan yanjiu ziliao* (莫言研究资料) [Research materials about Mo Yan], edited by He Lihua and Yang Shousen, 221–226. Jinan: Shandong daxue chubanshe, 1992.

Xiansheng Lu Xun (先生鲁迅) [Mr. Lu Xun]. Documentary series. Beijing: CCTV, 2007–2008. WWW.CCTV-YX.com.

Xie, Youshun (谢有顺). "Dang siwang bi huozhe geng kunnan: *Tanxiang xing* zhong de renxing fenxi" (当死亡比活着更困难：《檀香刑》中的人性分析) [When death is harder than life: An analysis of human nature in *Sandalwood Punishment*]. In *Mo Yan yanjiu ziliao* (莫言研究资料) [Research materials about Mo Yan], edited by Yang Yang, 270–284. Tianjin: Tianjin renmin chubanshe, 2005.

Xu, Huaizhong (徐怀中), Mo Yan, et al. "You zhuiqiu cai you tese: guanyu '*Toumingde hongluobo*' de duihua" (有追求才有特色：关于《透明的红萝卜》的对话) [Seeking brings uniqueness: A conversation about "A Transparent Red Radish"]. In *Mo Yan yanjiu ziliao* (莫言研究资料) [Research materials about Mo Yan], edited by He Lihua and Yang Shousen, 81–89. Jinan: Shandong daxue chubanshe, 1992.

Yan, Jiaqi (严家其), and Gao Gao (高皋). *Turbulent Decade: A History of the Cultural Revolution*. Translated and edited by D. W. Y. Kwok. Honolulu: University of Hawaii Press, 1996.

Yang, Xiaobin (杨小滨). *"The Republic of Wine*: An Extravaganza of Decline." *positions* 6, no. 1 (Spring 1998): 7–31.

Yang Yang (杨扬), ed. *Mo Yan yanjiu ziliao* (莫言研究资料) [Research materials about Mo Yan]. Tianjin: Tianjin renmin chubanshe, 2005.

Yue, Gang (乐刚). *The Mouth That Begs: Hunger, Cannibalism, and the Politics of Eating in Modern China*. Durham, NC: Duke University Press, 1999.

Zhang, Hong (张闳). *"Jiuguo* sanlun" (酒国散论) [Random discussions on *The Republic of Wine*]. *Jintian* (今天) [Today], no. 1 (1996): 87–98.

Zhongliu baiqi wencui (中流百期文萃) [Best essays of the one hundred issues of *Zhongliu*]. Beijing: Jincheng chubanshe, 1998.

Zhu, Binzhong (朱宾忠). *Kuayue shikong de duihua: Fukena yu Mo Yan bijiao yanjiu* (跨越时空的对话：福克纳与莫言比较研究) [A dialogue crossing time and space: A comparison study on Faulkner and Mo Yan]. Wuchang: Wuhan daxue chubanshe, 2006.

Zwingmann, Charles A. A. " 'Heimweh' or 'Nostalgic Reaction': A Conceptual Analysis and Interpretation of a Medico-Psychological Phenomenon." PhD dissertation. Stanford University, 1959.

INDEX